INSIDE

CONNECTICUT

and the

CIVIL WAR

INSIDE CONNECTICUT and the CIVIL WAR

Essays on One State's Struggles

MATTHEW WARSHAUER, editor

WESLEYAN UNIVERSITY PRESS

Middletown, Connecticut

WESLEYAN UNIVERSITY PRESS

Middletown CT 06459

www.wesleyan.edu/wespress

© 2014 Wesleyan University Press

All rights reserved

Manufactured in the United States of America

Designed by Richard Hendel

Typeset in Miller and Didot by

Tseng Information Systems, Inc.

Wesleyan University Press is a member of the
Green Press Initiative. The paper used in this book meets
their minimum requirement for recycled paper.

Library of Congress Cataloging-in-Publication Data

Inside Connecticut and the Civil War : essays on one
state's struggles / Matthew Warshauer, editor.

pages cm

Includes index.

ISBN 978-0-8195-7395-7 (cloth: alk. paper) —
ISBN 978-0-8195-7396-4 (pbk. : alk. paper) —
ISBN 978-0-8195-7397-1 (ebook)

1. Connecticut—History—Civil War, 1861–1865.

I. Warshauer, Matthew, 1965– editor of compilation.

E499.I67 2013

974.6′03—dc23   2013020094

5 4 3 2 1

TO MARC BASSOS

The Connecticut Civil War Commemoration Commission

Reenactor Liaison Extraordinaire

CONTENTS

Acknowledgments ix

Introduction 1
   Matthew Warshauer

1 Guns and Butter: How Connecticut Financed the Civil War 6
   James E. Brown

2 Mystic Shipbuilding and the Union Navy 45
   Diana Moraco

3 Patriotism and Abolitionism in Civil War–Era Windham County 69
   Carol Patterson-Martineau

4 Untried to Unrivaled: The Fourteenth Regiment,
   Connecticut Volunteer Infantry 101
   David C. W. Batch

5 The Colt Armory Fire: Connecticut and the
   Great Confederate Conspiracy 140
   Luke G. Boyd

6 Post-Traumatic Stress Disorder in the Civil War:
   Connecticut Casualties and a Look into the Mind 159
   Michael Sturges

7 Patriot, Soldier, Statesman: General Joseph R. Hawley and
   Civil War Commemoration in Connecticut 181
   Todd Jones

8 From Decoration Day to the Centennial Commission:
   Civil War Commemoration in Connecticut, 1868–1965 205
   Emily E. Gifford

9 Teaching the Past's Perspective of the Past:
   Civil War Reenactors in Connecticut 228
       Michael Conlin

   Contributors 259

   Index 263

ACKNOWLEDGMENTS

A book like this one requires thanks to many people. First and foremost, of course, is to the authors. Without their amazing research, motivation, and outstanding work ethic this book would be impossible. They are each and every one of them talented historians to whom we should look for much more in the future. Thanks also goes to the Connecticut Civil War Commemoration Commission, a group of some of the finest history/humanities professionals in the state, all of whom I am proud to call colleagues and friends. The commission's efforts to develop events and pro- ✓ grams for the Civil War sesquicentennial have helped to make Connecticut's history come alive. Telling the stories of who we are as a people and how we arrived at where we are today is what history and the humanities are all about. This has been our focus for commemorating the Civil War.

With this in mind special thanks go to Connecticut Humanities (CH), which is the principal representative of, and grant-funder for, the humanities in the state of Connecticut. CH has been a wonderful supporter of the commemoration in both spirit and funding. Thanks also go to the Connecticut State University–American Association of University Professors Faculty Research Grant Program, which provided important funding for this book. The Central Connecticut State University (CCSU) Alumni Association also provided tremendous support for the book's publication as well as for a wide variety of Civil War programming at the university and throughout the state of Connecticut. Indeed, the alumni association has been interested in the commemoration project since it began and recognized it as both an important part of Connecticut's history and a way to engage alumni and current students from CCSU. Top honors also go to Dr. Susan Pease, dean of the Carol A. Ammon School of Arts & Sciences, who generously contributed funding to make this book a reality. Susan has always recognized the importance of nurturing our students so that they feel like and become professionals. The publication of this book is a testament to that belief and her support.

Thanks also go to the Connecticut and New England reenactor communities. They have been steadfast in their devotion to Civil War history long before the sesquicentennial arrived, and since it began, they have taken on the important responsibility of representing through living history the Civil War generation. Marc Bassos, to whom this book is dedicated, has served as an extraordinary liaison to the many reenactment organizations and in doing so made the 150th anniversary so much more than it would have otherwise been. It is also important to mention Tad Sattler and Frank Niederwerfer, reenactors from Company G, Fourteenth Regiment Connecticut Volunteer Infantry 1862–1865, Inc. Both shared their detailed knowledge of the Fourteenth and helped to make the chapter on that subject more accurate. Tad has an extensive personal collection of images and other sources from the regiment and generously shared them whenever asked.

It is important to take special notice of Travelers Insurance, an organization that has not only generously contributed to funding the Civil War commemoration, but has gone far beyond a financial commitment. The company's involvement began with a Civil War connection to the Travelers' founder, James G. Batterson—who was one of the principal monument builders in Connecticut and around the nation, as well as a major supporter of Governor William A. Buckingham and President Abraham Lincoln—and blossomed into a genuine interest and partnership in telling Connecticut's story.

I also need to thank my friends and family, who have put up with my Civil War commemoration–obsessed life. The commemoration will soon be over, and I will get some rest. Three cheers for my girls, Emma, Samantha, and Jessica, who have been growing up amid lectures, book talks, and encampments, all the while coming to understand why this history is important and how it relates to our society today. Finally, thanks go to my wife, Wanda, who is the nicest person I know.

INSIDE

CONNECTICUT

and the

CIVIL WAR

INTRODUCTION

n October 11, 2012, the *Hartford Courant* announced in a news story that "Civil War sesquicentennial fever is gripping Connecticut."[1] How true that is. Since 2008, historical societies, museums, libraries, and universities across the state have been planning and now executing amazingly varied Civil War commemoration events. From encampments, both large and small, to symposia, book talks, living history events, historical debates, and much more, Connecticut has been bombarded with its connection to the nation's greatest struggle for survival. This is as it should be. The Civil War continues to occupy a place of often shocking reverence in our culture. The death toll was, and remains, unimaginable. It is not that we fail to recognize the numbers. Rather, we often cannot fully comprehend them, which is so evident when a packed room in a local library or museum hushes or murmurs at the ghastly body count. And that figure has, in fact, increased. The latest research reveals that instead of the fairly steady figure of 620,000 dead (5.9 million for today's population ratio), a number that has been with us for almost a century, the actual figure is somewhere between 650,000 and 850,000. Because we will never know for sure, the middle mark of 750,000 is the new death toll.[2]

The most lasting legacy of this death toll's impact is the myriad Civil War monuments that stretch out across Connecticut's landscape. At the start of the sesquicentennial, historians were certain that 139 monuments existed, this based on David Ransom's wonderful 1993 study of these tributes to a bygone era. As with our expanding understanding of the war's human destruction, we are also coming to realize that our count of the memorials to the war was inaccurate as well. There are at least 150, some of which were created after Ransom's study was completed, but a few that have been around since the late nineteenth century. Equally important is that historians are now certain that the Kensington Congregational Church Monument, dedicated on July 28, 1863, is the oldest permanent Civil War monument in the entire nation, not just in the North, as previously thought.[3]

The Kensington Monument, and all of our memorials, rightly places

Connecticut in an important place both historically and contemporarily. So many of the state's and nation's residents have no idea of the essential role this little New England powerhouse played in the war. They are thus equally surprised to see so many Civil War commemorative events happening during the sesquicentennial. Connecticut has been active and awarded in many areas: the Avon Free Library's National Endowment for the Humanities/American Library Association sponsored "Let's Talk about It" series; the Washington, Connecticut, Gunn Museum's "Letters from the Battlefield: Stories of Washington's Civil War Soldiers" exhibit, lecture series, and middle school social studies project, which won the only national Award in Excellence in Public History from the Society of Civil War Historians in 2011, a Leadership in History Award from the American Library Association for State and Local History, and an Award of Merit from the Connecticut League of History Organizations; as well as the Association for the Study of Connecticut History's first ever Bruce Fraser Award in public history given to the Connecticut Civil War Commemoration Commission.

Although this is clearly a bit of horn tooting, it is mainly to demonstrate the lengths to which Connecticut history organizations have gone and their success in telling the story of the Civil War. We have endeavored through scholarship and public engagement to teach our state's residents. Consideration and reflection have been our goal. A commemoration is meant to be a retrospective look back, not a celebration. It provides historians and the public an opportunity to think about what has gone before us, how it has impacted the nation both then and now, and what we did not know or may have gotten wrong over the course of time. This last component is particularly important.

During the Centennial Commemoration of the Civil War, both national and state commissions focused almost exclusively on "reconciliation" between the North and South.[4] This meant that the controversial issues of slavery and race were off the historical table. No one, especially in the midst of the tumultuous civil rights era, wanted to engage the core difficulties that launched America into an orgy of bloodshed. The focus of the sesquicentennial has been altogether different. Slavery has been at the core of the story. Connecticut residents are shocked to learn that their state was not the bastion of abolitionist liberalism that they had always assumed. Rather, it was, as the famed abolitionist William Lloyd Garrison derisively remarked, the "Georgia of New England."[5] This "new" history, however, is learned slowly and only with great effort. The aforementioned *Hart-*

ford Courant article on sesquicentennial fever, though getting the overall mood of Connecticut correct, begins with Harriet Beecher Stowe and John Brown, noting that "Connecticut may have lit the fuse igniting the powder keg of conflict."[6] Although they were certainly important figures in the state's and nation's history, Stowe and Brown are too often misrepresented as representative of Connecticut's mindset. The sesquicentennial has attempted to correct this misconception.

And just as commemorations offer the opportunity for consideration and reconsideration, they should spur new historical inquiry and insights. That is the goal of this volume. *Inside Connecticut and the Civil War: Essays on One State's Struggles* provides readers with a deeper look at a wide variety of Connecticut topics, from issues that faced the state in the midst of the conflict to how we chose to memorialize and tell the history. James E. Brown begins the book with "Guns and Butter: How Connecticut Financed the Civil War." An all too often neglected topic, the economics of how the nation and the state of Connecticut paid for the war will fascinate readers, as we have found ourselves in a similar predicament with the longstanding Iraq and Afghanistan wars. The next chapter carries readers through Connecticut's remarkable war industry. Rather than the standard account of firearms, brass, and uniforms, however, Diana Moraco engages the shipbuilding industry of Mystic, detailing the explosion of production that led to one of the nation's first ironclad war ships, the uss *Galena*. Next comes Carol Patterson-Martineau's "Patriotism and Abolitionism in Civil War–Era Windham County," which reveals both the difficulty and rewards of attempting to understand a particular region during the war. As small as Connecticut was, and remains, it was also a remarkably diverse place that defies easy summary. Each town and county must be studied on its own, and that is rarely done. True, we have learned a great deal about the lives of individual soldiers from a given town, but rarely do we have an opportunity to explore a region's overall outlook on the motivations for fighting. Patterson-Martineau provides us with that, helping to delineate Windham County's traditionally patriotic, Revolutionary appeal along with its not-so-traditional, reactionary, abolitionist mindset.

David C. W. Batch brings readers back to a focused account of one Connecticut regiment, the famed Fourteenth. In "Untried to Unrivaled: The Fourteenth Regiment, Connecticut Volunteer Infantry," Batch tells the story of these soldiers' inauspicious beginning at the Battle of Antietam to their remarkable victory at Gettysburg, then their slow and slogging continuation of the war, through Robert E. Lee's surrender at Appomattox to a triumphal march upon returning home to Hartford. We then enter the world of the Connecticut home front and the fears of Confederate conspiracy that rattled the state when Samuel Colt's famous armory burst into flames in early 1864. Luke G. Boyd's "The Colt Armory Fire: Connecticut and the Great Confederate Conspiracy" reveals just how much the southern war influenced the minds of Connecticut residents and gets to the bottom of the great "conspiracy." Michael Sturges's "Post-Traumatic Stress Disorder in the Civil War: Connecticut Casualties and a Look into the Mind" represents some of the most cutting-edge research on the impact of the Civil War on soldiers. PTSD is a twentieth-century concept, unknown to the physicians of an earlier era. Yet Sturges does an extraordinary job of connecting the often disparate understandings of the mind over time and dives into soldiers' home and hospital records that had remained uninvestigated for generations.

The last three chapters of *Inside Connecticut and the Civil War* focus on the war's aftermath. Todd Jones, in "Patriot, Soldier, Statesman: General Joseph R. Hawley and Civil War Commemoration in Connecticut," recounts the efforts of Hawley, a Civil War general, Connecticut governor, congressional representative, and senator, to honor veterans and educate the people about the requisite sacrifices made in defense of the nation. Hawley was ubiquitous at monument-dedication ceremonies and is rightly recognized as the first Connecticut man to volunteer for service following the Confederate bombardment of Fort Sumter. Emily E. Gifford carries the reader decades forward, from the beginnings of Decoration Day, which became Memorial Day, to the Centennial Commemoration of the war and the difficulties that ensued both nationally and within the state. "From Decoration Day to the Centennial Commission: Civil War Commemoration in Connecticut, 1868–1965" provides insights into the difficulties of remembering war and how contemporary politics infuse historical understanding. Finally, Michael Conlin's "Teaching the Past's Perspective of the Past: Civil War Reenactors in Connecticut" provides a fascinating look at the living historians who make Civil War encampments the centerpieces of the Sesquicentennial Commemoration. Nothing provides Connecticut residents with such visceral sights, sounds, and smells as do the encampments. They have served to drive further interest and study of the Civil War era. Conlin attempts to understand what makes the reenactors tick historically. Do they get the story right, wrong, or somewhere in between? The chapter brings the Civil War story right to our doorsteps and will surely be a bit controversial among the reenactors themselves.

Inside Connecticut and the Civil War represents the very active historical research that is going on in the state. The Connecticut Civil War Commemoration Commission's goal since the first stages of planning has been
"what will historians in another fifty years, at the Bicentennial Commemoration, say about what we did during the sesquicentennial?" Our abiding
desire has been to tell as much of the story as possible and to enliven the
study of history in Connecticut. This volume is part of that endeavor. It is
also particularly satisfying to me as a scholar, because each of the authors
was at one time a graduate student of mine and began his or her initial
research in my sometimes loved and sometimes dreaded History 501, The
Professional Historian. The goal in that course from day one is to get students engaged and immediately thinking of themselves as professionals.
The authors who have contributed to this book are each talented historians, great people, and wonderful representatives of Central Connecticut
State University's commitment to producing excellent graduates who contribute to their field and community.

NOTES

1. David K. Leff, "Connecticut Chock-Full of Civil War Sites," *Hartford Courant*,
October 11, 2012, A15.

2. J. David Hacker, "A Census-Based Count of the Civil War Dead," *Civil War
History* 57.4 (December 2011): 306–47; Guy Gugliotta, "New Estimate Raises
Civil War Death Toll," *New York Times*, April 3, 2012, D1.

3. David F. Ransom, "Civil War Monuments of Connecticut," *Connecticut Historical Society Bulletin* 58 (1993): 1–4; 59 (1994): 1–4. This important study is
available online as "Connecticut's Civil War Monuments," Connecticut Historical
Society, http://www.chs.org/finding_aides/ransom/introd.htm. The three additional monuments are the Burlington Monument (dedicated in 1998), the Connecticut Twenty-Ninth Regiment Monument in New Haven (dedicated 2008), and
the Bristol Soldiers Monument (dedicated 2011); there are also plans for a new
monument in Shelton. I discuss the Kensington Monument in *Connecticut in the
American Civil War: Slavery, Sacrifice, and Survival* (Middletown, CT: Wesleyan
University Press, 2011), 189–91. The Kensington Monument was thought to have
been second to the Hazen's Brigade Monument at Stones River Battlefield in Tennessee. An unpublished paper, Daniel A. Brown, "Marked for Future Generations:
The Hazen Brigade Monument, 1863–1929," located in the Stones River National
Park Service files, reveals that the monument was not completed until December
1863, making the Kensington Monument the nation's oldest permanent memorial.

4. Robert J. Cook, *Troubled Commemoration: The American Civil War Centennial, 1961–1965* (Baton Rouge: Louisiana State University Press, 2007). See also,
Warshauer, *Connecticut in the American Civil War*, chapter 6.

5. See Warshauer, *Connecticut in the American Civil War*.

6. Leff, "Connecticut Chock-Full of Civil War Sites."

1 : Guns and Butter

HOW CONNECTICUT FINANCED
THE CIVIL WAR

The phrase "guns and butter" is probably most often associated with President Lyndon Johnson's efforts to escalate the u.s. military presence in Vietnam while simultaneously implementing the Medicare program. Yet it aptly applies to any war, and specifically to the task of funding war-related expenditures while maintaining the day-to-day functions of government.

In Connecticut, the most important cost of the Civil War was immeasurable: of the more than 50,000 Connecticut soldiers who fought for the Union, 10 percent died as battle casualties or, indirectly, from wounds or disease, and so many more suffered horrible wounds and psychological trauma. Of the measurable costs, the state's budget must have seemed mind-boggling to Connecticut residents. In the fiscal year ending March 31, 1861, prior to the start of the war, total expenditures from Connecticut's General Fund came to $220,000. By the end of the war, Connecticut had expended more than $20 million, including more than $5 million spent by Connecticut's towns.[1]

When one considers the means of Union victory, the obvious focus is on battles and military strategy. Yet the military outcome was necessarily affected by the strengths and weaknesses of northern and southern financial resources and fiscal strategies.[2] In that regard, Connecticut officials faced many of the same public policy issues that President Abraham Lincoln and Congress dealt with at the national level: how to identify and gather resources; whether to pay for those resources by raising taxes, by borrowing, or by some other means; how to balance the competing interests of individuals, farmers, and small businesses on the one hand, and the state's corporations on the other; and how to do all of this while minimizing conflict and dissention and assuring broad-based support for the war effort.

These were complex decisions, whether addressed in Washington or in Connecticut. This chapter explores the background and implementation of financial strategies utilized during the Civil War, nationally and in Connecticut—recognizing that fiscal decisions were necessarily made in the context of military battles and politics. At the national level, the war facilitated a permanently larger role for the federal government. These financial decisions provided an experience base for dealing with similar strategic problems faced in subsequent wars. In Connecticut, the war tested the mettle of state residents, the bravery of our soldiers, and, most assuredly, the practicality and political skill of our state governmental leaders. In the end, Connecticut proved up to the task on all fronts.

FEDERAL FINANCING STRATEGIES

Financial historian Bray Hammond suggested that the Union's initial problem in confronting financing issues was the fundamental disconnection between the federal government and private business. Though any commercial business could borrow from a bank, by self-imposed rules the federal government could not. While the private economy had grown substantially in size and complexity, the federal government was essentially a primitive structure. In addition, the federal government insisted on conducting all of its business in "specie"—gold and silver. This was inefficient at best. Hammond found it ironic that despite all of the advantages the Union enjoyed at the start of the conflict, such as a larger population and far greater industry, the North could win the war only if it was a prolonged conflict—if it lasted long enough for the federal government to establish a financial infrastructure that could reap the benefit of such advantages. "It became essential to raise the vast sums required in a way that avoided exacerbating the underlying regional and class divisions," explained Hammond. "Lincoln, Chase and Congress had to soothe competing factions in order to meet urgent Civil War financing requirements and strengthen Northern political unity.[3]

There were essentially three possible sources of funds to meet war-related and non-war-related expenditures: taxing, borrowing, issuing new money. The Union utilized all three, by borrowing about 65 percent of the amount needed, looking to taxes for 20 percent, and to the issuance of new money for 15 percent.[4]

Prior to 1861, the federal government obtained its revenue almost exclusively from tariffs, or custom duties, and from the proceeds of public land sales. There existed no federal income tax of either individuals or businesses. Borrowing funds was time-consuming and difficult, as virtually every detail had to be approved by Congress.[5] In terms of how money flowed through the economy at the start of the war, the answer is simple: slowly. There were no federal banks, no centralized banking process, and

TABLE 1. *Sources of Federal Funds*

	Union	Confederacy
Borrowing	65%	40%
Taxation	20%	5%
Printing of money	15%	55%

Source: James M. McPherson, *Battle Cry of Freedom: The Civil War Era*
(New York: Oxford University Press, 1983), 443.

no national currency system. In fact, the government had intentionally avoided ongoing business interactions with banks for two decades. It conducted its financial business directly, and only in gold and silver. Private banking was conducted by more than 1,600 state banks, and transactions across the nation involved more than 7,000 different kinds of bank notes.[6]

The Lincoln administration entered the war with the financial philosophy that the generation fighting the war would not bear the primary burden of paying for it. Thus, raising funds through borrowing was emphasized over the imposition of taxes or the issuance of new money. There was a clear political element to this strategy. Many banks and financial institutions, as well as politicians, insisted that increased taxes were unnecessary because the war would be short in duration and because they feared that taxation might adversely influence public support. This approach was reflected in Treasury Secretary Salmon Chase's report to Congress in July 1861. Based on the assumption that the war would not drag on, Chase said, ". . . it seemed wisest to obtain the means for nearly the whole of the extraordinary expenditures by bonds, and thus avoid the necessity of any considerable increase of burdens of the people at a time when the sudden outbreak of flagitious rebellion had deranged their business and temporarily diminished their incomes."[7]

Lincoln's appointment of Chase was not a function of his expertise, but rather political expediency. The president wanted his rivals close at hand, and packed his cabinet with foes, as historian Doris Kearns Goodwin has so aptly described in *Team of Rivals*. Chase had no experience in finance and was eminently comfortable with the government's noninvolvement in banking and its reliance on specie.[8]

When Lincoln was inaugurated in March 1861, the national debt stood at $75 million, just under a quarter of which had been added since South

Carolina's secession had created the need to quickly raise a northern army. During the early months of the war, revenues of $5.8 million from tariffs and public sales were no match against expenditures of $23.5 million. Congress met in a special session in July 1861. Chase recommended that taxes be increased as necessary, but only for non-war-related expenditures and interest on the federal debt. War expenditures, he insisted should be funded by borrowing. He thus urged Congress to fund estimated expenditures of $318 million for the year, with $80 million in taxes and $240 million to be borrowed. Congress acted on Chase's advice and, on July 16, 1861, authorized up to $250 million in borrowing. One month later, Congress passed a related revenue bill, which included $20 million in taxes on real estate, a 3 percent tax on personal income over $600, and higher tariffs.[9]

Concerned late in the summer of 1861 that Congress had not by then acted on the pending tax bill, and specifically concerned that reluctance to raise taxes might be the cause of the delay, the New York Chamber of Commerce, revealing its misgivings about the financial war policies, adopted a resolution and forwarded it to Washington:

> Whereas, The Government of the United States is engaged in a contest for the suppression of rebellion, . . . which is destined to make a large demand upon the pecuniary resources of the Country, and the demand must chiefly be met by means of repeated loans,

> Resolved, That in the judgment of this Chamber, the success of the proposed loans will depend upon the enactment by Congress, now in session, of revenue and internal tax bills adapted to the existing emergency; and that if the government should succeed in procuring money without making wise provision for the reimbursement of principal and interest, it would be upon terms discreditable to the national name and prejudicial to the national interest.[10]

The Chamber thus chastised Congress for failing to address the delicate need of balancing borrowing and taxation as means of generating revenue. For individuals, businesses, or governmental entities to be comfortable investing in federal bonds, they would have to be assured that interest was paid on a timely basis and the principal redeemed when due; the federal government's image as a creditor could only be enhanced if potential borrowers were aware that the government had another ongoing source of funds to be used for these purposes. Congressman Thaddeus Stevens put it this way: "The capitalists must be assured that we have laid taxes which we can enforce, and which we must pledge to them in payment of interest on their loans, or we shall get no money."[11]

Just four months later, in December 1861, the financial crisis deepened. Secretary Chase revised his estimate of anticipated expenditures for the year, from $318 million to $532 million. Without any specific recommendations, Chase suggested additional taxation. He also recommended that Congress consider establishing a national banking system. That same month, private banks stopped making payments in gold and silver, and the federal government followed the same practice shortly thereafter. The result was general bewilderment. Debate in Congress resulted in the Legal Tender Act on February 25, 1862, which allowed the Treasury to issue non-interest-bearing notes that served as legal tender in all transactions. Though originally limited to $150 million in Treasury notes—called "Greenbacks"—another $150 million was authorized in July 1862, and yet another $150 million in early 1863.[12]

Reflecting the "don't be afraid of taxes" warning issued the previous year by the New York Chamber of Commerce, the *New York Times* issued a similar, impassioned plea for fiscal responsibility in January 1862, showing particular concern about how the Union's financial quandary and mettle might be viewed from Europe:

> The absurd fear of calling upon the people for the means to preserve the National integrity, which seems to bewilder a certain class of public men, is worthy only of the political demagogue whose whole ambition centers in the attainment of place, and whose estimate of the popular intelligence is so low that he is unwilling to trust it to sustain a money measure, let it be called for no matter what exigency. Congress is getting over this nonsense quite rapidly. And so it should, for, if the people were not ready to pay the necessary expenses of sustaining the Government which they are brought directly home to them, the sooner it is known the better.
>
> Hitherto taxation has been so light in this favored land, that our people have not yet learned the lesson long patent to every other on earth. But we must come to it, and that speedily. Liberal taxation is the only sound basis we can offer for the vast loans that will be needed to carry our existing war to a successful conclusion, and prove to the

world that American institutions have within them the elements of vigorous and enduring life. *Capitalists at home and abroad will take Government bonds in any required amount if we only show them that we are a tax-paying people.*

. . . [L]et us establish the policy of abundant taxation to meet all possible contingencies, and there will no longer be any trouble about the finances. When it is evident that the country will pay taxes heavy enough to yield the interest on the public debt, and leave a handsome margin for other extraordinary demands that may arise, not only will Government obtain all the money it may need, either at home or abroad, but the fact will satisfy Europe . . . that it has both the will and the power to survive the crisis which is now testing the stability of republican institutions.[13]

Congress did respond, enacting a complex tax bill in July 1862. The base for taxation was broadened by focusing on many more sources of revenue. Moreover, in recognition that many forms of taxation were regressive, and thus had an inordinate impact on those least able to bear the burden, the new income tax took on a progressive tilt: 3 percent on income between $600 and $10,000, and 5 percent on income over $10,000. Subsequent additional modifications brought the tax rate to 5 percent on income between $600 and $5,000, 7.5 percent on income between $5,000 and $10,000, and 10 percent on any income over $10,000. Furthermore, in anticipating requests for reducing taxes owed by states because of their own war expenses, Congress provided a credit against the direct tax on real estate. As a practical matter, because of the time delay involved in collection of the income tax and also because of the new state credits for property, neither tax proved to be a meaningful source of revenue during the war. The income tax provided no revenue in 1861 or 1862 and less than $3 million in 1863, before growing to $20.3 million in 1864 and $61 million in 1865. The direct tax on property raised only $1.8 million in 1862 and even less in subsequent years. Whereas taxes accounted for only 10 percent of revenue in 1862, they accounted for 25 percent in 1864 and 1865.[14] The new structure took time to develop.

The government also turned to bonds. In October 1862, Secretary Chase contracted with private banker Jay Cooke to market government bonds and hired some 2,500 subagents. Bonds were sold in amounts as small as $50. By mid-1863, Cooke had sold $157 million, and by Janu-

TABLE 2. *Federal Revenues — Taxes (in millions of dollars)*

	Total	Customs duties	Income tax	Direct (real estate) tax	Excise tax	Miscellaneous revenue
1861	$41.5	$39.6	$0	$0	$0	$1.9
1862	$52.0	$49.1	$0	$1.8	$0	$1.2
1863	$112.7	$69.1	$2.7	$1.5	$34.9	$4.5
1864	$264.6	$102.3	$20.3	$0.5	$89.4	$52.1
1865	$333.7	$84.9	$61.0	$1.2	$48.5	$38.1

Source: Paul Studenski and Herman E. Krooss, *Financial History of the United States: Fiscal, Monetary, Banking and Tariff, Including Financial Administration and State and Local Finance* (New York: McGraw-Hill, 1963), 152, table 19.

ary 1864, a total of $362 million in bonds had been sold. Cooke's success served as the foundation for World War I and World War II bond-selling campaigns.[15]

Table 2 depicts how the federal government's revenue from taxes evolved during the war. During the war years, the federal government collected just over $800 million in taxes, while borrowing $2.6 billion by marketing bonds. Despite the creation of new internal taxes, that is, taxes on items sold or activities occurring within the United States, the bulk of tax revenue throughout the war years continued to come from tariffs, or customs duties, on foreign goods. Before the war, a philosophy of free trade prevailed; the tariff served as a revenue-generating device and not as a tool of protectionism. Following southern secession, however, the tariff was used both to raise funds and to protect American industry. Tariff rates went from 19 percent in 1857 to 47 percent in 1864.[16]

Table 3 shows the evolution of federal expenditures during the war. War-related expenditures clearly dominated. Civilian government spending and spending on foreign affairs did not grow significantly. Because of the extensive borrowing to fund the war effort, interest expense grew continuously. Indeed, in the fiscal year that ended on March 31, 1865, interest expense exceeded the entire federal budget for the fiscal year that ended on March 31, 1861.

Table 4 shows the overall picture of the federal government's revenues

TABLE 3. *Federal Expenditures (in millions of dollars)*

	Total	Civil	Foreign	War	Interest	Miscellaneous
1861	$66.6	$6.1	$1.1	$35.4	$4.0	$20.0
1862	$469.6	$5.9	$1.3	$431.8	$13.2	$17.4
1863	$718.7	$6.3	$1.2	$666.6	$24.7	$20.0
1864	$865.0	$8.0	$1.2	$776.1	$53.7	$29.6
1865	$1,296.8	$10.6	$1.3	$1,153.3	$77.4	$54.2

Source: Paul Studenski and Herman E. Krooss, *Financial History of the United States: Fiscal, Monetary, Banking and Tariff, Including Financial Administration and State and Local Finance* (New York: McGraw-Hill, 1963), 152, table 19.

TABLE 4. *Federal Revenues, Expenses, and Debt (in millions of dollars)*

	Revenue	Expenditures	Surplus (deficit)	Cumulative debt
1861	$41.5	$66.6	($25.1)	$90.6
1862	$52.0	$469.6	($417.6)	$524.2
1863	$112.7	$718.7	($606.0)	$1,119.8
1864	$264.6	$865.0	($600.4)	$1,815.8
1865	$333.7	$1,296.8	($963.1)	$2,680.0

Source: Paul Studenski and Herman E. Krooss, *Financial History of the United States: Fiscal, Monetary, Banking and Tariff, Including Financial Administration and State and Local Finance* (New York: McGraw-Hill, 1963), 152, table 19.

and expenditures during the war. The federal budget experienced "financial embarrassment" in the form of deficits in every year of the war. Except in 1864, the deficit each year exceeded the deficit from the preceding year, growing in the aggregate from $90.6 million in 1861 to $2.7 billion at the end of the war. The federal debt peaked at $2.75 billion in 1866. Overall, federal debt decreased every year thereafter for the next decade.[17]

In February 1863, Congress passed "An Act to Provide a National Currency," which was revised in 1864 to become "The National Banking Act," authorizing the establishment and regulation of national banks. By October of that year, only sixty-six banks had opted for a federal charter. Twelve months later, there were 508 federal banks. Subsequently, with the "incentive" of a 10 percent tax on state bank notes enacted in March 1865, the number of federal banks increased to 1,513 by October 1865 and 1,644 by October 1866.[18]

CONNECTICUT'S POLITICAL LANDSCAPE

With the exception of the option to print money, virtually all of the financing issues that arose in Washington during the Civil War had to be addressed in Connecticut as well. The state's first Republican governor, William Buckingham, was forced to confront these issues. First elected in 1858, Buckingham was reelected annually thereafter, through 1865. With the benefit of hindsight, one can readily understand why he was labeled "Connecticut's War Governor" and "Connecticut's Lincoln." Yet no one entertained such thoughts as Connecticut recovered from the panic of 1857 and the relatively new Republican Party chose Buckingham as its candidate. A native of Norwich, Buckingham had previously been involved in purely local politics. Both the absence of political baggage and his reputation as a respected and successful businessman attracted voters.[19]

As he led Connecticut through the thicket of decisions forced by the war, Buckingham proved to be the right man for the job. As historian John Niven wrote, "One year of wartime responsibilities had made a surprisingly astute politician out of a cautious businessman. The stresses of mobilizing an unprepared people had also developed qualities of leadership which he exerted in a quiet but forceful manner." Buckingham mobilized and motivated the citizenry, coordinated with leadership in the General Assembly on important fiscal and nonfiscal policy decisions, traveled frequently to Washington, communicated directly with President Lincoln, and demonstrated concern and compassion for Connecticut troops.[20]

Buckingham's popularity and success during the war years was followed by Republican gubernatorial victories for several years thereafter. In contrast, disputes among antebellum Democrats on a national level were replicated in Connecticut and contributed to a weakening of the party throughout the war. Democrats were split into one of two camps: "Peace Democrats" or "War Democrats."

Peace Democrats seemed to be in denial of the northern industrialization. Nostalgic for an idealized southern society, politically they were strongly Jeffersonian. They believed in the right of southern states to secede from the Union, insisted there was no need for war, and feared that northern victory would result in the trampling of individual liberties and states' rights. An intrusive federal government would arise. This group was led by one of Connecticut's most popular Democrats, Thomas Seymour. He had served as governor from 1850 to 1853 and thereafter as u.s. ambassador to Russia. His stalwart ally was Hartford Assembly Representative William Eaton.[21]

War Democrats, generally, but not aggressively, supported the war effort once it became apparent that conflict was unavoidable. Still, they opposed many of Lincoln's war measures, and along with Peace Democrats attacked among other things the administration's fiscal policies. As historian Joanna Cowden explained, Democrats "bitterly assailed the Emancipation Proclamation, conscription, suspensions of the writ of *habeas corpus*, wartime taxes, and inflated currency."[22] In Connecticut, Eaton and his allies challenged the Buckingham administration on the nature and amount of costs incurred and the options for financing war expenditures.

CONNECTICUT'S FINANCING STRATEGIES
Year by Year: 1861

The day after President Lincoln issued a call for troops following the fall of Fort Sumter, Governor Buckingham followed suit, requesting volunteers to form a regiment in Hartford; the following day he issued a similar call for a regiment in New Haven. His immediate concern was how to pay for the troops. With the General Assembly not in session and no funds available for war expenditures, Buckingham applied for a $50,000 loan from the Thames Bank of Norwich. Within days, numerous other banks offered to loan funds to the state, and in short order the governor had more than $1 million at his disposal. Taking advantage of these offers, Buckingham gave the banks the following document: "Sir— This will be presented by _____ through whom I propose to avail myself of your patriotic offer of money to aid the State amid the present national calamities. Honor such drafts as he may draw on you and charge the same to the State, for the final payment of which I hold myself personally responsible." Buckingham thus borrowed substantially at the beginning of the conflict on his own personal security.[23]

Connecticut towns also began soliciting volunteers and addressing the need for funds. By the first day of May, for example, a committee in Stafford had been organized and voted to pay $20 to each volunteer and to assist local families as necessary. In Enfield and Waterbury, $10,000 was appropriated for similar purposes. In Woodbury, $5,000 in family aid was collected. Similar activity was reported in Coventry, Middletown, West Hartford, and other Connecticut towns.[24]

When the General Assembly convened in regular session in May, the governor informed legislators that volunteers comprising forty companies were being organized into regiments. He asked the General Assembly to address on a timely basis the state's needs in preparation for war. Realizing the impending federal need for money, Buckingham recommended that Connecticut borrow funds and then loan them to the federal government.[25] Although the Assembly did not go this far, it did quickly address the fiscal crisis that mirrored the military emergency. During May, the Assembly addressed a variety of fiscal issues, including,

- authorizing the governor to raise 10,000 volunteer soldiers;
- authorizing additional compensation of $10 per month to be paid to every volunteer soldier upon commencement of his service for the United States;
- authorizing towns to appropriate sums for organizing and arming troops, and to make provisions for the families of such soldiers, clarifying that the $10 additional compensation to be provided by the state would be in lieu of any similar payments made by the towns; and
- appropriating $2 million for war expenditures and authorizing the state treasurer to borrow funds by issuing bonds to defray these expenses.[26]

Reporting on this action by the General Assembly, the *Hartford Courant* noted, "The bill reposes much confidence in the Governor, and relieves him from heavy responsibilities incurred without express law, but from the best of motives. It indicates respect for the man and is a practical compliment which a Connecticut General Assembly rarely pays. The whole bill is a departure from ordinary policy warranted only by the solemn exigency of the occasion it indicates, unmistakably, that Connecticut is ready to do her utmost."[27]

A month later, the General Assembly modified this law, with the first of a number of confusing changes to the bounty, or incentive compensation, process. It replaced the $10 per month payment to volunteers with a $30 per year payment, while at the same time establishing a payment of up to $10 per month to the families of volunteers—$6 per month for a volunteer's wife, and $2 per month for each of up to two children. This was the first time such payments were referred to as "bounties," intended as incentive for enlisting. The same law authorized reimbursement to towns and committees who had provided uniforms to local soldiers.[28]

In October, after President Lincoln called for 500,000 additional troops, of which Connecticut's quota was 12,000, the General Assembly lifted the cap of 10,000 it had previously established in May. The same law authorized the state treasurer to pay up to an additional $10 per month to the family of any soldier taken prisoner for so long as he remained imprisoned. The Assembly also appropriated another $2 million and authorized the state treasurer to issue bonds of up to that amount to fund the increase.[29]

Year by Year: 1862
Despite the ongoing challenges of the war, by the time Governor Buckingham addressed the General Assembly in May 1862, both were more comfortable in dealing with the crisis. The shock of the first months had worn off, and Connecticut went about the business of accomplishing what had to be done to meet the needs of the war and simultaneously to maintain the state's economy.[30]

By May 1862, Connecticut had contributed more than 13,500 troops, expended more than $1.5 million, and secured from the federal government an interest-bearing certificate of indebtedness (essentially an IOU) in the amount of $600,000. In his annual message to the General Assembly, Governor Buckingham expressed confidence in the citizens of Connecticut and reported an estimated deficit for the year of approximately $1.6 million. He also spoke about the new federal income tax and the importance of Connecticut's meeting its obligations to the Union:

> Of the many questions of public interest which will require your attention, there will be none more important than those which relate to the finances of the state . . . It will probably be necessary to raise the sum mentioned above, which can be done either by taxation or a loan, or by both. . . . But we have abundant ability to meet these claims. A very small part of the profits of our industry will be sufficient to supply the public treasure with ample means to prosecute the war, and furnish a good foundation for public credit. Sound policy dictates that you should avail yourselves of this self-sacrificing patriotism by making liberal provision to meet our existing obligations.[31]

The General Assembly responded. In July 1862, it enacted legislation addressing taxation for the first time during the war. The measure no doubt reflected criticism from Democrats leveled at the administration for perceived overreliance on borrowing to fund war expenditures. It also

Hartford War Debt Bond, 1863. Courtesy of the Connecticut Historical Society, Hartford reflected the push and pull of Connecticut politics—the "tax him, not me" approach to proposed legislation.[32]

That same month, the General Assembly unintentionally created a competition of sorts among Connecticut towns by authorizing any town to appropriate funds to encourage voluntary enlistments.[33] This not only created a market for enlistment brokers, but added to the number of financial issues that had to be dealt with.

Among those issues was the continuing disappearance of coins from the economy. Like other states, Connecticut in 1862 experienced the hoarding of coins in response to private and public suspension of using gold and silver. This caused serious inconvenience in retail trade. Whereas in Philadelphia, old Spanish quarter dollars were used, and in New York City, some retailers simply declined to give change for paper bills, in Connecticut, dollar bills were cut into halves or quarters and used as currency. It was said that in Hartford, some $20,000 worth of bills issued by the Aetna Bank were cut in two and in circulation. In response, Congress authorized the use of stamps as currency, and subsequently approved the issuance of fractional currency—"paper coins" were issued in denominations as low as three, five, and ten cents.[34]

Year by Year: 1863

Connecticut's recruiting activities were in high gear when Congress enacted the Federal Conscription Act, the first federal draft legislation in the nation's history, on March 3, 1863. Unless sufficient volunteers could be found to meet new quotas, the shortfall would have to be addressed through the draft, which took effect in Connecticut on July 18, 1863.[35]

During the regular session in May, the General Assembly extended payments to the families of soldiers who became disabled and as a result were discharged from service. They also extended payments to the families of soldiers drafted under the federal draft; previously these payments were available only to families of soldiers who had volunteered. To cover these costs, the General Assembly authorized another $2 million in bonds. Interest, however, was to be paid at 5 percent, rather than at 6 percent, and the resulting difficulty of marketing these bonds led to repeal of the law in January 1864.[36]

The bounty issue was yet again addressed at a special session of the General Assembly held in November 1863. Several changes were motivated by new pressures on Connecticut as a result of the federal draft. One law enacted during this special session authorized a one-time payment of

$300 to any soldier who enlisted in Connecticut on or before January 5, 1864, and subsequently transferred into service of the United States under the federal draft. To address the costly issue of recruiting volunteer soldiers by competitive bounty, the new law also repealed previous legislation that had authorized towns to pay bounties to volunteers, and it specifically prohibited towns from doing so. Another law enacted during the November session authorized payment to black soldiers who were included in the count of soldiers credited to Connecticut's quota under the federal draft; the purpose of such payment was to supplement the black soldiers' federal pay, thus providing them with the same amount white soldiers received.[37]

Though Democrats, through William Eaton, voiced opposition to the state's growing debt and urged the General Assembly to take a "pay-as-you-go" approach to financing, taxes were not modified in 1863. Nevertheless, these pleas did not go unheard; Governor Buckingham supported raising taxes during the last two years of the war.[38]

Year by Year: 1864

The work of the General Assembly necessitated by the war peaked in 1864. In January, it authorized another $2 million in bonds and enacted a law calling for payments to soldiers who served as substitutes for men drafted under federal law.[39]

Several war-related laws were also enacted in June and July 1864. The General Assembly authorized towns that had incurred expenses for the benefit of drafted men to issues bonds to cover those expenses. A bounty of $300 was authorized to be paid to any person who furnished a substitute for himself prior to being drafted, and family payments were extended to families of substitutes. Under another law enacted in July, bounties and family payments previously applicable only to soldiers serving in the army were extended to those serving in the navy; similarly, payments authorized for army recruiters were extended to navy recruiters.[40]

In his annual message to the General Assembly, Governor Buckingham demonstrated that his philosophy on financing had changed during the course of the war. Although it was now late in the process, he had come to see the benefits of a larger "pay-as-you-go" component to balance the issuance of bonds: "From present indications the military campaign is to be prosecuted with great vigor, and we may anticipate an early requisition for more troops. . . . During the present inflated condition of the currency, which affords a time peculiarly favorable for meeting pecuniary obligations, I would recommend largely increased taxation, and authority to

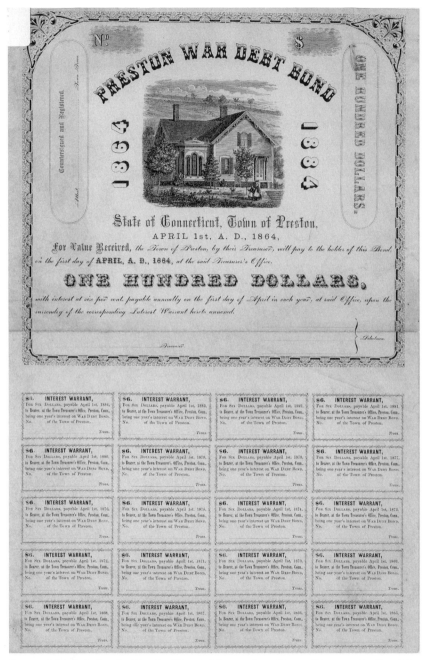

Preston War Debt Bond, 1864–84. "State of Connecticut, Town of Preston, April 1, A.D., 1864." Courtesy of the Connecticut Historical Society, Hartford

AN

INQUIRY

INTO THE

Prospective Financial Condition

OF OUR COUNTRY,

AS AFFECTED BY

THE WAR AND ITS DEBT.

NEW HAVEN:

THOMAS J. STAFFORD, PRINTER, 235 STATE STREET.

1864.

An Inquiry into the Prospective Financial Condition of Our Country, as Affected by the War and Its Debt, *attributed to Alfred Walker, 1864. Courtesy of the Connecticut Historical Society, Hartford* make loans required to supply any deficiency for appropriations."[41] During the May session, the General Assembly authorized another $2 million in bonds and modified the taxing structure it had put in place in 1863.[42]

Year by Year: 1865

Governor Buckingham's message to the General Assembly used typically eloquent language to speak about alternative views of the expenditures Connecticut had to make during the war: "The amount of State indebtedness appears like a heavy burden when we feel that it has been imposed upon us by crime; but when we consider that these expenditures have been incurred to conserve rights which we hold under the national government, and that they have successfully contributed to that object, the burden is removed and the necessary tax becomes a cheerful offering. The burden also appears light when compared with our ability to bear it." With regard to Connecticut's ability to pay, Buckingham went on to advise that the grand list (the total value of all taxable property) had seen a meaningful increase during the year and that the total amount of Connecticut's debt was less than two-thirds of that annual increased value, and less than 4.25 percent of the value of the grand list.[43]

During this final session of the General Assembly during the war, an additional $3 million in bonds was authorized, and new taxes affected the stock of any Connecticut corporation that did not fall within the groups of businesses already specifically taxed. Railroad companies, telegraph companies, mutual insurance companies, and express companies were also the subject of tax legislation.[44] The *Harford Courant* captured the mood at the General Assembly: "All rejoice who have borne the monotony and fatigue of the longest session on record."[45]

CONNECTICUT'S FINANCING STRATEGIES BY THE NUMBERS

Table 5 shows Connecticut's revenues, expenditures, surplus/deficit, and cumulative debt during the course of the war. It should be noted that Connecticut's General Fund revenue and expenditures did not include funds and expenses for public schools, which was separately addressed in the School Fund. Table 5 shows a dramatic rise in the budget between 1861 and 1862, with revenues increasing from $254,500 to $2.4 million. Approximately $2 million of the latter figure came from the sale of state bonds. In the same period, expenditures increased from $227,000 to $2.1 million, more than $1.5 million of which went to bounty payments, payments to soldiers' families, and to the purchase of equipment, supplies, and food for

TABLE 5. *Connecticut's Revenue and Expenditures, 1861–1865*

	Revenue	Expenditures	Surplus (deficit)	Cumulative debt
1861	$254,500	$227,000	$27,500	$50,000
1862	$2,400,000	$2,100,000	$300,000	$2,000,000
1863	$2,300,000	$2,500,000	($200,000)	$3,400,000
1864	$4,800,000	$4,900,000	($100,000)	$7,200,000
1865	$5,000,000	$4,700,000	$300,000	$10,500,000

Source: Annual Reports of the Treasurer and of the Comptroller, *Public Documents of the General Assembly of Connecticut*, 1861–1865.

the troops. By March 1865, annual revenues and expenses were each approximately $5 million; the state debt, which had been $50,000 in 1861, had risen to a whopping $10.5 million during the war.

Table 6 breaks down the sources of revenues and expenditures during one year of the war (1863). On the revenue side of the budget, 65 percent came from the sale of state bonds and from temporary loans; the remainder was derived from taxes. The largest generator of tax revenue was the tax on towns, which was the property tax. Next came the tax on banks, which included a tax on deposits in savings banks and a tax on stock dividends from commercial banks. The tax on insurers taxed agents of out-of-state insurance companies and the capital of mutual insurance companies. There was no tax on insurers based in Connecticut.

Table 7 breaks down state expenditures during the war between those that were war-related and those connected with the standard operation of state government. Table 8 divides the war-related expenditures into several categories. War-related expenditures accounted for 90 percent of the state budget from 1862 through the end of the war. Other state expenses did not undergo retrenchment during the war but rather grew modestly from 1861 through 1864. Non-war expenditures nevertheless grew substantially in 1865, as more revenue became available when taxes increased. With regard to war-related costs, 90 percent of the paymaster general's expenditures and all of the monies for families of volunteers were the result of soldier bounties. The quartermaster general's expenditures, for equipment and supplies, dropped substantially after 1862, as the federal government assumed responsibility for these payments.

TABLE 6. *Connecticut's General Fund Budget, 1863*

REVENUE		EXPENSES	
Source	*Amount*	*Expense*	*Amount*
Bonds	$1,100,000	Paymaster	$ 1,095,000
Temporary loans	$400,000	Families	$583,000
Tax on towns	$530,000	Quartermaster	$405,000
Tax on banks	$147,000	Judicial	$72,000
Tax on railroads	$50,000	Contingent	$70,000
Tax on insurers	$19,000	General Assembly	$51,000
Tax on stock	$17,000	Salaries	$25,000
Miscellaneous	$37,000	Public buildings	$28,000
		Other	$171,000
Total	$2,300,000	Total	$2,500,000

Source: Annual Report of the Comptroller, *Public Documents of the General Assembly of Connecticut*, 1863.

TABLE 7. *Connecticut's Expenditures (War-Related and Non-War-Related)*

	Total	Ordinary expenditures (non-war)	War expenditures	War expenditures as percentage of total
1861	$221,821	$214,341	$7,480	3%
1862	$2,104,481	$238,320	$1,866,161	88%
1863	$2,336,372	$251,010	$2,085,362	89%
1864	$4,897,820	$278,071	$4,619,749	94%
1865	$5,064,338	$417,818	$4,646,520	91%
1866	$1,066,581	$472,465	$594,116	56%
Total	$15,691,413	$1,871,725	$13,819,388	88%

Source: Annual Reports of the Treasurer and of the Comptroller, *Public Documents of the General Assembly of Connecticut*, 1861–1866.

TABLE 8. *Connecticut's War-Related Expenditures*

	Total	Paymaster general	Families of volunteers	Quarter-master general	Other
1861	$7,480	$0	$0	$7,480	$0
1862	$1,866,161	$403,330	$110,099	$1,169,778	$182,954
1863	$2,085,362	$1,095,000	$582,785	$405,000	$2,657
1864	$4,619,749	$3,640,000	$726,908	$15,000	$237,841
1865	$4,646,520	$3,550,000	$689,517	$25,350	$381,653
1866	$594,116	$170,000	$304,109	$110,000	$10,007
Total	$13,819,388	$8,858,330	$2,413,338	$1,732,608	$815,112

Source: Annual Reports of the Treasurer and of the Comptroller, *Public Documents of the General Assembly of Connecticut*, 1861–1866.

TABLE 9. *Towns' Expenditures for War Purposes*

Counties	Towns' expenditures for bounties, commutations, and family support	Estimated amount paid by individuals for bounties to volunteers and substitutes	Estimated amount paid by individuals for commutation
Hartford	$1,217,966.19	$163,153.98	$49,020
New Haven	$932,892.87	$181,466.03	$33,110
Fairfield	$903,276,79	$123,940.00	$82,450
New London	$730,067.65	$192,553.12	$35,900
Litchfield	$551,211.61	$192,998.94	$23,400
Middlesex	$305,785.71	$163,066.73	$27,500
Windham	$281,750.70	$75,494.00	$32,460
Tolland	$272,926.28	$42,090.00	$9,100
Total	$5,195,877.80	$1,134,762.80	$292,940

Source: "War Expenses" tabulation, General Assembly's Finance Committee, 1865, RG 002, box 71, Connecticut State Library.

Table 9 shows expenditures by Connecticut towns, grouped by county, during the war for war-related purposes. The bulk of these payments were for bounties to volunteer soldiers, payments to soldiers' families, and payments for commutations, that is, for substitutes in the draft.

CONNECTICUT SEEKS REIMBURSEMENT FOR WAR CLAIMS

Governor Buckingham reported to the General Assembly in May 1862 that as of March 1862, Connecticut had submitted claims of $1,516,565.74 to the federal government. He indicated that with the exception of extra compensation provided by the state to volunteers and their families, this claim was intended to embrace all expenses incurred by the state for arms, clothing, and all appointments, together with the wages, paid from the time the troops entered the service of the state to the time they were mustered into the service of the United States. At the time of his report to the Assembly, the federal government had not yet processed the claim, but it had provided Connecticut with a certificate of indebtedness, an IOU, in the amount of $600,000.[46]

Governor Buckingham's Annual Report for May 1866 noted that supplemental claims in the amount of $356,317.10 and $75,805.95 had been submitted in March 1863 and January 1865, respectively. He advised that, to date, Connecticut had received $1,656,301.28 from the original claim and the March 1863 claim combined, and indicated that the most recent claim had yet to be addressed. He advised that the amount disallowed from the 1862 and 1863 claims, $175,217.73, included all costs for interest; costs incurred in arresting deserters; damages to property rented; transportation and subsistence of men who enrolled and were ready to serve for the United States but were not called; any costs for purposes not authorized by army regulations; and a portion of claims for advertising and telegraphing.[47]

Thirty years later, following an 1895 decision of the U.S. Supreme Court (which took the position that Congress intended to include states' claims for interest expense within the scope of the 1861 statute authorizing the payment of states' war claims), Connecticut contracted with Samuel Fessenden, states attorney for Fairfield County, to pursue Connecticut's claim for interest on a contingency basis: Fessenden was entitled to keep 25 percent of recovered monies. This effort was successful. In 1903, Connecticut recovered $606,569, of which $151,642 was paid to Fessenden, leaving $454,927 to defray the state's interest expense. This brought the total amount Connecticut recovered in war claims to $2,111,228.[48]

CONCLUSION

In *The Price of Liberty: Paying for America's Wars*, historian Robert D. Hormats concludes:

> American history offers many political and economic lessons. But looking back over this nation's more than two hundred years, one central, constant theme emerges: sound national finances have proved to be indispensable to the country's military strength. Without the former, it is difficult over an extended period of time to sustain the latter. . . .
>
> Most (of America's wartime leaders) have recognized that it is not enough to have a large number of troops, sound military strategy, and able generals to fight a war; the country also needed a sound financial strategy and skillful leaders at the Treasury and in Congress to ensure that the money was available to meet extraordinary military expenses. The techniques American officials have employed to generate these funds under the duress of war have produced dramatic innovations in the nation's tax and borrowing policies, innovations that lasted long beyond the conflict during which they were introduced and many of which remain in effect today. America's wars have been fiscally as well as politically transforming events; changes that could not have gained public acceptance in quieter times won support when they answered the urgent requirements of war.[49]

This rings true from the Civil War. At the national level, changes were made that continue to affect us today—the initiation of a federal income tax, the establishment of an Internal Revenue Bureau, the adoption of a national banking system and a national currency—all were realized only because of the needs of the war.

In Connecticut, even though it was the Democrats who were most critical of relying too heavily on borrowing, Republican Governor Buckingham and the General Assembly nevertheless increased taxes substantially in 1864 and 1865. The state's decisions in this regard were in line with those of the federal government, whose 9:1 ratio of borrowing to taxes in 1861 dropped to 6:1 in 1862 and closer to 3:1 in the last two years of the war. Moreover, though the overall size of the debt Connecticut took on during the war ($10.5 million) was by any measure significant, it was well within Connecticut's ability to pay. The debt represented just 4.25 percent of Connecticut's grand list, which had increased by $40 million since 1861 and by $17 million during 1865 alone. The cumulative debt was thus less than two-thirds the size of one year's increase in the value of Connecticut real estate.[50] On the negative side, inflation during the war disproportionately hurt workers and soldiers on fixed incomes. The average worker's income in 1865 was equal in purchasing power to what it had been in 1832.[51]

Considering both the financial benefits and the financial burdens of the war, one may reasonably conclude that able leadership in Connecticut rose to the occasion, motivated the state's citizens, and adopted financial strategies that reasonably balanced the interests of varied constituencies. At the conclusion of the war, Connecticut's government was poised to respond to a diverse and rapidly evolving economy.[52]

Appendix 1
FEDERAL WAR CLAIMS RECOVERY PROCESS

At the start of the war, the state of Connecticut was in no condition to fund all the expenses of recruiting and outfitting a volunteer military and relied instead on the extraordinary efforts of towns, committees, and individuals. The federal government was similarly unprepared, and relied to a great degree on expenditures made by the individual states. Early on, no objections were made by the states. Refusing a War Department offer to purchase supplies for Rhode Island troops, for example, Rhode Island's governor responded that they "needed nothing . . . from the federal government; Rhode Island and her governor will attend to their wants." Such bravado was not prevalent, however, particularly when it became apparent that the war was not going to be either short or inexpensive.[53]

There was precedent for the government's indemnifying various parties for amounts expended on the nation's behalf. More than $20 million had been reimbursed to the states for expenses incurred during the American Revolution, and before the Civil War, $17 million in cash grants had been made to states to defray various types of costs, including some $3 million under appropriations to pay for states' war claims related to Indian uprisings.[54]

Despite substantial precedent and the government's having in place a rudimentary process for addressing states' war claims, the claim issues raised as a result of the Civil War were of a new dimension. By one estimate at the close of the war, the states could reasonably make claims against the federal government in amounts that would reach at least $468 million, if not more, and this estimate did not take into consideration the particular claims of Union states in the war zone, which might include destruction of property.[55]

On July 27, 1861, a week following the Union defeat at Manassas, Congress enacted "An Act to Indemnify the States for Expenses Incurred by Them in Defense of the United States." There was no debate, and passage of the bill, from introduction to the final vote, took less than twenty-four hours. As described to the House of Representatives, the purpose of the bill was to "direct the Secretary of the Treasury to pay to the Governor of any State, or to his duly authorized agents, the cost, charges and expenses, properly incurred by such State for enrolling, subsisting, clothing, supplying, arming, equipping, paying and transporting its troops employed in aiding to suppress the present insurrection against the United States, to be settled upon proper vouchers to be filed and passed upon by the proper accounting officers of the Treasury."[56]

Though the legislation itself seemed to provide broad authorization for indemnification, Treasury Secretary Chase adopted tight claim submission rules. By mid-1862, fifteen states had filed claims totaling $24 million. Though legislation was proposed to loosen the rules and allow the Treasury Department to pay based on certification by state governors, thus eliminating the need for proof of claims by vouchers, the bill was not passed. Secretary Chase's screening rules prevailed, and the result was a complicated, mind-numbing process:

> For states presenting their claims, the paper trail started in the Treasury's Office of the Third Auditor. After accounting clerks officially logged the claims, the paperwork passed to the War Department to determine the general validity of the claim. For claims pertaining to state volunteer units, examiners searched for evidence of each unit's actual time of muster. For claims pertaining to militia, the examination searched for evidence that the governor had the proper authorization from Washington to call out the militia. When the clerks and assigned special duty army officers in the War Department completed this screening, the claims traveled back to the Treasury Department and the third auditor's office.[57]

Assuming that the War Department certified the validity of a state's claims, the most difficult and time-consuming part of the process had now begun. Clerks examined every expenditure contained within a state's claim. The level of scrutiny was painstaking because the states had to provide—among other things—physical proof of each expenditure, as well as its necessity. Accordingly, the clerks examined everything that a military unit in the nineteenth century needed to become organized and then operational, including ice, lightning rods, recruiting posters, candlesticks, coffins, tobacco, food, and munitions. It was a time-honored, yet wearisome process. Nonetheless, the clerks persevered and sorted each expense into the categories of approved, disallowed, and suspended claims. Subsequently, the third auditor allowed the states to investigate further each of the disallowed or suspended claims in order to provide evidence that would answer the objections of the accounting clerks. The auditor then forwarded to the office of the second comptroller all of those claims that had been approved. In this office another set of clerks descended on the claims, checking the work of the previous office. For those claims that survived this process of attrition, the comptroller forwarded them to the secretary of the treasury for final approval.

In 1871, legislation was considered in Congress to allow indemnification of interest paid by states to borrow funds for war expenditures. This generated debate over the equity of such a provision. Connecticut's Civil War governor, William Buckingham, by then a United States senator, joined the debate. Perhaps time had caused Senator Buckingham to forget that Connecticut had issued bonds and incurred interest expense in the war effort. Whatever the reason, he argued that reimbursement of interest would not be equitable, at least with respect to interest incurred after the state had already received payment on its war claims from the Treasury: "Suppose a State is in debt; has become indebted for the very purpose of aiding the Government, and is paying interest annually on that account. Suppose the adjoining State has taxed its citizens and paid all its war debt. What propriety and justice is there in imposing an additional tax upon that adjoining State to pay the present indebtedness of the one by its side?"[58]

Earlier in the same discussion, Buckingham had argued against reimbursement of loss a state may have incurred by virtue of having issued bonds at a discount: "It would impose a heavier burden, an unjust burden, upon the people of Indiana [which had not discounted its bonds], thus to make up the losses sustained by the State of Minnesota [a state that had discounted bonds], because the State of Minnesota did not happen to have as good credit as the State of Indiana. I should be perfectly satisfied to have this bill provide for paying the interest on debts which the States incurred from the time the States paid them up to the time the money was refunded by the United States Government."[59]

Twelve years later, at the request of the state of New York, the United States attorney general issued an opinion clarifying that the law allow-ing states to be indemnified for Civil War claims did not encompass a claim for interest. New York sued the secretary of the treasury over this issue, and the court determined that interest claims were in fact encompassed within the scope of the law. The federal government appealed to the United States Supreme Court, which upheld the lower court's decision in 1895.[60]

Appendix 2
CONNECTICUT'S WAR-RELATED LEGISLATION, 1861–1865

May Session, 1861
Chapter 1: "An Act to Provide for the Organization and Equipment of a Volunteer Militia, and to Provide for the Public Defense," approved May 8, 1861

- Authorized the governor to raise 10,000 volunteer soldiers (cap was lifted by the October session, 1861, chap. 4)
- Stipulated that soldiers were to be paid until mustered into u.s. service
- Required that all expenditures for arms, supplies, etc. were to be made under the direction of the governor; all bills were to be audited by the governor, treasurer, and comptroller
- Ratified prior war actions taken by the governor
- Required payment of $10 per month as additional compensation for each soldier accepted into u.s. service
- Authorized towns to appropriate sums for "organizing, arming, equipping or providing any soldiers" and to make provisions for the families of such soldiers, provided that any extra compensation provided by the state was in lieu of any provided by the towns
- Appropriated $2 million for war expenses and authorized the treasurer to borrow for this purpose

Chapter 28: "An Act Authorizing the Treasurer to Borrow Money for the Equipment and Payment of the Volunteer Militia, and to Issue State Bonds," approved June 18, 1861

- Authorized the treasurer to issue bonds in connection with authorized borrowing of up to $2 million (chap. 1) at interest of 6 percent to be paid in January and June, principal to be paid in twenty years (or after ten years, at the discretion of the General Assembly)

- Authorized the treasurer to advertise and sell portions of such bonds as the governor decided was necessary and to accept the most favorable proposals offered by bidders, provided that none were sold at less than par

Chapter 36: "An Act in Addition to 'An Act to Provide for the Organization and Equipment of a Volunteer Militia, and to Provide for the Public Defense,'" approved June 27, 1861

- Replaced the $10 per month bounty with a $30 per year bounty and added family payment of up to $10 per month for soldiers' families—$6 per month for the wife and $2 for each child under the age of fourteen, subject to a family maximum of $10. (The $30 bounty was extended to nonresidents enlisting in Connecticut by the May session, 1862, chap. 60)
- Required towns to report to the comptroller the names of all soldiers resident in the town accepted into u.s. service, including the names of wives and children, plus the dates and terms of enlistment
- Required the comptroller to pay towns, quarterly, amounts due from the state to families; if the town had already paid, to be reimbursed by the state
- Authorized reimbursement to individuals and committees that had provided uniforms

Special October Session, 1861
Chapter 3: "An Act Relating to the Direct Tax Imposed by the Congress of the United States," approved October 15, 1861

- Confirmed that Connecticut would pay its share of the federal direct real estate tax, in part, by offsetting any war claims Connecticut had against the federal government.

Chapter 4: "An Act in Addition to 'An Act to Provide for the Organization and Equipment of a Volunteer Militia, and to Provide for the Public Defense,'" approved October 16, 1861

- Removed the cap (10,000) on the number of volunteer soldiers
- Authorized payment to families of soldiers taken prisoner, while imprisoned, of $6 per month for the wife and $2 for each child under the age of fourteen, subject to a family maximum of $10

- Appropriated another $2 million and authorized the treasurer to borrow and to issue bonds, subject to terms of the act of June 18, 1861

May Session, 1862

Chapter 55: "An Act in Addition to and in Alteration of 'An Act for the Assessment and Collection of Taxes,'" approved July 10, 1862

- Savings banks: 0.5 percent tax on deposits and stock, in lieu of all taxes except real estate
- Railroad companies: 0.75 percent tax on value of stock
- Telegraph companies: 0.75 percent tax on value of property in Connecticut
- Commercial banks and insurance companies incorporated in Connecticut: 0.75 percent tax on stock held by nonresidents
- Mutual insurers: 0.5 percent tax on capital, in lieu of all other taxes except real estate
- Out-of-state insurers: 2 percent tax on Connecticut premiums

Chapter 66: "An Act in Addition to an Act, Entitled 'An Act in Addition to "An Act to Provide for the Organization and Equipment of a Volunteer Militia, and to Provide for the Public Defense,"'" approved July 10, 1862

- For any bonds issued after July 10, 1862, authorized the legislature to repay principal after five years, rather than after ten years

Chapter 71: "An Act in Addition to Provide for the Organization of a Volunteer Militia, and for the Public Defense," approved July 10, 1862

- Authorized any town to make appropriation to encourage the enlistment of volunteers as deemed proper

"Resolution Directing the Payment of a Bounty of Fifty Dollars to Volunteers Enlisted before August 20th, 1862," approved July 10, 1862

- Authorized a one-time payment of $50 to any soldier enlisted after May 1, 1862, and before August 20, 1862, and who was mustered into u.s. service
- Authorized the governor to extend the August 20, 1862, date at his discretion

Special Session, December 1862

Chapter 5: "An Act to Authorize Towns, Cities and Boroughs to Issue Bonds or Other Obligations for War Purposes," approved December 18, 1862

- Authorized towns to issue bonds to cover actual military expenses, but not more, at 6 percent interest, provided that none were sold at less than par

Chapter 9: "An Act in Addition to an Act, Entitled 'An Act in Addition to "An Act to Provide for the Organization and Equipment of a Volunteer Militia, and to Provide for the Public Defense,"'" approved December 24, 1862

- Amended the act of June 27, 1861, to extend family support to families residing outside of Connecticut as long as they had resided in Connecticut at the time of enlistment

Chapter 16: "An Act to Authorize the Issuing of State Bonds," approved December 24, 1862

- Similar to the act of June 18, 1861, which related to the first $2 million bond authorization; the same terms were applicable to this, the second $2 million bond authorization
- Different in that this act authorized the treasurer to offer the bonds in New York City or Boston, provided that none were sold at less than par

Chapter 19: "An Act in Alteration of an Act, Entitled 'An Act to Provide for the Organization and Equipment of a Volunteer Militia, and to Provide for the Public Defense,'" approved December 24, 1862

- Authorized payment of the family payment for soldiers enlisting after May 1, 1862, specifically for the time after their enlistment and before they were transferred to u.s. service
- Authorized family pay to soldiers who were drafted, in addition to those who had volunteered

May Session, 1863

Chapter 46: "An Act in Addition to 'An Act to Provide for the Organization and Equipment of a Volunteer Militia, and to Provide for the Public Defense,'" approved July 10, 1863

- Provided that the family support for soldiers who became disabled, and as a result were discharged, should continue while they were disabled and end when the disability ended

Chapter 61: "An Act in Addition to 'An Act to Provide for the Organization and Equipment of a Volunteer Militia, and to Provide for the Public Defense,'" approved July 11, 1863

- Authorized payment of family support for any soldier drafted under the federal draft

Chapter 62: "An Act Authorizing the Further Issue of State Bonds," approved July 11, 1863 (repealed by the January session, 1864, chap. 2)

- Appropriated another $2 million
- Authorized the sale of $2 million in bonds at 5 percent
- Appropriated $400,000 of the amount to be reimbursed by the federal government to go into a "sinking fund" to redeem bonds issued under this act

Special Session, November 1863
Chapter 1: "An Act to Provide for the Payment of a Bounty to Volunteers," approved November 13, 1863

- Awarded $300 in addition to any other compensation, to be paid to any soldier who enlisted on or before January 5, 1864 (or later, if that date was pushed back by the governor), and mustered into u.s. service under the then most recent call of the president for volunteers
- Required the adjutant general to establish town-by-town quotas under the federal draft and to give each town credit against that quota for soldiers enlisting voluntarily
- Repealed a prior act authorizing towns to pay bounties to volunteers, and prohibited towns from doing so (but this was ignored in practice)

Chapter 6: "An Act in Addition to 'An Act to Provide Payment of a Bounty to Volunteers, and to Organize an Additional Militia Force,'" approved November 13, 1863

- Authorized payment to black soldiers who enlisted, and were counted toward Connecticut's federal quota, of an amount

necessary to bring their pay up to the level that white soldiers received, plus $3.50 for clothing
- Authorized payment of $10 per man to anyone who recruits volunteer soldiers as part of Connecticut's quota
- Appropriated up to $200,000 for expenses under this act
- Authorized the governor to recruit black soldiers, who would receive the same pay as white soldiers

Adjourned Special Session, January 1864
Chapter 2: "An Act Authorizing the Further Issue of State Bonds," approved January 15, 1864

- Authorized another $2 million in bonds, which could be sold without coupons, if requested

Chapter 3: "An Act to Provide for the Payment of Bounty to Volunteers and for Other Purposes," approved January 15, 1864

- Extended the provisions of the acts of June 27, 1861, and December 24, 1862, to soldiers who were substitutes for others who were drafted per the federal draft
- Authorized payment of a bounty of $300 to any soldier mustered into u.s. service and applied to the Connecticut quota per the president's October 17, 1863, call, even if Connecticut's quota was exceeded
- Authorized payment of a bounty of $300 to any soldier mustered into u.s. service on or before May 16, 1864, and applied to any quota required of Connecticut, provided the governor could order the cessation of such payments before May 16, 1864

May Session, 1864
Chapter 20: "An Act in Addition to an Act Entitled 'An Act to Authorize Towns, Cities and Boroughs to Issue Bonds or Other Obligations for War Purposes,'" approved June 30, 1864

- Authorized towns that had incurred expenses for the benefit of drafted men to issue bonds

Chapter 56: "An Act in Addition to An Act Entitled 'An Act to Provide for the Payment of a Bounty to Volunteers and for Other Purposes,'" approved July 9, 1864

- Authorized payment of $300 to any person who furnished a substitute for himself prior to being drafted
- Extended family payments to families of substitutes

Chapter 63: "An Act in Addition to 'An Act to Provide for the Payment of a Bounty to Volunteers and for Other Purposes,'" approved July 9, 1864

- Authorized payment of $300 to those enlisting after July 1, 1863, though not credited to towns where they reside, provided they had not intentionally done so seeking a greater bounty

Chapter 65: "An Act in Addition to 'An Act Provide for the Payment of a Bounty and for Other Purposes,'" approved July 9, 1864

- Authorized the same bounties and family payments for persons enlisting in the navy as in the military
- Authorized the same payment to a person recruiting for the navy as for the military

Chapter 70: "An Act in Addition to 'An Act to Provide for the Payment of a Bounty to Volunteers, and for Other Purposes,'" approved July 9, 1864 (repealed July 11, 1865)

- Authorized the governor to appoint agents to recruit soldiers in southern states, who would count toward Connecticut's federal quota; said agents to receive up to $100 per volunteer

Chapter 74: "An Act Entitled 'An Act in Addition to and in Alteration of "An Act for the Assessment and Collection of Taxes,"'" approved July 9, 1864

- Savings banks: 0.75 percent tax on deposits and stock, in lieu of all taxes except real estate
- Railroad companies: 1 percent tax on market value of stock
- Telegraph companies: One cent tax per message sent in Connecticut
- Commercial banks and insurance companies incorporated in Connecticut: 0.25 percent tax on market value of stock
- Mutual insurers: 1.5 percent tax on capital, in lieu of all other taxes except real estate
- Out-of-state insurers: Continued the 2 percent tax on Connecticut premiums, but special provision was made for companies incorporated in states that tax Connecticut insurers

- Express companies: 1 percent tax on gross charges
- Auctioneers: 1 percent tax on gross sales

Chapter 80: "An Act to Authorize the Issue of State Bonds, and to Borrow Money," approved July 9, 1864

- Authorized the sale of another $2 million in bonds at 6 percent

May Session, 1865
Chapter 27: "An Act Confirming the Action of Towns in Relation to Bounties," approved June 29, 1865

- Approved actions by towns in giving bounties (even though the General Assembly had specifically prohibited town bounties in the November 1863 special session, chap. 1)

Chapter 43: "An Act Taxing Certain Corporations," approved July 11, 1865

- Tax of 0.5 percent on market value of stock of Connecticut corporations other than those already specifically taxed

Chapter 89: "An Act to Authorize the Issue of State Bonds, and to Borrow Money," approved July 14, 1865

- Authorized the sale of $3 million in bonds at 6 percent

Chapter 96: "An Act Entitled 'An Act in Addition to and in Alteration of "An Act for the Assessment and Collection of Taxes,"'" approved July 21, 1865

- Railroad companies: 1 percent tax on value of stock and debt
- Telegraph companies: 2 percent tax on gross receipts from messages sent in Connecticut
- Mutual insurers: 1 percent tax on capital, in lieu of all other taxes except real estate
- Express companies: 2 percent tax on gross charges

NOTES
1. See table 5, "Connecticut's Revenue and Expenditures, 1861–1865"; table 7, "Connecticut's Expenditures (War-Related and Non-War-Related)"; table 8, "Connecticut's War-Related Expenditures"; and table 9, "Towns' Expenditures for War Purposes."
2. Paul Studenski and Herman E. Krooss, *Financial History of the United States: Fiscal, Monetary, Banking and Tariff, Including Financial Administra-*

tion and State and Local Finance (New York: McGraw-Hill, 1963), 137; Robert D. Hormats, *The Price of Liberty: Paying for America's Wars from the Revolution to the War on Terror* (New York: Henry Holt, 2007), 83: "The Union's greater creditworthiness, bolstered in substantial measure by its capacity to raise vastly greater amounts of tax revenues, provided it with an enormous advantage over the Confederacy, undergirding its ability to prevail in the war."

3. Bray Hammand, *Sovereignty and an Empty Purse: Banks and Politics in the Civil War* (Princeton, NJ: Princeton University Press, 1957), 719–20; Hormats, The Price of Liberty, 58.

4. James M. McPherson, *Battle Cry of Freedom: The Civil War Era* (New York: Oxford University Press, 1983), 443. The ratio of funds borrowed versus taxes assessed changed during the course of the war—from 9:1 in 1861, to 6:1 in 1862, and closer to 3:1 in the last two years of the war. This change reflected recognition of the need to avoid overreliance on borrowing. In contrast to the Union, the Confederacy had no taxing history or structure in place. It relied primarily on the issuance of new money (55 percent of its costs), looked to borrowing for about 40 percent, and derived only 5 percent from taxes. See Hormats, *The Price of Liberty*, 83.

5. Studenski and Krooss, *Financial History of the United States*, 137.

6. Studenski and Krooss, *Financial History of the United States*, 137–38.

7. Chase quoted in Albert S. Booles, *The Financial History of the United States from 1861 to 1865* (New York: D. Appleton, 1886), 159.

8. Doris Kearns Goodwin, *Team of Rivals: The Political Genius of Abraham Lincoln* (New York: Simon & Schuster, 2005), 290; Studenski and Krooss, *Financial History of the United States*, 139.

9. Average income in 1861 was $150; less than 3 percent of individuals would be affected by the income tax (Hormats, *The Price of Liberty*, 62). See also Studenski and Krooss, *Financial History of the United States*, 139–41; Arthur C. Bining, *The Rise of American Economic Life* (New York: Charles Scribner's Sons, 1955), 318; Leonard Curry, *Blueprint for Modern America: Nonmilitary Legislation of the First Civil War Congress* (Nashville, TN: Vanderbilt University Press, 1968), 150.

10. *New York Times*, August 2, 1861, 5.

11. Stevens quoted in Hormats, *The Price of Liberty*, 63.

12. Studenski and Krooss, *Financial History of the United States*, 142–44; Bining, *The Rise of American Economic Life*, 319. The new legal tender was printed with green ink on one side, thus the name, "greenbacks." Confederate currency, printed with blue-gray ink, earned the name "bluebacks" (Hormats, *The Price of Liberty*, 77).

13. *New York Times*, January 3, 1862, 9.

14. Studenski and Krooss, *Financial History of the United States*, 150–53.

15. Studenski and Krooss, *Financial History of the United States*, 153.

16. Charles Beard and Mary R. Beard, *The Rise of American Civilization* (New York: MacMillan, 1937), 107.

17. Jeffrey G. Williamson, "Watersheds and Turning Pointes: Conjecture on the Long-Term Impact of Civil War Financing," *Journal of Economic History* 34.3 (September 1974): 642.

18. Studenski and Krooss, *Financial History of the United States*, 155; Bining, *The Rise of American Economic Life*, 318.

19. Under the Fundamental Orders of 1639 and subsequently under the constitutions of 1818 and 1965, gubernatorial elections were held annually until 1876, every two years from 1876 until 1950, and every four years since 1950. For Buckingham, see Samuel Giles Buckingham, *The Life of William A. Buckingham: The War Governor of Connecticut* (Springfield, CT: W. F. Adams Co., 1894); David Drury, "Gov. William Buckingham, Faded from History, Played National Role during Civil War," *Hartford Courant*, April 7, 2012.

20. John Niven, *Connecticut for the Union: The Role of the State in the Civil War* (New Haven, CT: Yale University Press, 1965), 72.

21. In 1860, Eaton presented consistently and inflexibly the Jeffersonian views of Connecticut's Peace Democrats. His position on the secession issue and on the possibility of war contrasted starkly and antagonistically with that of Governor Buckingham, who argued that when the states ratified the Constitution, they surrendered their sovereignty and any right to secede. Eaton believed that the states voluntarily chose to coexist within the framework of a republic and did not surrender their sovereignty. See William W. Eaton, "The Union: Past, Present and Future," City Hall, Hartford, CT, Democratic State Central Committee, March 3, 1860, Connecticut State Library, Hartford, State Archives. Ironically, Eaton replaced u.s. Senator (and Civil War Governor) Buckingham upon the latter's death in 1875 and was subsequently also elected to the u.s. House of Representatives.

22. Joanna D. Cowden, "The Politics of Dissent: Civil War Democrats in Connecticut," New England Quarterly 56.4 (December 1983): 539–40 and 551–52. See also Joanna D. Cowden, "Sovereignty and Secession: Peace Democrats and Antislavery Republicans in Connecticut during the Civil War Years," *Connecticut History* 30 (1989): 41–47; John E. Talmadge, "A Peace Movement in Civil War Connecticut," *New England Quarterly* 28.3 (September 1964): 306–21; and Matthew Warshauer, *Connecticut in the American Civil War: Slavery, Sacrifice, and Survival* (Middletown, CT: Wesleyan University Press, 2011).

23. Buckingham, *The Life of William A. Buckingham*, 129–31. Throughout the war, the governor's salary was $1,100 per year. At the same time, justices of the Connecticut Supreme Court were paid $2,000 per year, and even the reporter of judicial decisions was paid $1,200 (Report of the Comptroller, Public Documents of the General Assembly of Connecticut, 1861–1865). Documents published by the General Assembly were done so under contract with a different company almost every year. What follows is a list of printers and dates, but hereafter these notes will simply list Public Documents of the General Assembly—New Haven: Carrington & Hotchkiss, State Printers, 1861; Hartford: J. R. Hawley & Co., State Printers, 1862; New Haven: Babcock & Sizer, State Printers, 1863; Hartford: J. M. Schofield & Co., State Printers, 1864; New Haven: Carrington & Hotchkiss, State Printers, 1865.

24. *Hartford Courant*, May 1, 1861, 2.

25. Buckingham, *The Life of William A. Buckingham*, 172.

26. "An Act to Provide for the Organization and Equipment of a Volunteer Mili-

tia, and to Provide for the Public Defense," approved May 8, 1861, chap. 1. Public Acts, Passed by the General Assembly of the State of Connecticut (Hartford: J. R. Hawley & Co., 1861). Hereafter, references to legislation will be shortened to refer to the applicable session of the General Assembly and the chapter number. A listing of all the laws referred to is included in appendix 2, "Connecticut's War-Related Legislation, 1861–1865."

27. *Hartford Courant*, May 4, 1861, 2.

28. May session, 1861, chap. 36.

29. Special October session, 1861, chap. 4.

30. The civilian economy continued to flourish, both in response to, and in spite of, the war. John Niven, Connecticut for the Union, 415, noted, "After the first year of the war, a general prosperity was evident in all economic activities. Credit sources—like banks of deposit and exchange, savings banks, and insurance companies—were unable to accumulate nonreserve funds for investment rapidly enough to accommodate the needs of an expanding war economy. . . . Though credit grew more expensive, industry and finance maintained a high level of prosperity."

31. Report of the State Treasurer to the General Assembly," Public Documents of the General Assembly of Connecticut (May session, 1862): 3–5.

32. The General Assembly settled on a law that targeted savings banks (0.5 percent tax on deposits and stock); commercial banks and insurance companies incorporated in Connecticut (0.75 percent tax on market value of stock held by nonresidents); mutual insurance companies (0.5 percent tax on capital); "foreign" insurance companies, i.e., those incorporated outside of Connecticut (2 percent tax on premiums collected in Connecticut); railroad companies (0.75 percent tax on market value of stock); and telegraph companies (0.75 percent tax on market value of property in Connecticut). Soon thereafter, the General Assembly also doubled the mill rate (from 2 to 4) for taxing real estate (May session, 1862, chap. 55; *Hartford Courant*, July 11, 1862, 2; *Hartford Courant*, July 14, 1862, 2).

33. May session, 1862, chap. 66.

34. Wesley C. Mitchell, "The Circulating Medium during the Civil War," *Journal of Political Economy* 10.4 (1902): 554; Hormats, *The Price of Liberty*, 78.

35. Niven, *Connecticut for the Union*, 88; Federal Conscription Act, u.s. Statutes at Large, vol. 12, p. 731, http://memory.loc.gov/cgi-bin/ampage?collId=llsl&fileName=012/llsl012.db&recNum=762.

36. May session, 1863, chaps. 46, 61, and 62; special January session, 1864, chap. 2.

37. Special November session, 1863, chaps. 1 and 6. Recruiting bounties continued nevertheless. See *Hartford Courant*, January 6, 1864, 3.

38. Harold J. Bingham, *History of Connecticut* (N.p.: Lewis Publishing, 1962), 606.

39. Adjourned special January session, 1864, chaps. 2 and 3.

40. May session, 1864, chaps. 20, 56, 63 and 65; Niven, *Connecticut for the Union*, 413; *New Haven Register*, June 23, 1864.

41. Message of Governor William A. Buckingham to the General Assembly, Public Documents of the General Assembly of Connecticut, 1864.

42. May session, 1864, chaps. 74 and 80. Taxes were increased on savings banks (from 0.5 percent to 0.75 percent on deposits and stock); mutual insurance companies (from 0.5 percent to 1.5 percent tax on capital); and railroad companies (from 1 percent to 1.5 percent of market value of stock). Taxes were modified on Connecticut-based commercial banks and insurance companies (from 0.75 percent of market value of stock held by nonresidents to 0.25 percent of market value held by any stockholder) and on telegraph companies (from 0.75 percent on market value of Connecticut property to one cent per message sent in Connecticut). Taxes were newly established on express companies (1 percent of gross charges in Connecticut) and on auctioneers (1 percent of gross sales in Connecticut).

43. Message of the Governor to the General Assembly, Public Documents of the General Assembly of Connecticut, 1865, 4–5.

44. May session, 1865, chap. 89 addressed borrowing; chaps. 43 and 96 addressed taxation.

45. *Hartford Courant*, July 15, 1865, 2.

46. Message of the Governor to the General Assembly, Public Documents of the General Assembly of Connecticut, 1864, 4. The handling of federal war claims is itself an interesting story. Details are provided in appendix 1, "Federal War Claims Recovery Process."

47. Message of the Governor to the General Assembly, Public Documents of the General Assembly of Connecticut, 1865, 3–5.

48. *Hartford Courant*, March 17, 1903, 14.

49. Hormats, *The Price of Liberty*, xiv–xv.

50. Bingham, *History of Connecticut*, 610; Message of the Governor to the General Assembly, Public Documents of the General Assembly of Connecticut, 1865, 5. Though the cumulative state debt ($10.5 million) seemed manageable in light of the continual growth in the grand list and tax measures adopted late in the war years, it declined only gradually in the postwar years, to $7.2 million in 1870 and $5.0 million in 1875. Annual Reports of the Treasurer and of the Comptroller, Public Documents of the General Assembly of Connecticut (New Haven: Safford Co., Printers, 1870; Hartford: Case, Lockwood & Co., Printers, 1875).

51. Niven, *Connecticut for the Union*, 344. The Union experienced inflation of approximately 80 percent during the war. Compare the Confederacy's Civil War inflation rate of 9,000 percent (Hormats, *The Price of Liberty*, 78).

52. The civilian side of Connecticut's financing structure—banking and insurance—contributed to and thrived during and after the war. Niven, *Connecticut for the Union*, 424–25, noted, "All financial institutions prospered during the war, particularly after 1863, when state restrictions on investment were relaxed. . . . . Though the mortgage mart became somewhat depressed due to the absence of so many potential home owners in the armed forces, savings banks were able to make up this loss by the relaxation of investment restriction at the close of 1862." See also 441–42: "Insurance had been a Hartford specialty long before 1861. . . . But it

was the war itself that elevated insurance to the status of big business and established Hartford's absolute supremacy as the center for the industry in the state and a challenger for first rank in the nation. . . . At first, the war administered a sharp setback to industry in Hartford and elsewhere. Premium revenue from the South, which accounted for a substantial share of the life insurance business and a lesser but still not insignificant part of the fire insurance business, ceased abruptly, forcing the industry to reorient its market policy. . . . By 1862, however, the insurance industry had more than made up its loss of southern business in the booming economy of the Middle West. Indeed, life insurance entered a period of spectacular growth that was to be sustained for the next twenty years."

53. Quoted in Kyle S. Sinisi, *Sacred Debts: State Civil War Claims and American Federalism, 1861–1880* (New York: Fordham University Press, 2003), 1.

54. Sinisi, *Sacred Debts*, 3–4.

55. Sinisi, *Sacred Debts*, xi; Booles, *The Financial History of the United States*, 245; *New York Times*, February 3, 1866, 8. Connecticut's potential share was approximately $17 million. This figure, however, was unrealistic in that it included types of expenses beyond those that would later be authorized for reimbursement by Congress.

56. U.S. *Statutes at Large*, vol. 12, p. 276, http://memory.loc.gov/cgi-bin/am page?collId=llsl&fileName=012/llsl012.db&recNum=307; Congressional Globe, 37th Cong., 1st sess., 253, http://memory.loc.gov/cgi-bin/ampage?collId=llcg&file Name=057/llcg057.db&recNum=270276, 362.

57. Sinisi, *Sacred Debts*, 12–13.

58. Congressional Globe, 41st Cong., 3rd sess., 551, http://memory.loc.gov/cgi -bin/ampage?collId=llcg&fileName=096/llcg096.db&recNum=566.

59. Congressional Globe, 41st Cong., 3rd sess., 550, http://memory.loc.gov/cgi -bin/ampage?collId=llcg&fileName=096/llcg096.db&recNum=565.

60. *New York Times*, August 11, 1883, 2. Curiously, though the U.S. attorney general's opinion went into great detail to confirm that there was no precedent from previous wars under which interest would be indemnified, he failed to note that in 1871 Congress considered but did not enact an amendment to address this issue. This could have been cited in support of his conclusion that in enacting the 1861 law, Congress did not intend to reimburse states for interest expense. The U.S. Supreme Court's opinion, United States v. State of New York, appears at 160 U.S. 598 (1895).

2 : Mystic Shipbuilding and the Union Navy

William Fowler writes in his book *Under Two Flags: The American Navy in the Civil War* that "without a powerful navy the North could not have won the war."[1] Vessels of all types, from gunships to transports, were needed to fortify the extensive coastal blockade and ferry Union troops to the South. The war also witnessed the advent of ironclad warships, which changed the very nature of sea warfare. Mystic, Connecticut, played an integral role in the Union's ability to fortify its navy. With the same rapid fervor that Samuel Colt, Eli Whitney, and other Connecticut arms producers turned out weapons and munitions for the Union Army, the small shipbuilding community of Mystic did likewise with gunboats and supply vessels for the Union Navy. Although the production and sale of seagoing vessels took place along the Connecticut coastline, Mystic excelled in shipbuilding, producing more ships for the navy than any other municipality in the North, with the exception of Boston.[2]

At the outbreak of Civil War, the town of Mystic had long been established as a thriving shipbuilding locality. During the war years, shipyards manufactured and sold steamer vessels to the Union government, including gunboats, supply crafts, and army transport vessels, demonstrating both dexterity in business relations with the Department of the Navy and expertise in the design and construction of ships. Mystic's ingenuity in converting existing ships to navy-worthy vessels and contracting for the production of new vessels established Connecticut as an avid and crucial contributor to the Union's commanding navy. Confidence in the construction abilities of Mystic shipyards and well-established business associations, not to mention political connections, also gained for Mystic a contract for one of the Union's first ironclad warships, the USS *Galena*.

When the Civil War started, Connecticut immediately readied itself for involvement. On April 15, 1861, Governor William Buckingham wrote to President Lincoln, expressing the state's loyalty and willingness to serve the Union. That same day Lincoln put out a call for 75,000 men, and

Buckingham called for regiments to gather at Hartford and New Haven. Historian John Niven wrote of the local response as a "rising of the people," and of how "the state was transformed overnight into a hive of military activity." Weapons production soared as new arms factories were established to supplement the existing arms industries in New Haven and Hartford.[3] This burst of manpower and industry put Connecticut at the beckoning call of the Union's needs. As with the arms industry, shipbuilding across the state responded considerably to the needs of the Union at war. When the Union government appealed for vessels to improve the navy, Mystic soon proved itself adaptable to these urgent requests.

The Union Navy at the beginning of the Civil War was unprepared for confrontation. In the "Report of the Secretary of the Navy," which updated Congress on the status of navy vessels, appropriations, and documented naval operations for the year, President Lincoln's secretary of the navy, Gideon Welles, of Glastonbury, Connecticut, attributed the navy's lack of readiness to its organization as "a peace establishment."[4] In 1865, Welles looked back on the navy's condition at the start of the war, remembering that "fifty years of peace," had diminished it to "a low standard of efficiency." He noted that the Union possessed "restricted and wholly insufficient navy yards for the construction and repair of vessels" but that "the resources of the country were equal to the emergency. . . . With only limited means at the command of the Department to begin with, the navy became suddenly an immense power."[5]

In April 1861, the Union fleet included only ninety warships, many of which were stationed in overseas ports and not immediately available for action. Other vessels were either unusable because of damage, were no longer in commission, or were of an outdated architectural model. On April 19, President Lincoln announced a plan to blockade the southern coast, but he soon expanded the blockade's range, after the Confederates captured Norfolk Navy Yard, to include the coasts of Virginia and North Carolina.[6] Though opposed to the blockade strategy, Secretary Welles ordered construction to begin on twenty-three new gunboats to enforce the blockade. He began planning as well for the purchase and construction of vessels from northern states to help implement the blockade. Owing to its long history of shipbuilding, Connecticut, in particular Mystic, had the resources the Union needed.[7]

In 1861, Mystic was a thriving shipbuilding community. William M. Peterson, author of *Mystic Built: Ships and Shipyards of the Mystic River, Connecticut, 1784–1919*, explores the history of the region's shipbuild-

Abraham Lincoln's secretary of the navy, Gideon Welles of Glastonbury, Connecticut. He served as secretary from 1861 to 1869. This portrait of Welles was created sometime between 1860 and 1870. Courtesy of Civil War Glass Negative Collection, Prints & Photographs Division, Library of Congress, LC-DIG-cwpb-04842

ing past and the factors that helped establish and maintain the industry. Noting the beginnings of shipbuilding in Mystic after the American Revolution, when the country badly required self-sufficiency in producing vessels, he then considers the sudden prosperity that Connecticut shipyards began to experience in the mid-nineteenth century as shipping demands began to overload New York shipyards. Mystic's location was highly favorable to the shipbuilding industry. Located only 125 miles from New York City on a navigable river protected by barrier islands, with an ample supply of timber, Mystic's position could not have been better.[8]

Between the 1820s and the start of the Civil War, Mystic-built ships designed for the cotton trade were part of the town's best business, and by the 1840s, the area produced ships for a number of New York shipping companies engaged in the southern cotton institution. Peterson concludes that cotton fueled the shipbuilding industry in Mystic.[9] When this source of revenue disappeared with the onset of the Civil War, Mystic shipbuilders quickly adapted by fulfilling government requests for steam vessels. Unused merchant vessels in Mystic shipyards were quickly eyed by the Department of the Navy.[10] In a general analysis of Mystic shipbuilding during the war, Peterson writes, "Mystic's fifty-seven steamers represented a full 5 percent of Northern steamships constructed during the war, and they were crucial to the war effort."[11] Over the course of the war years, shipbuilding in Mystic found itself to be one of the most prosperous and valuable businesses in Connecticut. The *Mystic Pioneer*, a local newspaper, remarked that visitors to the town "could not fail to be struck with the importance of this place as a shipbuilding and ship owning locality."[12]

There existed in Mystic three principal shipbuilding concerns—Charles Mallory & Sons, George Greenman & Company, and Maxson, Fish & Company. Each produced steam-powered vessels used in a variety of naval applications. The story of Charles Mallory strolling into town on Christmas Day in 1816 with only $1.25 in his pocket is a familiar account among the histories of the Charles Mallory & Sons shipyard. At his death in 1882, Mallory was the wealthiest man in Mystic.[13] The anecdote of these humble beginnings that transformed into successful entrepreneurship and a prominent shipbuilding company recognizes the thriving shipbuilding industry in mid-nineteenth century Mystic and the business opportunities that quickly developed in the midst of the war. In his "business biography" *The Mallorys of Mystic: Six Generations in American Maritime Enterprise*, James P. Baughman summarized the Mallorys' decision at the start of the war to build only steamers for sale to private and government entities and to make attempts to gain contracts for building naval vessels. Referring to it as the company's "wartime business strategy," Baughman remarked, "The Mallorys' enterprises had been inseparable from the Union war effort for four years." As a result, Mallory's shipyard was the most productive for the Union Navy, launching roughly one vessel every two months. So prominent were Mallory vessels that on May 31, 1862, the

Mystic Pioneer ran a list of "famous" ships produced at the Mallory yard, including the *Stars and Stripes, Varuna, Owasco, Falcon, Eagle, Haze,* and the *Bushnell*.[14] The newspaper also provided brief weekly updates of the Mallory company, reporting the launching of vessels and new contracts.

In addition to the Mallory shipyard, George Greenman & Company manufactured vessels for the Union, and, said Peterson, during the Civil War years the company "may have had the longest and most successful career as a builder of ships at Mystic." In *George Greenman & Co.: Shipbuilders of Mystic, Connecticut,* Thomas Stevens and Charles Stillman, founders of the Marine Historical Association in Mystic, classify the Greenmans as "principal builders" during the war years, along with the Mallorys. In total, the Greenmans launched eighteen steam vessels during the war years. They too were featured prominently in the *Mystic Pioneer.* Additionally, two of the Greenman ships, the *Albatross* and *New London,* both built before the start of the war, were sold for government use.[15]

The third prominent shipbuilding business in Mystic during the Civil War was the yard of Maxson, Fish & Company. The most recently established of the Mystic shipyards and owned by business partners William Ellery Maxson and Nathan G. Fish, it too experienced its best business during the conflict, producing fourteen steam vessels, including the gunboat *Vicksburg* and the first ironclad steam vessel built in the United States, the USS *Galena*.[16]

The industrial base in Mystic was not limited solely to shipbuilding itself. The vital structural components of vessels, such as engines, boilers, and other integral parts were also created in this naval hub. Mystic Iron Works, for example, was established in 1862 directly in response to the building boom created by the Civil War. The busy shipbuilding community was a natural market for the company, which produced engines for Mystic vessels as well as those built elsewhere for the Union. Charles Mallory patronized ship repair services at Mystic Iron Works as well. In addition, the company could claim more than just engines and boilers—it constructed a steam vessel in 1863, the only iron-hulled vessel to be built at Mystic. Another firm, the Reliance Machine Company, began operations in 1848 as a manufacturer of agricultural machines, such as cotton gins. With the outbreak of the war and the decline of the cotton trade, Reliance shifted production to steam engines and boilers.[17]

Vessels launched by the Mallory, Maxson, and Greenman yards that went in to naval service took on various types of roles for the Union Navy. The gunboats *Galena* and *Vicksburg*, built by the Maxson yard, were de-

A drawing by artist Alfred Waud of the Albatross, *built prior to the start of the war by George Greenman & Company and sold to the U.S. Navy for conversion to a gunboat. The writing on the drawing reads: N.B. 'The "Penguin" is precisely like 'the "Albatross." Courtesy of Morgan Collection of Civil War Drawings, Prints & Photographs Division, Library of Congress, LC-DIG-ppmsca-20329*

A deck scene onboard the ironclad USS Galena. *There is a large hole in the smoke stack, a result of Confederate cannon fire. Courtesy of Selected Civil War Photographs Collection, Prints & Photographs Division, Library of Congress, LC-DIG-ppmsca-19335*

signed as warships, as were the Greenman steamers, *Albatross* and *New London*, which were converted into gunboats by the navy. The Mallory yard sent to the navy the gunboats *Owasco*, *Stars and Stripes*, and *Varuna*, which gained the most attention during the war. Each shipyard also provided vessels that served as transport and supply ships. In 1861 alone, the Greenmans produced three steam transports for the navy. The Maxson, Fish & Company steamer *Nightingale* acted as a naval supply ship in the Gulf of Mexico, while the clipper ship *B. F. Hoxie* was captured and burned in 1862, its property loss being the heaviest that Mystic experienced during the war.[18]

The weekly *Mystic Pioneer* provided detailed coverage of the shipbuilding scene in Mystic during the war, explaining the progress of ship construction, launch information, and the roles vessels had in the war. A weekly "List of Vessels," or "Memoranda of Mystic Vessels," gave brief status updates on Mystic-owned vessels or those captained by Mystic men. In August 1861, the newspaper reported that a number of propellers were being built in the town and even published special reports on the history of various shipyards. Notice of launches and new contracts also frequently spotted the pages, though the only real detail given was reserved generally for those from government contracts, such as the *Varuna* and *Owasco*.[19] Still, from the coverage provided by the *Mystic Pioneer*, it is clear that the "big three" shipyards in the town were constantly building.

All of this shipbuilding, however, took time. As with armaments and munitions for the Union Army, production of naval ships by shipyards like those in Mystic did not get into full production at the immediate outset of the war. Yet the Union's need for a strong naval response to the beginning of the rebellion remained strong. In the first months of the war, Secretary Welles found himself in the position of rapidly increasing a scant supply of armed vessels. He wrote, "the necessity of an augmentation of our Navy, in order to meet the crisis, and assist in causing the laws to be executed at all ports, was immediately felt."[20] Richard S. West's biography on Gideon Welles characterizes the purchasing and chartering of vessels as Welles's "greatest single task," and one he moved quickly to accomplish.[21]

Acting as purchasing agent for merchant vessels was George D. Morgan, a New York merchant and also Welles's brother-in-law. His instructions were to purchase vessels that could easily be converted for blockade duty. Welles wrote in the 1861 "Report of the Secretary of the Navy" of his directives to "purchase or charter, arm, equip, and man steamers which, upon examination, might be found fit, or easily convertible into armed vessels suitable for the public service."[22] Morgan's first purchase for the navy was the *Varuna* in the spring of 1861, built by Charles Mallory & Sons. John Niven recounts in *Connecticut for the Union* the somewhat desperate steps taken by the government to procure ships for naval service that were not particularly built for such tasks. The *Varuna*, for instance, was constructed in 1861 for passenger and freight uses, but after government purchase it was armed with overweight weapons. The urgent need of the navy for warships frequently warranted these unfit conversions at the start of the war.[23]

Also authorized to purchase and charter for the navy was New Haven businessman Cornelius S. Bushnell, who had gained success as a railroad magnate and in 1861 founded the New Haven Propeller Company. Welles and Bushnell had been business associates before Welles became part of Lincoln's cabinet. Although W. A. Croffut and John Morris proclaim in their study of Connecticut in the immediate aftermath of the war that Bushnell was "an enterprising and public-spirited citizen of New Haven," historian John Niven expresses a more negative view, questioning the respectability of his business dealings.[24] Niven's opinion stems in part from Bushnell's method of acquiring the newly built vessel *Stars and Stripes* from the Mallory shipyard. Whereas Mystic historian William Peterson writes indifferently that Bushnell purchased the steamer from Charles Mallory & Sons for $35,000 for the New Haven Propeller Company, and leased it to the navy for $15,000 for two months before selling it to the government for $55,000, Niven adds that Bushnell had acquired for himself a $10,000 commission, in addition to the leasing and sales revenue, for the purchase.[25] Whatever the ethics of such a deal, it did not deter Welles from future dealings with Bushnell.

While officers and agents traveled throughout the northern states to negotiate for the lease and purchase of vessels, Welles prepared for the construction of ships as well. In charge of designing a blockade fleet of steamer gunboats was John Lenthall, naval architect for the Department of the Navy, and Benjamin Isherwood, engineer in chief. Twenty-three gunboats were planned for construction at various shipyards, and nicknamed ninety-day gunboats for the quick turnaround time expected for their construction.[26] A contract for one of these vessels was awarded to Mystic's Maxson, Fish & Company, though not without significant confusion over its assignment. William Maxson's frustration was apparent, and he noted his continued waiting to hear "whether I get a gunboat to build or not."[27] Though the contract for one of the ninety-day gunboats was granted to the Maxson shipyard, it was soon after subcontracted to the Mallory company for construction. The *Mystic Pioneer* reported, "We are informed that a contract for one of the Gun-boats has been awarded to Messrs. Maxson, Fish & Co., of this place, and that it will be constructed in the yard of Charles Mallory, Esq."[28]

Maxson explained the reasoning for the subcontracting in his diary: "We get it being obligated to transfer the contract to Mr. Mallory his having (proposals) been withdrawn being lower than ours so to get a higher price it being determined that there was to be but one built in Mystic."[29] Jeffrey Remling writes in "Patterns of Procurement and Politics: Building Ships in the Civil War" that because the Department of the Navy was willing to grant only one contract to the town of Mystic, Horace Bushnell may have suggested a plan by which both of the Mystic yards could reap a profit; that the Maxson yard subcontract its $53,000 government contract to the Mallory yard for $50,000 (Mallory's original government bid was $47,000), gaining Maxson $3,000 for little more than transferring the contract. At the same time, two shipyards would accumulate revenue for Mystic. Remling suggests that Bushnell may have asked for $1,500 for brokering the deal between the two shipyards, though evidence for that is not definite.[30] Considering Bushnell's business practices in the lease, sale, and commission of the *Stars and Stripes*, it is certainly plausible that he wrote in a reward for himself in negotiating a contract. The gunboat under construction at the Mallory yard was the *Owasco*. The *Mystic Pioneer* reported the progress on its construction, noting across three weekly issues the building of a "government gun boat," a large work force of one hundred men, and the boat's launching, with a highly detailed story on the details and specifications for the ship.[31]

The business dealing with Bushnell for the *Owasco* was an important precursor to another significant role that Mystic shipyards played in naval construction during the Civil War—the construction of an ironclad warship. The uss *Galena*, built by the Maxson, Fish Company, was among the first such vessels. Though a total failure as a warship and ultimately stripped of its armor plating, the *Galena* nonetheless represented a new technological innovation in naval construction—one that changed the nature of war on the seas forever. The need for a formidable Union warship came when the prized frigate uss *Merrimac* fell into Confederate hands when they overtook the Norfolk Navy Yard in Virginia in April 1861.

Secretary Welles faced the daunting task of matching an imminent threat that was now being constructed under the direction of the Confederate Secretary of the Navy Stephen Mallory. Interestingly, Stephen was a cousin of Charles Mallory and had at the outset of the war sent a letter asking if Charles could provide "any light draft strong fast ship of this design (a screw ship) for sale," or "a first rate ship carpenter." Charles responded that he would remain "strictly legitimate and above board" and that he hoped for a peaceable settlement as opposed to the horror of "a collision between the two sections of my beloved country."[32] Obviously, once war began in earnest, Charles lent his efforts and that of his company to the Union. His cousin Stephen knew the Confederate States Navy could not match the Union without a formidable weapon, in the form of an ironclad warship. Writing to the Confederate chairman of the House Committee on Naval Affairs, Mallory announced, "I regard the possession of an iron-armored ship as a matter of the first necessity. Such a vessel at this time could traverse the entire coast of the United States, prevent all blockades, and encounter, with fair prospect of success, their entire Navy."[33] With this goal in mind, the captured USS *Merrimac* was being transformed into the CSS *Virginia*.

Originally, Secretary Welles had little interest in building ironclad vessels for the navy, but upon learning that the Confederacy's ironclad was in progress, he promptly changed his mind.[34] Welles himself drafted a bill asking Congress to grant funding for an ironclad construction program. In the meantime, he relied greatly on Bushnell to lobby Congress in favor of the project, and on July 19, 1861, the Senate introduced the bill "to provide for the construction of one or more armored ships and floating batteries, and for other purposes." It authorized Secretary Welles to appoint an Ironclad Board—three naval officers who would be tasked with reviewing plans for various ironclad gunboat designs.[35] The bill appropriated $1.5 million for the project, and on August 4, 1861, President Lincoln signed it into law. No time was wasted in gathering submissions for ironclad designs. Three days later, the Department of the Navy published an advertisement requesting bids for "the construction of one or more iron-clad steam vessels of war, either of iron or of wood and iron combined, for sea or river service."[36]

Welles's Ironclad Board reviewed the submissions and provided recommendations on September 16. Once again, Bushnell's perhaps questionable business practices resulted in opportunities and profit for Mystic. Not only did he lobby for the bill, but he also submitted a design for an ironclad vessel and was granted one of the contracts.[37] In "Mystic River Builds an Ironclad," James Christley writes that Welles had difficulty at first convincing senior officers of the need for an ironclad, and therefore approached Bushnell to lobby on behalf of the project. Bushnell also approached naval architect Samuel H. Pook of Boston and iron manufacturers in Troy, New York, about designing an ironclad warship.[38] It is likely that these communications with Pook took place during the time that Bushnell was lobbying for the ironclad bill, before the bill had been passed, and that Bushnell had a design ready for submittal to the Ironclad Board before the advertisement for ironclad designs was even made public.[39] Mention of an ironclad vessel in a June diary entry from William Maxson further supports the idea that Bushnell's design was in progress before President Lincoln had signed the ironclad bill.[40] It is reasonable to assume that Bushnell was expecting to be granted a contract. His communications with Mystic shipbuilders in the months before the ironclad bill was approved regarding the contract support this assumption. Equally interesting, prior to the awarding of any contracts, Bushnell had contacted John Ericsson, a respected inventor and mechanical engineer, and presented his design for the ironclad ship, asking Ericsson if the wooden vessel would support the iron plating. Bushnell, in turn, presented to Secretary Welles Ericsson's own design for an ironclad. It ultimately became the famous uss *Monitor*.[41]

Bushnell's first attempt to build the ironclad in Mystic was directed at Charles Mallory. In June, prior to the approval of congressional appropriations, Bushnell asked Mallory for a price on an "Iron cased gun boat." Mallory demurred at the new idea for iron plating, responding that he would be happy to build another gunboat similar to the *Owasco*.[42] Always a businessman, Bushnell also approached the Maxson yard in June. His dealings with the company had begun several years earlier, in 1858, when Bushnell acquired ownership of a financially unsettled railroad company. He arranged for a rail line to run directly through the Maxson work yard and allowed the ship company to operate the local station.[43] On the same day that he commented on the subcontracting of the *Owasco* contract, William Maxson wrote, "We are requested to give a price for building another class of Gun Boat to be plated and shot proof got up by Mr. Bushnell of New Haven and another man." Bushnell may have, in part, been attempting to appease Maxon for giving up the contract for the *Owasco* to Mallory, by requesting the quote for the ironclad. Maxson continued his entry, "We feel rather bad to have to give up the contract," referring to the *Owasco*. Whatever Bushnell's reasoning, the offer to Maxon proved fruitful. Baughman noted that when the time came to officially delegate the contract, the Maxson yard not only had a better understanding of the ironclad design but also, when it received the contract in August 1861, the company had no other vessels under construction and could therefore begin the project immediately.[44]

On August 19, both William Maxson and Nathan Fish noted in their diaries that Bushnell had approached them about a quote for an ironclad gunboat.[45] The following day, Maxson wrote, "Mr. Bushnell made a conditional contract to build the vessel." Fish added in his diary in regard to the contract, "We expect to decide tomorrow." On August 22, 1861, Maxson officially signed on to build the ironclad for Bushnell and the Union Navy.[46] Ever the enterprising entrepreneur, Bushnell assured big profits for himself. The government contract awarded $235,250, yet Maxson, Fish & Company built the vessel for a mere $65,000.[47]

The *Mystic Pioneer* reported on September 7, 1861, that Maxson, Fish & Company had secured a contract with the government to build "an ironclad bomb-proof steamer." Local and regional publications followed construction of the vessel through its launch in early 1862. By September 21, 1861, the *Mystic Pioneer* reported that one hundred men were employed at the shipyard. Reporters visited the site on October 19 to observe the progress and made a variety of interesting observations. They compared the new iron-plated vessel with past innovative naval designs, reminding readers that the screw propeller had at first been mocked and suggesting that the same was happening to the ironclad. Yet the paper also hedged its bets, telling readers, "It would not be well to expect too much from any efforts which may be made in advance. . . . Armor ships (for war steamers) are decidedly a step in advance."[48]

Historian Carl Cutler writes, "While under construction the *Galena* was an object of intense interest to the community and to the country in general. . . . [It was] condemned or praised according to the predilection of the observer."[49] Opinions on the design of the ship and how it would perform in naval combat were mixed. The well-respected *Scientific American* published numerous positive articles during the vessel's construction and launch period, providing accounts of the design and specifications. Before the vessel ever hit the water, the magazine wrote, "We really believe it will be the most novel craft that was ever sent forth upon American waters."[50] After the launch in February 1862, the journal again praised its innovation: "Such is the peculiar construction of the vessel, however, with her beautiful rounded stern, sharp bow and convex sides, that this thickness will be amply sufficient to sustain the shock of the heaviest projectiles without injury." Two weeks later it wrote, "We have little doubt that she will prove a very efficient and serviceable vessel of war." *Harper's Weekly* was not as excited about the new vessel but did note the "special service" the Mystic ironclad would provide for the navy.[51]

The USS *Galena* was launched February 14, 1862, with the ceremony attended by between 1,000 and 2,000 area residents from Mystic, Norwich, New London, Stonington, and Westerly, Rhode Island. The *Mystic Pioneer* applauded Maxson, Fish & Company, saying, "The whole work in detail gives evidence of an earnest endeavor to do justice to the government." The paper also noted that the vessel "floats like a duck and must give satisfaction to Uncle Sam's naval agents."[52] An important note, however, is that Maxson was concerned enough about the ship's stability at the launch that its full armor was not installed until the vessel arrived at the Continental Works shipyard in New York, where it would also receive two boilers. On April 21, 1862, the *Galena* was commissioned and ready for war.[53]

From early on, there were many who expressed concerns over the *Galena*'s seaworthiness and ability in combat. After visiting the vessel in April shortly after its commissioning, Flag Officer Louis Goldsborough of the North Atlantic Blockading Squadron felt strongly that the gunboat was "a most miserable contrivance—entirely beneath Naval criticism." He added, "She is a sad affair. Her projectors & builders ought to be ashamed of her."[54] Commander John Rodgers, who led the *Galena* on its first major naval operation, also had his doubts, writing, "I do not think she fully comes up to the idea of an iron-plated craft," but also noted "she is very much safer than an ordinary vessel."[55] Historian Carl Cutler wrote that the significance of the *Galena* for Connecticut lay in the fact that "one of our smallest seaports was chosen to build a new, revolutionary, and critically important vessel."[56]

The controversial *Galena* was prepared for service after its commissioning in April 1862. General George McClellan awaited the ship's arrival to assist his movement to Yorktown, Virginia, writing on April 23, 1862, "I expect great aid from the Galena."[57] He did not, however, receive any aid from the *Galena*; it was standing guard at Hampton Roads while the CSS *Virginia* was on the hunt for the USS *Monitor*.[58] In early May, Commander Rodgers convinced President Lincoln to let him lead the *Galena*, *Monitor*, and a number of wooden war vessels up the James River to cut off Confederate supply ships.[59] The mission led him to Drewry's Bluff, where the *Galena* engaged in its first battle, and a Confederate artillery battery that sealed the *Galena*'s fate as a failed ironclad. In a letter to Flag Officer Goldsborough, Rodgers reported the unsuccessful operation that

The uss Galena *and its crew after receiving damage from Confederate shots.*
Courtesy of Civil War Glass Negative Collection, Prints & Photographs Division,
Library of Congress, lc-dig-cwpbh-00826

took place on May 15 involving the *Galena*, stating that the ironclad was unable to defend itself and that by late morning 13 men were killed and 11 wounded. He wrote, "We demonstrated she is not shot-proof. Balls came through, and many men were killed with fragments of her own iron."[60] Rodgers is often criticized for the physical position in which he placed the *Galena*. Historian James Christley noted the commander's "tactical blunder" and explained, "The armor so carefully applied in the Maxson & Fish yard was subjected to punishment for which it was never intended. . . . The ship did not fail people, people failed the ship."[61]

William Maxson had followed the path of his gunboat after it left his yard, writing in his diary, "The Galena has gone up the James River," and

"The Galena silenced the two forts or batteries at the mouth of the James River with 12 guns in a ½ day without harm to herself." When news of the failed Drewry's Bluff operation reached Mystic, Maxson made note of it then ceased to make any further mention of the *Galena*.[62] The *Mystic Pioneer* similarly never made mention of the vessel again. Still, the USS *Galena* was not yet finished with the Union Navy. Although it failed as an ironclad, there was still hope that it could perform as a wooden warship. The *Galena* stayed on the James River in ironclad form until early 1863 as part of the North Atlantic Blockading Squadron, providing sporadic support for McClellan's peninsular campaign. In 1863, its armor was stripped, and the *Galena* finished out the war as a wooden gunboat, performing nobly in 1864 as part of Admiral Farragut's battle for Mobile Bay as a guardian vessel for the USS *Oneida*.[63] On the morning of August 5, the *Oneida* and *Galena* were engaged in battle, and when the *Oneida* became damaged and an explosion made it unable to respond, the *Galena* stepped in to assist, providing not only firepower but also medical assistance from its surgeon. According to Lieutenant Charles Huntington of the *Oneida*, "the safety of the ship after the explosion depended upon the Galena." The *New York Times* reported the ship's service, but though the *Mystic Pioneer* in the weeks following the operation at Mobile Bay reported on eight ironclads, it made no mention of the *Galena*.[64]

Other Mystic-built vessels fared much better than the *Galena*, gaining national recognition and signifying the strength and versatility of the town's built ships. The *Varuna*, which in mid-1861 was at the center of purchasing agent George Morgan and Cornelius Bushnell's business transaction with the Mallory shipyard, participated valiantly in the capture of New Orleans in April 1862 and gained for itself a place in what might be called folklore of Mystic shipbuilding. Published first in the *Philadelphia Press* and republished by the *Mystic Pioneer*, press reports announced, "Who has not heard of the dauntless *Varuna*? Who has not heard of the deeds she has done?"[65] The vessel's first major assignment was to escort the *Monitor* to Hampton Roads and replace the frigate *Congress*, though when the *Varuna* arrived, the *Congress* had already been destroyed by the *Virginia*.[66]

In the battle for New Orleans, the *Varuna* is best known for its service in sinking six Confederate gunboats before itself being damaged in battle and sunk on April 24, 1862.[67] After six days of battle, the Union squadron underwent intense fire from Confederate vessels as it moved up the Mississippi River, but it succeeded in destroying eighteen enemy vessels, six of which were attributed to the *Varuna*. Secretary Welles wrote that the capture of New Orleans was "an undertaking of the greatest difficulty and of the greatest importance. The city itself was the largest and wealthiest in the southern portion of the Union, and from its position it was the most vitally interesting in the whole insurrectionary region."[68]

Nor did the *Varuna*'s accomplishments go unnoticed by Welles. In a letter written by Welles and published in the *Hartford Daily Courant* to Honorable E. B. Washburne, Chairman of the Committee on Government Contracts, Welles wrote of the "gallant 'vessel Varuna,'" and the "great victory in which she bore so conspicuous a part." He continued, "After rendering service never surpassed, perhaps, by any vessel of her capacity afloat, and sinking six of the enemy's steamers—two of which were iron clad— was herself finally borne down and now lies buried beneath the waters of the Mississippi." Welles continued that, without doubt, "the public have a patriotic feeling in all that concerns that extraordinary vessel." Published alongside Welles's letter was a letter from the *Varuna*'s commander: "Her model for speed and all the qualities necessary for a sea-steamer I have never seen surpassed, having proved the fastest vessel of the fleet. . . . I consider that she was among the best of the additions to the navy from the merchant marine."[69]

The *Mystic Pioneer* mentioned only that the gunboat sank when it was fighting "rebels," but noted that the vessel's boilers came from the Reliance Machine Company in Mystic. Cutler wrote in regard to the capture of New Orleans and the *Varuna*'s accomplishments, "Altogether the episode of the *Varuna* constituted one of the pluckiest and most spectacular naval contests of the war. The news of the action was received with marked enthusiasm throughout the North."[70] From the correspondence that took place regarding the *Varuna*'s final naval engagement, it becomes clear that the gunboat was vital to the capture of New Orleans, a feat that Secretary Welles commended. It is also feasible to speculate that had the *Varuna* not been present to defeat the six Confederate steamers that it did, the city might not have been taken by the Union. Also impressive is the fact that the *Varuna* accomplished these feats as a commercial steam vessel that had been improvised into a naval gunboat early in the war. Of all the vessels produced by Mystic for the Navy, it can be argued that the *Varuna* was one of the most successful and effective.

Stars and Stripes, the other gunboat at the center of Bushnell's business dealings with the Mallory shipyard, found action off the coast of the

Carolinas as part of the Union blockade in the North Atlantic Blockading Squadron. Over the course of a little more than one month, the gunboat was involved in the amphibious attacks on both Roanoke Island and Newbern, North Carolina.[71] The amphibious operation against Roanoke Island commenced on February 5, 1862, with the approach to the island, and on the morning of February 7 the actual battle began. By midnight, 10,000 Union Army troops had landed on Roanoke Island in a successful operation of the navy and army. *Stars and Stripes* again participated in an amphibious operation from March 12 through March 14, when a naval battle opened a route for troops to land on the shores of Newbern. Both operations were successful; Admiral David D. Porter wrote in his *Naval History of the Civil War*, "History will show that, throughout the war, whenever the Army and Navy cooperated harmoniously success followed."[72]

Stars and Stripes did not play as significant a role as the *Varuna* in New Orleans and did not get the written praise allotted to the *Varuna*, but after the amphibious battle it was tasked with traveling to Fort Monroe in Virginia to deliver communications from Flag Officer Goldsborough and to bring back ammunition to Roanoke Island.[73] The gunboat did receive some minor consideration from the *Hartford Daily Courant* on its excursion to Fort Monroe and back to Roanoke, and the *Mystic Pioneer* reported on the operation at Roanoke but did not mention the *Stars and Stripes* by name. At the end of May, the paper did include the gunboat in a list of "famous" vessels from Mystic.[74]

The George Greenman & Company shipyard also produced a successful gunboat that saw action on the Mississippi River in 1863. Sold to the Union Navy on March 23, 1861, it was armed at the New York Navy Yard and sent into duty. On March 12, 1863, the USS *Albatross*, as part of Admiral Farragut's squadron, partnered with the admiral's ship, the USS *Hartford*, in an advance past Port Hudson toward the Red River. In battle in front of Port Hudson, the *Albatross* returned fire and made it through the conflict, joining the blockade of the Red River and preventing supplies for Confederate vessels and troops from leaving the area. One month later, as the *Albatross* moved up the Red River with accompanying vessels, it engaged several Confederate vessels found stripping ordnance from a sunken Union ship. The *Albatross* initiated the engagement and suffered extensive damage.[75] Though there was no local mention of the gunboat in the newspapers from its home port, the *Albatross*'s part in Farragut's campaign, particularly in its position as a sort of guardian for Farragut's own vessel, demonstrates once more the varying roles with which Mystic vessels were challenged.[76]

The other steamer gunboat produced by the Greenman shipyard, the USS *New London*, was sold to the government in 1861 and was stationed as part of the Gulf Squadron, where it became known for capturing a number of Confederate vessels. In mid-January 1862, both the *New York Times* and the *Hartford Daily Courant* reported that the *New London* had pursued a number of Confederate vessels and captured three. It was also responsible for capturing twelve Confederate sloops in Mississippi, all of which were suspected blockade runners. In 1863, it was transferred to the West Gulf Squadron under Admiral Farragut. The gunboat was attacked in July 1863 while traveling to announce the surrender of Port Hudson on the Mississippi River. As a result of the attack, the *New London* was engulfed in steam and grounded, and it had to be towed while still under fire.[77]

Another gunboat that gained the attention of the Mystic locals was launched from the Maxson, Fish, and Company yard in August 1863. The *Vicksburg* was requested via government contract for blockade duty. On May 2, 1863, the *Mystic Pioneer* reported, "Maxson Fish & Co. have contracted to build a first class steamer for parties of this place. Her engine and boiler are to be built at the Mystic Iron Works." Though there is no mention of the gunboat's name, it can be assumed this report is in reference to the *Vicksburg*, when compared to the vessel's launch date of August 27. After the launch, the *Mystic Pioneer* complimented the ship's design: "Judging from appearance [the *Vicksburg*] will probably be one of the fastest gunboats in the United States service." It was commissioned on December 12, 1863, and sailed from New York in February 1864, serving through the end of the war.[78]

One of the earliest Mystic gunboats, the *Owasco*, was active for virtually the entire war. Purchased from the Mallorys in mid-1861, the majority of its time was spent in the Gulf of Mexico. It was known to have captured and destroyed several blockade runners, and on October 4, 1862, along with a several other Union vessels, it captured the harbor and city of Galveston, Texas, with little resistance.[79] Despite the controversy that surrounded the contract for its construction, the *Owasco* turned out to be a worthy venture for the Department of the Navy.

The story of the Union Navy often gets second billing when it comes to Civil War history. The massive army and bloody land battles that scarred the countryside remain foremost in many people's minds. Yet the ability of the Union Army to engage in tactical operations required a significant, formidable naval presence. From the extensive coastal blockade, to ferrying soldiers and supplies, to the very important role naval vessels played in destroying Confederate-occupied forts, taking southern cities, and controlling the Mississippi, seagoing warships were instrumental to winning the war. Few cities throughout the Union contributed more to that effort than Mystic, Connecticut. Historians Thomas Stevens and Charles Stillman wrote that "during the Civil War period, 1861–1865, Mystic became one of the most important shipbuilding centers of the country."[80]

Mystic led the state in supplying the navy with some fifty-seven steam vessels for the Union war effort. A combination of smart business dealings and a tremendous aptitude for ship design and construction led Mystic to be a frontrunner in producing these vessels. When the community was selected as the construction location for the first seaworthy ironclad vessel to be built in the country, Mystic's versatility and ingenuity in the shipbuilding domain was immediately acknowledged. From the Mallory Company, to Maxon, Fish, to the Greenman shipyards, as well as the many shipbuilding-related companies that existed in the area, Mystic proved, along with the various firearm companies such as Colt, Sharps, and many others, that Connecticut was indeed an arsenal for the Union.

NOTES

1. William M. Fowler, Jr., *Under Two Flags: The American Navy in the Civil War* (New York: W. W. Norton, 1990), 10.

2. John Niven, *Connecticut for the Union: The Role of the State in the Civil War* (New Haven, CT: Yale University Press, 1965), 353, 391. Ships for the Union Navy were produced in localities such as East Haddam, Fair Haven, and Norwich.

3. William A. Buckingham to Abraham Lincoln, April 15, 1861, in The Abraham Lincoln Papers at the Library of Congress, http://lcweb2.loc.gov/cgi-bin/query /r?ammem/mal:@field(DOCID+@lit(d0908800); Samuel G. Buckingham, *The Life of William A. Buckingham: War Governor of Connecticut* (Springfield, CT: W. F. Adams Co., 1894), 128–29; Niven, *Connecticut for the Union*, 47, 353–54.

4. U.S. Department of the Navy, "Report of the Secretary of the Navy, July 4, 1861," in Appendix to the Congressional Globe, 37th Cong., 1st sess., 7. http://memory .loc.gov/cgi-bin/ampage?collId=llcg&fileName=057/llcg057.db&recNum=500. Hereafter referred to as "Report of the Secretary of the Navy, July 1861."

5. U.S. Department of the Navy, "Report of the Secretary of the Navy with an Appendix Containing Reports from Officers" (Washington, DC: Government Printing Office, 1865), xii. Hereafter referred to as "Report of the Secretary of the Navy, 1865."

6. Bruce Catton, *The Civil War* (1960; repr., New York: Mariner Books, 2004), 69–70; Stephen Howarth, *To Shining Sea: A History of the United States Navy,*

1775–1991 (New York: Random House, 1991), 182–83. For Welles's detailed description of the types of vessels available as of March 9, 1861, and the problems with the vessels that made them unfit, see "Report of the Secretary of the Navy, July 1861."

7. John Niven, *Gideon Welles: Lincoln's Secretary of the Navy* (New York: Oxford University Press, 1973), 356–57, 359. Secretary Welles's concern over the blockade rested on the fact it would encourage foreign nations to recognize the Confederacy with belligerent privileges. Welles favored closing ports in the Confederate states to enable Union officials to seize vessels entering those ports. Regarding the Blockade Proclamation and Welles's doubts, see also Howarth, *To Shining Sea*, 183; and Richard S. West, Jr., *Gideon Welles: Lincoln's Navy Department* (New York: Bobbs-Merrill, 1943), 117. For more on Welles's plans to accumulate vessels for the navy, see Fowler, *Under Two Flags*, 51; Howarth, *To Shining Sea*, 185; and "Report of the Secretary of the Navy, July 1861." For a brief, yet inclusive, history of the Mystic shipyards, see also Carl C. Cutler, *Mystic: The Story of a Small New England Seaport* (Mystic, CT: Marine Historical Association, 1945).

8. William N. Peterson, *Mystic Built: Ships and Shipyards of the Mystic River, Connecticut, 1784–1919* (Mystic, CT: Mystic Seaport Museum, 1989), 1, 5, 13.

9. Peterson, *Mystic Built*, 5–6.

10. Fowler, *Under Two Flags*, 51. See also Howarth, *To Shining Sea*, 185–86; and Niven, *Connecticut for the Union*, 388. Connecticut's use of steam before the war included steam vessels for trade and commercial purposes, but the need for steam vessels for the navy prompted many steam vessel owners to sell to the government, leading the trade business to rely on the older technology of schooners and sloops.

11. Peterson, *Mystic Built*, 8.

12. *Mystic Pioneer*, August 24, 1861.

13. Peterson, *Mystic Built*, 47. The story of Charles Mallory's humble beginnings is also told by Cutler, *Mystic*, 145; and James P. Baughman, *Mallorys of Mystic: Six Generations in American Maritime Enterprise* (Middletown, CT: Wesleyan University Press, 1972), 100.

14. Baughman, *Mallorys of Mystic*, 106, 122; Peterson, *Mystic Built*, 48; *Mystic Pioneer*, May 31, 1862. For an in-depth study of the Mallory family's involvement in selling vessels to the government during the war, see Jeffrey Remling, "The Procurement of Vessels by the United States Military during the American Civil War as an Output of Fiscal Policy: The Mallory Family, A Case Study," Manuscripts Division, G. W. Blunt White Library, Mystic Seaport Museum, Mystic, CT. Remling's study focuses only on dealings within Connecticut and does not involve the use of the vessels during the war. It is useful for gaining a general sense of how the Mallory family conducted business regarding vessels for the Department of the Navy.

15. Peterson, *Mystic Built*, 3; Thomas A. Stevens and Charles K. Stillman, *George Greenman & Co.: Shipbuilders of Mystic, Connecticut* (Mystic, CT: Marine Historical Association, 1938), 21; Peterson, *Mystic Built*, 38.

16. Peterson, *Mystic Built*, 56–57.

17. Peterson, *Mystic Built*, 60; Carl C. Cutler, "History by Carl C. Cutler," Mallory Family Papers, coll. 5, Manuscripts Division, G. W. Blunt White Library, Mystic Seaport Museum, Mystic, CT.

18. Peterson, *Mystic Built*, 38, 48, 57; Stevens and Stillman, *George Greenman & Co.*, 19; Peterson, *Mystic Built*, 168; "History of Maxson, Fish & Co. Shipbuilders," Manuscripts Collection, RF 238, G. W. Blunt White Library, Mystic Seaport Museum, Mystic, CT. *Owasco* was built as a gunboat, whereas the *Stars and Stripes* and the *Varuna* were converted into gunboats by the navy. The *Greenman's Blackstone* was the first and largest transport vessel built for the navy, in 1861.

19. *Mystic Pioneer*, 1861–1865.

20. U.S. Department of the Navy, "Report of the Secretary of the Navy, July 1861," 8.

21. West, *Gideon Welles*, 120.

22. U.S. Department of the Navy, "Report of the Secretary of the Navy, July 1861," 8.

23. Niven, *Gideon Welles*, 362; Niven, *Connecticut for the Union*, 389.

24. W. A. Croffut and John M. Morris, *Military and Civil History of Connecticut during the War of 1861–1865* (New York: Ledyard Bill, 1868), 190; Niven, *Connecticut for the Union*, 392.

25. Peterson, *Mystic Built*, 232; Niven, *Connecticut for the Union*, 392–93. Niven lists the purchase price for the *Stars and Stripes* from the Mallory shipyard as $36,000, with a monthly leasing profit of $8,200. Bushnell was later questioned by a government committee investigating government contracts, pertaining to his $10,000 commission for the sale of the *Stars and Stripes*, and also a $25,000 commission he received from the sale of the *Varuna*, which he owned together with the Mallorys, and for which he brokered the sale between purchasing agent George D. Morgan and the Charles Mallory & Sons.

26. Niven, *Gideon Welles*, 359; Fowler, *Under Two Flags*, 53.

27. Diary of William Ellery Maxson, June 12, 1861, coll. 166, Manuscripts Division, G. W. Blunt White Library, Mystic Seaport Museum, Mystic, CT.

28. *Mystic Pioneer*, June 29, 1861.

29. Diary of William Ellery Maxson, June 24, 1861.

30. Jeffrey Remling, "Patterns of Procurement and Politics: Building Ships in the Civil War," *Northern Mariner: Journal of the Canadian Nautical Research Society* 17 (January 2008): 21–22.

31. *Mystic Pioneer*, August 21, September 21, and October 5, 1861.

32. Mallory Family Papers, G. W. Blunt Library, Mystic Seaport Museum; also in James Baughman, *The Mallorys of Mystic* (Middletown, CT: Wesleyan University Press, 1972), 105.

33. Steven Mallory to Charles M. Conrad, May 10, 1861, quoted in Fowler, *Under Two Flags*, 45.

34. Niven, *Gideon Welles*, 364.

35. Niven, *Gideon Welles*, 365; "A Bill to provide for the construction of one or more armored ships and floating batteries, and for other purposes," S. 36,

37th Cong., 1st sess., in *A Century of Lawmaking for a New Nation: U.S. Congressional Documents and Debates, 1774–1875: Bills and Resolutions* (June 19, 1861), http://memory.loc.gov/cgi-bin/ampage?collId=llsb&fileName=037/llsb037 .db&recNum=203.

36. U.S. Department of the Navy, "Report of the Secretary of the Navy in Relation to Armored Vessels" (Washington, DC: Government Printing Office, 1864), 2. (Within the 1864 report are reprinted passages from the earlier 1861 report. This quotation originally appeared in the 1861 report but was reprinted in the 1864 report.)

37. U.S. Navy Department, "Report of the Secretary of the Navy in Relation to Armored Vessels," 3, 5–6. The other two contracts were given to John Ericsson, for his design of the USS *Monitor*, and to Merrick & Sons of Philadelphia, who would construct the USS *New Ironsides*. For a careful analysis of Gideon Welles's new ironclad program and Bushnell's involvement, see also James Phinney Baxter, *The Introduction of the Ironclad Warship* (1933; repr., Boston: Archon Books, 1968), 238–84.

38. James L. Christley, "Mystic River Builds an Ironclad," *Log of Mystic Seaport* 32.4 (1981): 130. Pook was a well-respected architect of clipper ships during the previous years, and the Troy, New York, ironworks company of Corning and Winslow worked with Bushnell when he was expanding his railroad business through Mystic.

39. The advertisement requesting designs and specifications for "iron-clad steam vessels" was published by the Department of the Navy on August 7, 1861, and run by publications such as *Scientific American*, August 24, 1861, and the *New York Times*, August 15, 1861.

40. Diary of William Ellery Maxson, June 24, 1861.

41. Christley, "Mystic River Builds an Ironclad," 130.

42. Baughman, *Mallorys of Mystic*, 111.

43. Remling, "Patterns of Procurement and Politics," 18.

44. Diary of William Ellery Maxson, June 24, 1861; Baughman, *Mallorys of Mystic*, 112; *Mystic Pioneer*, August 24, 1861.

45. Diary of William Ellery Maxson, August 19, 1861; Diary of Nathan G. Fish, August 19, 1861, coll. 252, Manuscripts Division, G. W. Blunt Library, Mystic Seaport Museum, Mystic, CT.

46. Diary of William Ellery Maxson, August 20, 1861; Diary of Nathan G. Fish, August 20, 1861; Diary of William Ellery Maxson, August 22, 1861.

47. U.S. Department of the Navy, "Report of the Secretary Navy in Relation to Armored Vessels," 7; Diary of William Ellery Maxson, September 16, 1861.

48. *Mystic Pioneer*, September 7, 21, and October 19, 1861.

49. Cutler, "History by Carl C. Cutler," 140.

50. "The New Iron-Clad Steamer for Our Navy," *Scientific American*, October 26, 1861, 265.

51. "New Iron Plated War Steamer," *Scientific American*, March 1, 1862, 131; "Naval Intelligence," *Scientific American*, March 15, 1862, 162; *Harper's Weekly*, April 5, 1862.

52. Diary of William Ellery Maxson, February 14, 1862; *Mystic Pioneer*, February 15, 22, 1862.

53. Steven Biller, "From the Drafting Table to the Front Lines: Designing, Building, and Utilizing the Ironclad uss *Galena*," *Log of Mystic Seaport* 53.1 (2001): 7.

54. Louis M. Goldsborough to Gustavus V. Fox, April 24, 1862, in *Confidential Correspondence of Gustavus Vasa Fox: Assistant Secretary of the Navy, 1861–1865*, ed. Robert Means Thompson and Richard Wainwright (New York: Naval Historical Society, 1920), 263; Goldsborough to Fox, 265.

55. Robert Erwin Johnson, *Rear Admiral John Rodgers, 1812–1882* (Annapolis, MD: United States Naval Institute, 1967), 194.

56. Cutler, *Mystic*, 157.

57. McClellan to Lincoln, April 23, 1862, http://lcweb2.loc.gov/cgi-bin/query /r?ammem/mal:@field(DOCID+@lit(d1565100)).

58. Johnson, *John Rodgers*, 195–96. On March 9, 1862, the *Monitor* and *Virginia* battled at Hampton Roads, Virginia, in the first battle between ironclads in the United States. The battle was inconclusive because neither side could pierce the other's armor.

59. John Rodgers to Ann Rodgers Macomb, May 8, 1862, quoted in Johnson, *John Rodgers*, 198.

60. u.s. Department of the Navy, "Report of the Secretary of the Navy in Relation to Armored Vessels," 25.

61. Christley, "Mystic River Builds an Ironclad," 137.

62. Diary of William Ellery Maxson, May 13, 16, 19, 1862.

63. Kurt Hackemer, "The Other Union Ironclad: The uss *Galena* and the Critical Summer of 1862," *Civil War History* 40.3 (1994): 243; Christley, "Mystic River Builds an Ironclad," 138.

64. Report of Lieutenant Charles Huntington, in u.s. Department of the Navy, "Report of the Secretary of the Navy, 1864" (Washington, DC: Government Printing Office, 1864), 444–45; *New York Times*, September 17, 1864. Between August and September the *New York Times* reported multiple times on the Battle at Mobile Bay, mentioning the *Galena* briefly in much of its coverage; *Mystic Pioneer*, August 13, 1861.

65. *Mystic Pioneer*, July 5, 1862.

66. Cutler, "History by Carl. C. Cutler," 129. Prior to engaging the *Monitor*, the *Virginia* took out the Union frigates *Cumberland* and *Congress*.

67. Peterson, *Mystic Built*, 236.

68. u.s. Department of the Navy, "Report of the Secretary of the Navy, December 1, 1862," in Appendix to the Congressional Globe, 37th Cong., 3rd sess., 13–14, http://memory.loc.gov/cgi-bin/ampage?collId=llcg&fileName=063/llcg063 .db&recNum=692. Hereafter referred to as "Report of the Secretary of the Navy, December 1862."

69. *Hartford Daily Courant*, May 21, 1862.

70. *Mystic Pioneer*, May 10, 1862; Cutler, "History by Carl C. Cutler," 129.

71. Peterson, *Mystic Built*, 232; B. S. Osbon, ed., *Handbook of the United States Navy, From April, 1861 to May, 1864* (New York: Trubner & Co., 1864), 249.

72. U.S. Department of the Navy, "Report of the Secretary of the Navy, December 1862," 12; David D. Porter, *The Naval History of the Civil War* (Secaucus, NJ: Castle, 1984), 114.

73. Louis M. Goldsborough to Gustavus V. Fox, April 24, 1862, in *Confidential Correspondence of Gustavus Vasa Fox*, 240.

74. *Hartford Daily Courant*, February 15, 20, 1862; *Mystic Pioneer*, February 15, May 31, 1862.

75. Myron J. Smith, "The Greenman's Forgotten Gunboat: The USS *Albatross*," *Log of Mystic Seaport* 24.2 (1972): 47–49; Porter, *Naval History of the Civil War*, 349, 464.

76. Peterson, *Mystic Built*, 201. The Mallory vessel, *Haze*, was also involved in the Red River campaign.

77. Porter, *Naval History of the Civil War*, 107; *New York Times*, January 21, 1862; *Hartford Daily Courant*, January 18, 1862; U.S. Department of the Navy, Civil War Naval Chronology, 1861–1865 (Washington, DC: Government Printing Office, 1971), II-25; Porter, *Naval History of the Civil War*, 351.

78. *Mystic Pioneer*, May 2, August 29, 1863; Diary of Nathan G. Fish, August 27, 1863; Osbon, *Handbook of the United States Navy*, 262.

79. Cutler, "History by Carl C. Cutler," 138; U.S. Department of the Navy, "Report of the Secretary of the Navy, December 1862," 14.

80. Stevens and Stillman, *George Greenman & Co.*, 19.

3 : Patriotism and Abolitionism in Civil War–Era Windham County

espite all the evidence, including Matthew Brady's graphic photographs, the carnage of the American Civil War is beyond modern conception. Sterile statistics that document the loss of well over a half million lives cannot accurately convey the horrific reality of tens of thousands of rotting corpses lying under the sweltering southern sun or the anguish of those whose horrendous wounds were far beyond the skills of nineteenth-century surgeons.[1] Why, then, did northern civilians rush to enter the ranks as soldiers in America's bloodiest war? Why did they fight valiantly, often in the face of almost certain death, and then reenlist to tempt fate and Rebel bullets yet again? Although these questions have fascinated contemporary scholars, including James McPherson and Edward Ayers, even as the war raged, Abraham Lincoln posited that "patriotism, political bias, ambition, personal courage, love of adventure [and] want of employment" drove the thousands who had rushed to early enlistment.[2]

The narrowly focused work that follows attempts to speak for those who volunteered from one sparsely populated area of Connecticut: Windham County, in the state's far northeastern corner. Windham was but one of the state's primarily rural areas, and this chapter does not purport to be universally representative of all such regions. Nor does it attempt extensive comparisons between the agrarian and urban war experiences. What it does do is to provide some understanding concerning the roots of Windham County's resounding Unionism, how it was grounded in both a traditional, Revolutionary legacy and a more modern conception of antislavery, abolitionist thought. In these respects, both the extensive pro-Union nationalism and the abolitionist leanings, made Windham County unique within the state.

While there existed significant, overt support for the South within many Democratic strongholds of the state—including rural Litchfield County in the far northwestern corner—Windham's support of the Lincoln administration and the war effort was unique in one important aspect: it was

Main Street, Danielsonville, Connecticut, 1861, following President Lincoln's call for volunteers. Courtesy of Killingly Historical & Genealogical Society

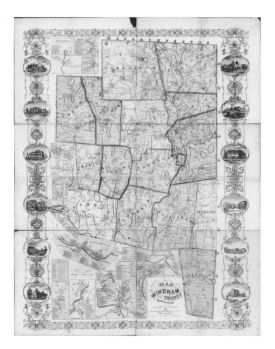

Map of Windham County, Connecticut, by E. M. Woodford (Philadelphia: Wagner & McGuigan), 1856. Courtesy of University of Connecticut Magic Project

virtually universal and unflagging. Windham was determined to send volunteers, not draftees, to war, and even as late as 1864, many towns in the
county still boasted enlistment numbers far higher than their cumulative quotas.[3] The sole, rather weak-kneed antiwar resolution tendered in
Windham County was immediately and permanently quashed by public
pressure.

To be sure, the county's farmers, blacksmiths, and weavers made up
only a small percentage of those from Connecticut who fought and died.
Yet their reasons for doing so illustrate how local history and community
perception customized the issues faced by all Connecticut citizens—and
all Americans—throughout the Civil War. In many respects, Windham
County's stalwart support for Lincoln and the Union grew out of the area's
seventeenth-century origins, coalesced in the decades of the early republic, and was undergirded by circumstances of the war itself.

Of the 2,288 men Windham County sent into Union service, 592 were
with the ill-fated Eighteenth Connecticut Volunteers who fought under
General Robert Huston Milroy at Second Winchester, Virginia, in June
1863. Although the regiment fought valiantly, the untried men had spent
their entire enlistment year guarding a railroad and were thus poorly prepared for battle against the Confederate forces that vastly outnumbered
them. Only 23 soldiers were killed in action, but more than 500 were taken
prisoner, including 41 who were badly injured. Enlisted men were paroled
relatively quickly, but the 24 captured officers languished in Libby Prison
under horrendous conditions until March 1864.[4] John Niven said the
Eighteenth "ceased to exist" after Second Winchester: an exaggeration,
perhaps, but the unit never fully recovered, and its numbers had dwindled
from more than 1,000 to about 600 by war's end.[5]

Killingly men formed the largest contingent of Windham forces within
the Eighteenth Regiment. Native son Major Ephraim Keech led 166 soldiers into the South. But given the scarcity of personal correspondence
from Windham soldiers, other enlistment patterns are impossible to explain. The First Regiment Heavy Artillery contained 233 county men, and
145 served with the First Cavalry.[6] The 29 horsemen from Woodstock who
jockeyed successfully for a place with the mounted unit howled in protest
that their town could easily raise several full companies of cavalry on its
own and should be allowed to do so.[7] In the Eleventh Regiment were 271
men from northeastern Connecticut towns, and the Fifth, Sixth, Seventh,
Eighth and Twelfth Regiments were also well-represented. The Twenty-
First included 221 Windham men: Brooklyn sent as many recruits to the

Twenty-First as it did to the Eighteenth, and Plainfield almost twice as many.[8]

The average desertion rate for Windham soldiers was 9 percent, far lower than the 14 percent for Connecticut as a whole. But even this figure is skewed upward by the inclusion of Mansfield's and Scotland's 17 percent. Except for Sterling (14 percent) and Windham (12 percent), desertion rates for the remaining twelve county towns were in the single digits—between 6 and 8 percent. Brooklyn, home to the bones of the indefatigable Israel Putnam, tied with Canaan in Litchfield County for the second-lowest rate in the state (4 percent), and only 3 percent of Canterbury men deserted—the lowest rate in Connecticut.[9] Why did more Windham men not walk away? Hines pointed out that many more desertions resulted from monotony, drudgery, and poor conditions in camp than were caused by cowardice; and certainly eastern Connecticut men were as bored, tired, and hungry as any other Connecticut soldiers.[10] Despite the best efforts of local recruiters, late in the war, some well-to-do county men did hire substitutes who, it is generally acknowledged, tended to desert at high rates, often even before reaching camp.[11] But even the unflinchingly pro-war *Transcript* did not condemn those who hired substitutes, observing rather succinctly, "All the able-bodied are already in the service of the country."[12]

History never provides pat answers. One contributing factor to these low desertion rates may have been that there were no large contingents of Windham soldiers killed in any one major battle, such as Chancellorsville, Antietam, or Gettysburg. A total of 366 county soldiers were lost to the war, either killed in action or by disease or accident.[13] But these deaths occurred gradually. Had 100 Killingly men perished at Bull Run, or 80 Thompson men at The Wilderness, morale within the community and in the ranks may have started down a path ultimately leading to much higher desertion rates. Stronger evidence, however, suggests that from the first shots at Fort Sumter, Windham County soldiers viewed the conflict as a mission, not only to preserve the Union, but also to end slavery.

Similarly, the region's nascent abolitionism was also rooted in its past, a more recent past, which included Prudence Crandall's attempt to create an all-black school for girls and residents' ugly reaction to it. The aftermath brought both remorse and abolition, in the form of William Lloyd Garrison and his many supporters.

Because the northeastern townships of Connecticut grew and developed under influences quite different from those that shaped the majority of the colony, the roots of the strong political consciousness that fortified Windham County's support of the Lincoln administration and the war effort originated in its seventeenth-century beginnings. When Thomas Hooker and his followers departed Massachusetts Bay Colony to found Hartford in 1636, they traveled what came to be known as the "Connecticut Path." At the time, however, they referred to it as a "hideous and trackless wilderness."[14] Those who trekked further, to Windham County, most certainly thought so, especially in comparison with the rich river bottom of the Connecticut River Valley. Anyone who has driven over the roller-coaster roads of Route 6, Route 44 or Route 101 should imagine the grades unbowed by bulldozer and covered in virgin forest; then envision the trip on foot, with wheelbarrows and handcarts. It is hardly surprising that no one immediately suggested planting crops. By 1682, however, white settlement of the area had begun. Large tracts were purchased by English entrepreneurs eager to transform forest into board-feet. The area also drew large numbers of Massachusetts Puritans seeking land and opportunity.[15] Their "Separatist mindset" flourished during the First Great Awakening and, as in so many other places, caused politics in the early northeastern townships to display an ideological approach to the development of partisanship. Far from the sea and with little to recommend it except recalcitrant farmland and extremely long church services, the area was deprived of the ethnic and economic diversity that developed so rapidly in the Connecticut River settlements from Windsor to New Haven following the Revolutionary War. Absent those influences, political awareness was formed primarily around constitutional and religious issues rather than economic concerns. Driven by this political perspective, Jeffersonian Republicanism grew more rapidly in the northeastern townships than in Connecticut as a whole.[16]

After 1805, the popular base from which the Federalist Party drew support began to decline in Windham County, owing largely to the Congregational bickering that heralded the Second Great Awakening. Strong separatist tradition manifested itself in the demand for a new state constitution and a definitive end to state-supported religion. By the end of the decade, almost one-third of Windham's residents had departed the confines of the Standing Order for Separatist, Methodist, Baptist and Episcopalian havens.[17] Religious dissent, however, was not the sole stimulus behind the growth of Democratic-Republicanism. Attaining the status of the Windham farming aristocracy, long-dominated by Federalists, was fast becoming impossible. Virtually all suitable land was already under cultivation, and even that which remained was selling at a premium. Manufacturing concerns were growing rapidly, and successful cotton entrepreneurs sought political power commensurate with their economic standing—and thus an end to overpowering Federalist patronage that pervaded local business interests. While motivated differently, Windham's businessmen and religious dissenters found common ground in their desire for a new state constitution and, as one historian put it, "the destruction of political ministry and the end to a state church."[18]

So while elsewhere in Connecticut, Republicans struggled mightily and suffered numerous setbacks until 1819, the fall election of 1806 marked the end of Federalism in Windham County.[19] The general attitudes toward *national* partisanship may well have retained some degree of belief that Republicans were, in fact, "atheists and Jacobins," as their enemies argued, but voters supported the party on state and local levels based on its commitment to constitutional and religious reform.[20] This was not a battle of small proportion, nor was it quickly forgotten. Years later, Gideon Welles, Lincoln's secretary of the navy, remembered bitterly the difficult birth of Republicanism in the Land of Steady Habits. Jeffersonians in Connecticut, he remembered, were "proscribed and regarded as an inferior caste, a degraded race like the Soodras in India, the Israelites in Egypt or the Jews in Europe . . . aliens and strangers in their native land."[21] Writing in 1905 for the *American Historical Review*, one scholar noted, "Connecticut men whose memories go back for only fifty years will recall anecdotes and traditions that they heard in their boyhood that show how bitter and how lasting was the feeling then engendered."[22]

Such a history, and memory, places Windham's rejection of Federalist aristocracy in favor of egalitarian republicanism squarely in the collective conscious of the mid-nineteenth century and helps to explain why residents proclaimed themselves the "Most Republican County" in the state—just as rejection of southern aristocracy and support of the Lincoln administration became synonymous with loyalty to the Union. Granted, during the antebellum period, Democratic strongholds had formed in the most heavily populated manufacturing towns of Killingly and Windham, and these did factor decisively in Thomas Seymour's successful bid for governor in the 1850s.[23] Yet absent any significant immigrant population, these Democratic pockets were composed overwhelmingly of native-born,

Protestant residents of English and Scottish ancestry whose economic interests just happened to have diverged from their virtually identically pedigreed agrarian Whig neighbors.[24] Furthermore, adoption of the state constitution, the end to religious infighting, and the metamorphosis of Windham's strong antislavery tradition into widespread abolitionist sentiment following the Prudence Crandall scandal in 1833 had all encouraged focus on issues held in common.[25]

As the Whig Party breathed its last and the attitude of the state's Democrats grew increasingly pro-southern, the political reconciliation of the homogeneous population under the banner of the modern Republican Party was accomplished. Indignant at Republican charges of vote-tampering in the bitter election of 1860, Connecticut Democrats pointed to Windham County, where the Republican vote had completely nullified the Democratic majority in New Haven. Voters, they charged, had obviously been brought in from Rhode Island and Massachusetts.[26] Considering that strangers attempting to cast ballots in towns where virtually "everyone knew everyone" would have been immediately challenged, if not summarily thrashed, these accusations bordered on ludicrous. Yet even in victory, the state's Republican officials saw little humor in the allegations. Ironically, that was left to the Democratic New Haven *Register*: "That the little 'one-horse' county of Windham, whose entire vote hardly exceeds the Democratic numbers of New Haven, should be the means of blocking the patriotic impulses of the whole state, is too bad! . . . If the Democrats ever get the power in Connecticut, we move that Windham County be 'set-off' to Massachusetts or Rhode Island."[27] A Republican voter replied: "Well, it *is* rather Un-Democratic, as Democracy runs now-a-days, to allow people to vote anything except the Administration ticket. What right have those men in Windham to go and fly in the face of the patriots who had arranged such a promising fraud in the cities?"[28] This notoriety—fleeting and mocking as it may have been—reinforced an already strong sense of political awareness and tightened communal bonds at a time when support for the government would soon mean support for the war effort.

Windham's antebellum political conscious was also nurtured by access to information. Contrary to assertions by historian John Niven that all of Connecticut's nineteenth-century farm families lived in poverty-ridden isolation, ate moldy vegetables, and read only the Bible and week-old copies of daily city newspapers, by 1861, Windham residents had been obtaining their state, national, and international news on a daily basis from both Norwich and Boston for more than twenty years, and from Hartford and Providence for more than a decade.[29] The significance of the railroad to nineteenth-century Windham County cannot be overestimated. In 1839, long before rail transportation to rural areas was a given, the opening of the Norwich & Worcester line summarily connected landlocked, rural Windham to both Boston and Long Island Sound along the corridor of today's I-395. In 1849, the Hartford & Providence Railroad ran eastward as far as Willimantic, and by 1854 connected Hartford with Providence.[30] At the war's outbreak, countless freight cars and at least seven passenger trains passed through Windham County every day. From Danielsonville, Boston was an easy hour's ride; Norwich, slightly less.[31] While this early access to rail transportation did not build large cities from mere outposts, as occurred postwar in the western territories, it did support an influx of ideas and philosophies that would have otherwise been lacking in an isolated, rural environment.

REVOLUTIONARY IDEOLOGY AND CIVIL WAR PATRIOTISM

Yet this sense of modernism, ushered in by transportation and thus access to the outside world, was not the primary philosophical momentum that caused Windham County men to join the ranks of Civil War regiments. There were other powerful influences. In 1861, twenty-five-year-old men were only three generations removed from the American Revolution, and it is widely accepted among contemporary scholars that the watershed event separating the American colonies from England was entrenched in the ideologies of both Union and Confederate soldiers.[32] In northeastern Connecticut, this was certainly no vague connection to a bygone history. Patriotism in Windham County was inextricably grounded in Revolutionary War–era *genealogies* of a population primarily of English and Scottish ancestry; when they spoke of their "forefathers" it was not in the abstract. Even in 1889, historian Richard Bayles posited that "[a] complete muster role of Windham's revolutionary soldiers would probably include the name of nearly every family in the county, while many families sent very large representations. It is said that seventeen cousins by the name of Fuller were in the service from Windham's Second Society. The Adamses and the Clevelands were almost without number. Peter Adams and Ephraim Fisk of Killingly each had six sons in the army and Barzillai Fisher and Lusher Gay each had four."[33]

This observation is confirmed by the fact that it is difficult to find a surname mentioned by Bayles or by nineteenth-century historian Ellen

Larned in conjunction with the Revolutionary War that does not also appear on the Civil War roster of the Connecticut Eighteenth Regiment or within the pages of the Windham County *Transcript* during the war years. Just as the railroad shuttled endless carloads of Civil War soldiers en route to Dixie from northern New England through Windham, the county's location on the "main thoroughfares of travel" brought eighteenth-century residents into very close and constant communication with the leading towns of the northern colonies throughout the Revolutionary War period.[34] "Filial and fraternal relations connected them with the flaming patriots of Boston and Providence," noted Bayles, and in colonial Windham County "[a] remarkable unity of sentiment existed among the people. . . . Tories were very few and those who did entertain sentiments in favor of the mother country were careful about flaunting those sentiments too strongly in the face of their neighbors."[35]

The connections to the fight for American independence were imbued in the 1861 collective conscious via the moldering remains of General Israel Putnam, long entombed in the town of Brooklyn. Killing the last wolf in Connecticut earned Putnam a reputation and, undoubtedly, the undying gratitude of Pomfret sheep,[36] but his military legacy began with "Don't fire until you see the whites of their eyes" at Ticonderoga.[37] It was Putnam who sent armed vigilantes from Windham and New London Counties to intercept King's Agent Jared Ingersoll as he traveled from Boston toward Hartford to assume his newly appointed position as stamp master—the first act of defiance against the 1765 Stamp Act in the Connecticut colony.[38] But it was Putnam's Revolutionary War command that assured "the hero of Bunker Hill" of immortality in northeastern Connecticut. General Putnam's breakneck ride from Brooklyn to Cambridge on April 18, 1775, was, to Windham County, as important, if not more so, than that which had been taken the night earlier by Paul Revere between Lexington and Concord. When the Royal Navy bottled up Boston Harbor, Windham was the first to respond with aid to the starving city: 258 descendants of those Pomfret sheep were driven to Cambridge. Three days later, Windham militia followed, the "first trained units to respond from outside their [Boston's] limits."[39]

Within the speeches and resolutions made in Windham during the first days of the Civil War, references to these common bonds, and the "noble history" and "ancient fame" of Windham County permeated every newspaper article. Men were urged to emulate "the example of our fathers and . . . show that we are not 'degenerate sons of noble sires.'"[40] So pervasive was this spirit of genealogical unity that a Baptist elder from Willimantic publicly apologized for having "no ancestry to lean on" as he pledged himself to enlistment at a countywide rally.[41] Brooklyn's successful fundraising caused the town to be "worthy to hold the ashes of Old Put," and quick enlistments in Woodstock inspired the observation that "[the] spirit of '76 still animates the hearts of her sons! . . . [T]he 'home of Putnam' will not [lag behind]."[42] Even Putnam's abandonment of his undoubtedly puzzled oxen in a Pomfret cornfield upon receiving word that the Revolution had come was considered patriotic fodder in 1861, as demonstrated by this cryptic and flowery resolution: "At the command of Joshua, the sun and moon stood still, of like potency was the news from Lexington, in 1775, to cause the plow to stand still in the furrow. And so shall Massachusetts blood, which now stains the streets of Baltimore [following the April 1861 attack on Massachusetts regiments in Maryland], of need be, dry up, in Windham County, every source of industry, until those stains are either deepened or avenged."[43]

Even Eastford-born General Nathaniel Lyon, fighting in faraway Missouri and the first Civil War general to perish in the conflict, could not escape the Putnam legacy. The *Transcript* noted on June 27, 1861, "He attended school [at] Brooklyn, where he probably inherited an increase of patriotism by paying homage to lofty courage at the shrine of the hero of Bunker Hill."[44] As late as December 1861, the editor, John Stone, responded to unfounded accusations in the *Norwich Bulletin* that Windham was lagging in enlistments by noting that the town had been "urged to more activity or we should not show ourselves worthy as noble ancestry."[45] Still, the ultimate, if somewhat bizarre, salute to their most favorite son — and to their own place in American history — was made by members of Windham's First Company of Union Guard during a flag raising at a Killingly mill. "[The canteen] . . . worn by General Putnam at Bunker Hill [was exhibited] . . . and each volunteer drank from it some pure native wine pressed from grapes raised on the Putnam farm in Brooklyn."[46] Eagerness to drink from an eighty-year-old canteen — even by nineteenth-century hygienic standards — surely spoke to the Civil War soldiers' firm grounding in Revolutionary War patriotism. Seventy years after his death, Israel Putnam went to war with Windham County soldiers one last time.

This patriotic legacy and Union-minded inspiration runs strongly against historian John Niven's assertion that hardships associated with Connecticut farming were integral factors in spurring early rural enlistments.[47] While there is little doubt that tilling the land — any land at any time—requires a level of dedication not easily understood by those otherwise inclined, Niven's position is incorrectly based on what David R. Meyer of Brown University refers to as the "impoverished agricultural theory": the assumption that mid-nineteenth-century Connecticut farmers remained mired in the struggles that traditionally characterize subsistence farming.[48] Long before the Civil War, the recalcitrant land of Windham County had forced farmers to diversify, creating what Brown refers to as a "synergy between agriculture and industrialization." By 1861, this transition to a cash crop economy had placed Windham farmers among northeastern Connecticut's most affluent citizens; their land and improvements were worth well over $9 million.[49] In a similar vein, Niven argued that the dreary, poverty-ridden lives of Windham's mill workers drove them into the ranks of the Eighteenth Connecticut Regiment.[50] Here, again, there is no question that factory work in a nonunionized, pre-OSHA America was inequitable and dangerous, but Niven's arguments are not convincing. For instance, he cited an "average" weekly wage of $5 for Connecticut textile workers during the 1850s. This figure is of questionable relevance because of the large discrepancies between what was paid to women and children—none of whom joined the army—and the salaries of far better paid male mechanics, carpenters, dyers, machinists, and firemen, who did join.[51] Did Windham's textile workers respond to the enlistment speeches of mill owners? Niven suggested that employees of Voluntown's Beachdale Mill were motivated to enlist by owner-manager Ira Briggs, a "self-made man" who commanded great respect. (One should note that the source Niven cited does not contain the anecdote he relied on).[52] Still, the argument seems contradictory, even to Niven's own position. Briggs may have been self-made, but he was also the one doling out the $5 per week pay envelopes that relegated workers to the despair Niven alleges. Briggs's credibility may have been questioned by his more perceptive workers. Additionally, in the first year of the war, it could not have been in the financial interest of mill managers to deplete their labor forces. Most had the foresight to stockpile raw cotton in 1860, as relations between North and South became increasingly tenuous, and some Windham mills had sufficient stores to remain in operation well into 1862.[53]

Another arm of the Niven argument stated that "[the] great religious revival that had begun in 1857 merged into the patriotic revivals of 1861 and 1862. These were to fill up the ranks of the 18th Connecticut."[54] Within the minutely documented religious history of Windham County, however, there is no evidence of such a concurrence. An enormous portion of both

Bayles's and Larned's late-nineteenth-century research was a painstaking examination of church records. Both historians meticulously detailed the changes brought about through both "Great Awakenings" in every congregation, of every denomination, in every Windham County township. After 1842, their histories reflect only minimal revivalist activity in northeastern Connecticut, and that which did take place was largely conducted in conjunction with the Temperance Movement, which was very active in the area.[55] Soldiers from Windham County were, for the most part, deeply religious and largely Congregational. Their faith in God is clearly evident in their published letters, and they do not appear to have been chafing under the constraints of nineteenth-century American Christianity, as Niven also asserts, nor do they seem to have been carried to war on a wave of post–Second Great Awakening revivalism.

THE SPIRIT OF CIVIL WAR WINDHAM

By 1861, Windham County's unique history, geography, and demography had worked in concert to shape a collective consciousness within the community—a principled consensus regarding the economic, political, and racial issues that would drive the Civil War. The best reflection of communal attitude appears within the pages of the local newspapers, which ran uninterrupted throughout the war and were sent regularly to every regiment in which Windham men were fighting.[56] War, by its nature, is isolating. But these publications dedicated themselves to becoming the conduits through which soldiers and civilians shared their experiences across a newly defined "local community" that now was scattered throughout the entire Confederacy, stimulating, as the paper announced, "county feeling and the bond of union between the several towns."[57] This is not to suggest that the papers abandoned advertisements for hair restoratives and cure-all purges or became paragons of unbiased journalism. But pro-war partisanship was consistently underwritten with editorial honesty, especially evident in the *Windham County Transcript*, owned and published by John Quincy Adams Stone. It was Stone's integrity and standing in the community—in conjunction with the coincidences inherent in war—that allowed his folio to shed the constraints of its more humble origins and become a bona fide instrument of education: a "power throughout the County," as one local historian put it, nurturing the patriotism and social values that undergirded enlistment and supported community morale.[58]

Stone purchased the *Telegraph*, a struggling local with a circulation of less than four hundred, in 1858. By 1861, he had abandoned the original hand-cranked printing press, and the rechristened *Transcript* boasted a pressman, a circulation manager, and two "departments," one in Danielsonville and the other in Putnam, headed by Associate Editor J. F. Wilkinson.[59] Stone was a temperance man, strongly disinclined toward the vicious politics that had preceded the war, and he took his responsibilities to the community very seriously. Throughout the secession crisis, and until the smoke rose over Fort Sumter on April 12, 1861, *Transcript* editorials bravely fought local public opinion: "We have ever spoken for peace, and labored in our humble sphere for it; but it was not to be and we submit. We have advocated concession in order to . . . avert the calamity of civil war."[60] From April 18 onward, however, Stone tasked himself and the paper with unflagging support of the community, the government's war effort, and the preservation of the Union.

The paper contains none of the poorly spelled, barely decipherable letters that are so often characteristic of the Civil War era. Stone openly solicited correspondence from many well-educated men before they even took the field.[61] As was the case among many soldiers writing for hometown publications, especially early in the war, most correspondents did not fully identify themselves by name; preferring to append initials or pen names.[62] Some were low-level officers and chaplains, but many were lowly privates.[63] One might question whether Stone freely edited or excluded some letters. Yet there are no obvious indications that letters from less-accomplished pens were corrected or ignored, and strong suggestions that the job of corresponding with the local newspaper was simply awarded to whichever Windham man was best suited for the task.

There were Windham County men in most Connecticut regiments, and statistically, it seems highly improbable that none questioned themselves or the strongly felt principles that drove enlistment—and reenlistment— especially early in the war. Yet whatever personal disillusionment may have overtaken them, they did not share it with the community-at-large. This was certainly not the case in many other newspapers.[64] The *Transcript* contains nothing even remotely comparable to that expressed by the *Hartford Times*, when it printed an anonymous letter from a soldier who wrote, "The feeling here is that the Rebels never can be conquered by fighting—the soldiers are disheartened."[65] Certainly, the soldiers from northeastern Connecticut never considered the war jolly good fun. Their letters to the *Transcript* are filled with death, mutilation, disease, exhaustion, exposure, hunger, and homesickness. They criticize Generals McClellan, Patterson, and Milroy; the prisoner parole system; draftees and malingerers; but none ever suggests that the war was wrong or that the effort should be abandoned.

Again, one might raise the question of potential editorial censorship on the part of newspapers dedicated to supporting the war effort and the morale of the readership—soldier and civilian alike. Yet examining the ways in which Stone and his counterpart, *Willimantic Journal* editor E. S. Simpson, set the tone and controlled the content of their respective publications suggests otherwise. Simpson was a bombastic, no-holds-barred newspaperman who responded unequivocally to the one antiwar resolution issued by Democrats in the town of Mansfield: "For shame, Mansfield! Wash yourselves of this foul reproach alike disgraceful to your manhood and to every principle of justice and humanity."[66] Such vehemence directed at an entire town strongly suggests that Simpson would have had no compunctions about publicly scalding any individual—soldier or civilian—he viewed as unpatriotic.

There are actually very few references to southern sympathizers within the community in the *Transcript*, although one account of a June 1861 flag-raising noted that "The [celebrating was] said to be heard by a 'Secesh,' who, unfortunately, was not way down on the 'Sacred soil' of Virginia, but [here in] Connecticut."[67] Stone's approach to editing was discretionary. He did, on occasion, withhold what he considered demoralizing or unproductive. Historians know this because he conscientiously printed acknowledgment of receiving such items and fully explained his reasoning for not publishing them. One such letter came from a soldier whose company had apparently been held in the rear and who apparently felt himself deprived of due glory. Stone wrote: "We have received quite a lengthy communication from 'A Sufferer' in the Eleventh Regiment complaining of the hardships which some of the men endured on the voyage and the unfortunate inactivity of the Regiment at the time of the victory on Roanoke Island. Some of the complaints indulged in by this writer may justly be made, but we believe no good will result from their publication at the present time. . . . Our County [has] many of her citizens in the Eleventh and . . . had opportunity been given, they all [would have fought nobly]. . . . All cannot be in the front rank."[68]

Yet Stone did not censor what he apparently believed was constructive, well-founded criticism. In December 1862, he published a letter recounting a spirited debate held in the camp of the Eighteenth Regiment on the proposition "Resolved: that President Lincoln had sufficient cause to remove General McClellan." The soldier reported, "After two hours of strong and able argument it was submitted to the judges, who brought in a verdict in favor of the negative. What would our President think, had he heard the arguments? Guess he would have ordered him back to command the army of the Potomac again. Hope not."[69]

Following the utter decimation of the Eighteenth Connecticut at the Second Battle of Winchester, one captured Windham man noted dryly, "We saw the 'Stonewall Brigade'; they told us they were going to Boston; guess they would if we had a few more Gen. Milroys."[70] Nor did Stone flinch at stronger complaint. Following the First Battle of Bull Run, he printed a diatribe from one soldier who assured the community that all "Windham boys" believed General Patterson to be nothing less than "a traitor and a secessionist."[71] As did most nineteenth-century newspapermen, Stone considered himself a guardian of community well-being simply by virtue of his education and position. Exactly what the *Transcript*'s editor found so damning in the letter from the disgruntled Eleventh Regiment soldier is long-lost. But Stone's commentary speaks to his character. He printed the names of those who failed their physical exams but flatly refused to publish their ailments.[72] This brand of journalistic integrity— apparent even in the presence of blatant partisanship—would have made it extremely difficult, if not impossible, for him to have simply ignored any significant amount of correspondence for any reason, and it renders the *Transcript* a reliable barometer of the community's attitude and soldiers' morale throughout the war. And what it reveals, through hundreds of pages over four years of war, is a community dedicated to the Union and Lincoln. There simply existed little dissent or Democratic fervor.

PRUDENCE CRANDALL AND
ABOLITION IN WINDHAM COUNTY

Although antebellum Windham County was certainly not as rabidly abolitionist as parts of Massachusetts, there is strong evidence that the sentiment was sufficiently ingrained in the greater collective consciousness to have both effectively suppressed public expression of proslavery sentiment and to have motivated even early Civil War enlistment. Furthermore, there seems to have been a level of egalitarianism underpinning antislavery sentiment in northeastern Connecticut, not unlike that which drew the most vituperative ravings from South Carolina directly at Massachusetts.

Generally, in Connecticut, being an abolitionist had little to do with believing in racial equality. Bigotry and prejudice based on physical appearance were the norm, not the exception: slaves might deserve freedom, but free or bonded, they were inferior to whites. Eastern Massachusetts abolitionists, on the other hand, drew the contempt of the South for their ultraliberal views. John Brown was a Torrington, Connecticut, native—a fact seriously underplayed in Litchfield County. It was Cambridge Transcendentalist Henry David Thoreau who painted Brown the martyr in his "Plea for Captain John Brown." William Lloyd Garrison's Boston *Liberator* printed correspondence from the Grimke sisters, former South Carolina slaveowners turned Quaker abolitionists, who advocated interracial marriage, which in turn enraged residents of the Palmetto State. But the best illustration of southern antiabolitionist ire directed northward was the caning of Bay State Senator Charles Sumner by South Carolina Congressman Preston Brooks.[73]

The condescending language of racism is missing from the *Windham County Transcript*. Transcribed, the letters submitted to the *Transcript* between 1861 and 1865 fill more than four hundred pages, but the word "nigger" appears fewer than five times. Personal interactions with the county's black population, as well as long-held antislavery sentiment within the community, shaped soldiers' war experiences from the opening days of the conflict and continued to evolve in the light of discussion and experience. Except for the famous Eighty-Fourth Regiment of the Massachusetts Voluntary Infantry, the Eighteenth Connecticut—half of which was from Windham County—provided more officers for Connecticut's two black regiments than any other.[74] According to the 1860 federal census records, free blacks accounted for only 1.4 percent of Windham County's total population: the same ratio that existed in Hartford County.[75] Although certainly lacking any degree of urban congestion, it seems likely that even this small number of free blacks in rural Windham would have been a visible presence within the community. Young Aaron Day of Danielsonville, encamped with the Fourth Connecticut in Maryland in June 1861, sent the *Transcript* a good-natured description of crawling around in the mud while on picket duty, noting, "The prowling around here o'nights is not quite as pleasant as the fun we had in old Killingly. We are all getting as black as our colored friend H—— P——."[76] Obviously, anyone who lived in Danielsonville or knew Aaron Day would have known exactly who "H.P." was, yet J.Q.A. Stone afforded him the same courteous anonymity as he did all private individuals mentioned in published correspondence.

It is as ironic as it is telling that an editorial published in the April 18,

1861, edition of the *Windham County Transcript*—until that very day, an advocate for "peace democracy"—acknowledged that the issues of slavery and disunion could not be separated. As Associate Editor J. F. Wilkinson fervently reconciled the paper with the community, he acknowledged the dissenting position of the majority:

> We have ever spoken for peace, and labored in our humble sphere
> for it; but it was not to be and we submit. We have advocated conces-
> sion in order to . . . avert the calamity of civil war. . . . [The] claim of
> [southern] leaders that "negro slavery is a divine institution" . . . never
> found an echo in our heart nor assent in our mind. . . . It was not
> because we look with favor upon negro slavery that we have differed
> with the majority of our fellow-townsmen . . . but because we believed
> that climate and . . . free state settlers. . . . were sufficient guaran-
> tees against the increase of slave states. With slavery in its present
> limits we have nothing to do. A majority of the northern people have
> held different views. . . . Two forces now stand opposed. . . . One has
> declared for disunion and slavery; the other for Union and free-
> dom. . . . What choice is there? We have decided.[77]

Contemporary scholars seem to generally agree that most Union soldiers did not perceive themselves fighting to end slavery until they had
moved into the "cotton and rice" Confederacy and witnessed its injustices
and cruelties firsthand. One such revelation came to the *Transcript* from
Louisiana in July 1862 from a colonel in the Thirteenth Connecticut, who
found three slaves chained by their necks in a "stock house" owned by a
New Orleans Confederate: "Never, never shall I forget the expression . . .
of those poor fellows. . . . I asked the keeper how long they had been there.
He said . . . two or three weeks. One of them answered 'I have been here
five weeks.' How long will a merciful God suffer such things to be enacted
in a country boasting of its Christian liberties?"[78]

Accounts like these began to appear frequently about this time, and
by the end of the war, they pervaded the newspaper's pages. Yet they had
come earlier as well. In a letter sent from Camp Welles in Washington,
dated June 13, 1861, J. T. Phillips of the Second Regiment wrote: "We may
close our eyes to the truth and assert that we are only attempting to crush
out treason [but] this rebellion is being waged for the perpetuation and
extension of slavery and that while we maintain the integrity of the government we settle forever the question of slavery."[79]

Just after Christmas 1861, "J.D.L," who had yet to travel further south

PRUDENCE CRANDALL,
Principal of the Canterbury, (Conn.) Female Boarding School,

RETURNS her most sincere thanks to those who have patronized her School, and would give information that on the first Monday of April next, her School will be opened for the reception of young Ladies and little Misses of color. The branches taught are as follows:—Reading, Writing, Arithmetic, English Grammar, Geography, History, Natural and Moral Philosophy, Chemistry, Astronomy, Drawing and Painting, Music on the Piano, together with the French language.

☞ The terms, including *board, washing,* and tuition, are $25 per quarter, one half paid in advance.

☞ Books and Stationary will be furnished

Advertisement in William Lloyd Garrison's The Liberator, *March 2, 1833.*

than Camp Tyler in West Meriden, expressed the belief that while the war was "to protect our families, our property and our lives," it was "all on account of that cursed institution called slavery. . . . [The] war will never [end] until this horrid institution is annihilated and driven from the soil of our nation."[80] Letters in the *Transcript* demonstrate that Windham soldiers were open-minded and interested in the slaves they encountered. When "six fine negroes" came into the camp of the Second Connecticut early in June 1861, "J.T.P" noted with satisfaction that "[our] boys, not having the fear of the fugitive slave law before them, soon supplied them with a liberal supply of food." When the planter appeared to reclaim his "property," the soldier continued, he was "informed that if he valued himself and horse he had better seek other quarters."[81] Following his first encounter with an escaped slave in January 1862, "F.M.S." reported "a portion of . . . the descendents of Ham . . . can claim more intelligence than we Yankees are wont to attribute to them. . . . [His] master's barn was set on fire last night . . . seven mules perished in it—not including the owner."[82]

Why would Windham County men display, so early in the war, what

SCHOOL FOR COLORED GIRLS

COLORED SCHOOLS BROKEN UP, IN THE FREE STATES.

When schools have been established for colored scholars, the law-makers and the mob have combined to destroy them ;—as at Canterbury, Ct., at Canaan, N. H., Aug. 10, 1835, at Zanesville and Brown Co., Ohio, in 1836.

"Colored Schools Broken Up, in the Free States," woodcut print, Anti-Slavery Almanac, *1839.*

seems to be a fervent antislavery bias? In his work *In The Presence of Mine Enemies* Edward Ayers observed that the long-standing conflicts over slavery that divided Americans prior to the Civil War were based on many different dynamics, including "rivalry . . . moral outrage . . . past insults [or] new events that inflamed the antagonism."[83] Ayers's explanation may fit Windham County quite well. The moral outrage and past insult of the region can be summed up in a name: Prudence Crandall. When she attempted in the early 1830s to create an all-black girls school in Canterbury, many of the town's residents engaged in wholesale terrorism. She ultimately closed the school and fled the state. What followed in Windham County effectively counteracted what was active, widespread support of the African colonization movement and spurred a rising abolitionism. The incident also created a legacy of shame that existed well into 1880, when historian Ellen Larned, from Thompson, and only eight years old in 1833, was still engaged in damage control: "Looking back upon this memorable episode after nearly half a century, we also can rejoice that in this as in numberless other instances 'the wrath of man' so signally subserved the highest interests of God and the highest interests of humanity. Miss Cran-

LENGTHY DIGRESSION

dall did not succeed in teaching many colored girls, but she educated the people of Windham County. Not only did every act of violence elicit corresponding sympathy, but in the resultant agitation mind and conscience were enlightened."[84]

By 1830, several pastoral towns in Windham County had become vacation destinations for beleaguered city dwellers. In all but the worst weather, the well-maintained Post Road between Hartford and Boston was easily traveled, and guest houses and hotels were a source of sought-after income. Thompson, in closest proximity to Boston, had become one of the wealthiest rural towns in Connecticut, and ambitious Canterbury town leaders saw in their own bucolic surroundings the potential for both renown and financial success.[85] Their plan to establish a prestigious female boarding school was at least superficially in keeping with the educational trend that had produced some 150 privately funded academies across the rural northeast during the early decades of the nineteenth century, including Woodstock, Ashford, Windham, and Plainfield Academies in Windham County and Norwich Academy in neighboring New London County.[86] It was against this backdrop that Prudence Crandall's decision to discharge her privileged white female students and enroll free black girls took place.[87] As there was no legal basis by which to prosecute Crandall, Congressman Andrew T. Judson, resident of Canterbury and a prominent member of the American Colonization Society, harangued the Connecticut General Assembly to pass the "Black Law," under which she was charged.[88] The two years that followed produced the nineteenth-century equivalent of a "media frenzy."[89]

The *New Bedford Mercury* termed Crandall "courageous and enthusiastic" but "running a little too fast into trouble."[90] The *Norwich Courier* asked, "The Public will now understand that it is a crime by the Law of Connecticut to give instructions to colored persons who are not inhabitants of the State. Will the Good People of this State countenance such a law?"[91] The London *Times*, perched safely across the Rubicon of Slavery on the Shore of Abolition, termed the prosecution "ludicrous."[92] An earlier effort to open a similar school for free blacks in New Haven had quickly been quashed, rendering the issue of an existing school a state test case. The larger legal issue, however, called into question the status of free blacks as citizens. If "citizens" could travel at will to attend school, they could also, at least theoretically, stay put at will to avoid colonization.[93]

Along with bad press, the Crandall trials brought social reformers to Windham County. Prominent New York abolitionist Arthur Tappan pledged $10,000 for the schoolteacher's defense. Before advertising for black pupils, Crandall had consulted with William Lloyd Garrison and Rev. Samuel Joseph May, then in his first pastorate at the Brooklyn Unitarian Church, only six miles from Canterbury. May had already embraced the temperance movement, and, with longtime Brooklyn abolitionist George Benson, founded the Windham Peace Society in 1826.[94] In support of Crandall, Garrison spent much of 1833 in Brooklyn, hosted by Benson, whose daughter, Helen Eliza, Garrison married the following year.[95] Crandall's case was dismissed for lack of evidence by the Connecticut Supreme Court of Errors.[96] When she resumed her teaching despite the standing Black Law, Canterbury citizens fouled her well, broke her windows, and tried to burn the school over the heads of the students, adding destruction of private property and attempted arson to the town's burgeoning reputation. Crandall capitulated to the violence, closed the school, and left Connecticut permanently.

With all prospects of infusion capital gone, Canterbury remained defiantly unrepentant.[97] By 1834, Garrison and the New England Anti-Slavery Society had come to realize that broadsides and pamphlets alone were not spreading their message, and they had begun to recruit "agents" to carry it personally to lyceums and churches throughout New England.[98] Garrison's establishment of family ties brought him to Brooklyn on a regular basis and provided antislavery agents with contacts throughout Windham County. It became a base of operations.[99]

The Plainfield Anti-Slavery Society, formed in August 1833 in the midst of Crandall's legal battles, was Connecticut's second such group, and May and Benson founded Connecticut's first abolitionist newspaper, the *Unionist* in Brooklyn that same year.[100] In 1836, six of the fifteen Connecticut antislavery societies were located in Windham County.[101] By 1837, there were a total of thirty-nine societies, a third of which were in Windham.[102] Documents held in the Siebert Underground Railroad Collection archives show that Plainfield, Pomfret, Woodstock, and Brooklyn were stops on the Railroad.[103] In 1838, Phillip Pearl, Hampton delegate to the Connecticut General Assembly and former chairman of the committee that passed the Black Law, led the drive to repeal it. He subsequently became the founding president of the Connecticut Anti-Slavery Society.[104] Woodstock citizens aided in the formation of the Liberty Party, whose platform included black suffrage and, in 1843, contributed 116 votes for the abolitionist congressional candidate. So powerful was the party that for three years it obstructed the choice of town representatives.[105] By the outbreak of the Civil War in 1861, abolitionism in Windham was inscribed into much of the local consciousness.

Still, if anyone—soldier or civilian—needed an "abolitionism booster," it came from one of the county's most prominent citizens. In July 1862, civilian Joseph Danielson—of Danielsonville—traveled to South Carolina to take a position as one of the superintendents of the Port Royal Experiment under the auspices of the National Freeman's Relief Association.[106] Prior to the war, Danielson's views on slavery were well known within the community: he was *not* an abolitionist. His change of heart while in the South, however, was noted with delight by *Transcript* editor John Stone, and it must have been a tonic for men in the field and encouragement for those contemplating enlistment.[107] Danielson's year-long tenure in Port Royal produced a thirteen-part newspaper series titled "Life among the Contrabands."[108] The highly educated superintendent was a true student of humanity, and his willingness to learn from those whose "moral and intellectual improvement" he was tasked with improving was clearly demonstrated in his enthusiastic, albeit flowery, narratives that appeared in the *Transcript*: "Every day's experience brings . . . something new in the life and character of the contraband. . . . I rather like him. He is so much smarter than myself (or would be, had he but been free), that I can't help respecting him and when he meets me with doffed hat and a low bow and the salutation of 'bos,' 'massa' 'obseer' and the like, with a reverential sir appended to each, I feel like telling him to hold up his head and show himself the man that he really is; but he can't do it, for he is a black man, and he knows it."[109] The good-humored Danielson's firm belief in the capabilities of the former slaves, and his interest in their religion, music, food, dress, language, and family life must have been welcome confirmation of long-held abstract abolitionist convictions in the face of the catastrophic Union losses early in the war.

Other prominent Windham County men also wrote from the theater of war. With the help of direct rail transportation, Windham officers returned home regularly to recruit—often for periods as short as a weekend. Two Windham men in particular bolstered enlistment and coalesced community spirit. J. F. Wilkinson, associate editor of the *Windham County Transcript*, must have left for Norwich to join the Buckingham Rifles before the ink was dry on his April 18 editorial. He embraced his role as "embedded journalist," and his early letters to the *Transcript* reflected the same desire for action felt by all untested soldiers. Instead, Wilkinson, who might have contended for the Pulitzer Prize or at least a spot on CNN (had either been in existence), was wounded and captured at First Bull Run. Evacuated from the area of fighting at a full gallop behind the saddle of a young Confederate lieutenant, he survived his yearlong captivity in four different prisons from Richmond to Tuscaloosa, and returned home to pen a sixteen-part series titled "Life among the Rebels."[110] The consummate newspaperman, Wilkinson's powers of observation and investigation served him amazingly well, and his ability to recall detail and maintain his objectivity are a testament to journalism in any century.

"Life among the Rebels" was full of detailed accounts of prison hardships and the camaraderie that held lives together. He sought out people, not only his fellow prisoners, but guards, doctors, slaves, and white civilians, and asked them questions—and people talked to him. He wrote about white southern illiteracy, the absence of public schooling, and the "good common sense" of the slaves he encountered.[111] He provided northeastern Connecticut with vivid pictures of the brutalities endured by southern Union sympathizers, the kindnesses of Confederate doctors, and the deterioration of the Confederate infrastructure and economy.[112] Many of his observations concerning the sociology of the war stand up to contemporary scholarship.[113]

Another prominent Windham man was Dr. John McGregor, a Thompson physician, who seems to have been the living stereotype of the "best-loved-but-irascible country doctor." As a regimental surgeon in the Third Connecticut, McGregor was also captured at First Bull Run after he refused to leave his field hospital when retreat was ordered. Promised a speedy exchange by General P.G.T. Beauregard, McGregor was allowed to continue treating first his own men and, later, wounded Confederates. Instead of release, he was transferred first to Libby Prison, then later, to Castle Pinckney, Columbia, and, finally, Salisbury. There he became very ill and fearful for his sanity, as he was held in complete isolation after guards discovered he had failed to report an escape attempt. Emaciated and unconscious, he was dumped on the banks of the James River and left for dead. Aided by an escaped slave, McGregor eventually flagged down a passing Union steamer and returned to Windham a bona fide hero.[114]

The treatment of these well-respected citizens elicited strong reaction from the community; binding it together in purpose. Both Wilkinson and McGregor had dramatic influence on enlistments and recruiting, the former as a recruiting officer and the latter as chief examining physician for Windham County. It was not only their credibility that rendered them valuable to the war effort; it was their timing. Both men suffered terribly while imprisoned in the South, but they returned home, whole, to tell about it in mid-1862, just in time to encourage the 500 men who volunteered for the Eighteenth Connecticut.

CONCLUSION

There were many factors that influenced Windham County's wholehearted support of the Union war effort. Windham was possessed of a healthy vision of itself, firmly grounded in its separatist mindset and its perception of its own Revolutionary War heritage. By the mid-nineteenth century, access to information and local political and social history had imbued the largely homogeneous population with a strong republican tradition. When war finally came, the people of Windham County wrapped themselves in their long-held Revolutionary heritage and marched to war as their fathers had done generations before. It was a significant factor in the region's Unionism.

So too was the role of the local press. John Quincy Adams Stone retasked his newspaper, not only to all-out support of the Lincoln administration, but also to the continuing education of the rural community and to Windham men spread out across the Confederacy while serving in the Union Army. Knowledge is empowerment, and empowered people do not casually doubt themselves.

Finally, the Prudence Crandall affair was the catalyst for refining longheld antislavery beliefs into an egalitarianism that supported early black suffrage and, ultimately, demanded that the South give up its most prized possessions. From the war's onset, abolitionism was viewed in Windham as inseparable from the Union cause, and the early war experiences of respected citizens cultivated and reinforced this belief. These ideas had been propelled forward by Crandall's ill-fated school and the shame felt by many over what had happened in their own midst. The steady abolitionist tide represented by William Lloyd Garrison's presence in Brooklyn also made an indelible impact.

Windham propelled itself through the hardships and tragedies of the Civil War on a wave of idealism liberally salted with Swamp Yankee stubbornness. As its men fanned out across the battlefields of the Confederacy, the county turned inward to its patriot identity to sustain itself, even as it joined with state and Union to preserve the government. Understanding how the people of Windham viewed themselves and their role in the war that redefined the nation enables us to better comprehend the collective American sacrifice that was the Civil War.

NOTES

1. See Drew Gilpin Faust, *This Republic of Suffering: Death and the American Civil War* (New York: Knopf, 2008); for a new study that argues for a full 20 percent increase in the number of Civil War casualties, see J. David Hacker, "A Census-Based Count of the Civil War Dead," *Civil War History* 57.4 (December 2011): 306–47; Guy Gugliotta, "New Estimate Raises Civil War Death Toll," *New York Times*, April 3, 2012, D1.

2. Abraham Lincoln, "Opinion on Draft, September 14, 1863," in *Collected Works of Abraham Lincoln*, vol. 6 (Ann Arbor: University of Michigan Digital Library Production Services, 2001), http://name.umdl.umich.edu/lincoln6, 446. For examples of contemporary scholarship, see James McPherson, *What They Fought For, 1861–1865* (Baton Rouge: Louisiana State University Press, 1994) and *For Cause and Comrades* (New York: Oxford University Press, 1998); Edward Ayers, *In the Presence of Mine Enemies* (New York: W. W. Norton, 2003).

3. *Windham County Transcript*, September 8, 1864. The study of the Civil War requires, in many instances, a town-by-town focus. For a small state, Connecticut was remarkably diverse in its outlook. For information on Civil War dissent in Connecticut, see Matthew Warshauer, *Connecticut in the American Civil War: Slavery, Sacrifice, and Survival* (Middletown, CT: Wesleyan University Press, 2011); Joanna D. Cowden, "The Politics of Dissent: Civil War Democrats in Connecticut," *New England Quarterly* 56.4 (December 1983): 538–54; see also J. Robert Lane, *A Political History of Connecticut during the Civil War* (Washington, DC: Catholic University of America Press, 1941); John E. Tallmadge, "A Peace Movement in Civil War Connecticut," *New England Quarterly* 37.3 (September 1964): 306–21.

4. Blaikie Hines, *Civil War Volunteer Sons of Connecticut* (Thomaston, ME: American Patriot Press, 2002), 196–99.

5. John Niven, *Connecticut for the Union: The Role of the State in the Civil War* (New Haven, CT: Yale University Press, 1965), 116.

6. Hines, *Civil War Volunteer Sons of Connecticut*, 426–27.

7. *Windham County Transcript*, December 21, 1861.

8. Hines, *Civil War Volunteer Sons of Connecticut*, 22–259.

9. Hines, *Civil War Volunteer Sons of Connecticut*, 292–372.

10. Hines, *Civil War Volunteer Sons of Connecticut*, xiii.

11. Henry Vernon Arnold, *The Making of Danielson, an Outline History of the Borough of Danielson, Connecticut* (self-published, 1905), 171. This author suggests that procuring substitutes and obtaining bogus medical exemptions in Killingly was very common beginning in late 1864. This position, however, is strongly contradicted by accounts published in the *Transcript* at the time and may be due to obvious personal dislike of a prominent civilian recruiter who was actually held in great esteem by the wartime community. See *Windham County Transcript*, December 10, 1863. Regarding hiring substitutes in Connecticut, see Warshauer, *Connecticut in the American Civil War*, 130–33, 142.

12. *Windham County Transcript*, August 27, 1863.

13. Hines, *Civil War Volunteer Sons of Connecticut*, 292–372.

14. Jason Newton, "Rediscovering the Old Connecticut Path," https://sites
.google.com/site/oldconnecticutpath.

15. Richard Bayles, *The History of Windham County* (New York: W. W. Preston,
1889), 23, 24, 27.

16. William F. Willingham, "Grass Root Politics in Windham, Connecticut during the Jeffersonian Era," *Journal of the Early Republic* 1.2 (Summer 1981): 127–
48.

17. Obviously, as in the remainder of Connecticut, Congregationalism remained
the predominant Protestant denomination in Windham. Still, my point rebuts
the theory that the suffocating nature of the Standing Order drove the men of
Windham to enlist in the Union Army. See Niven, *Connecticut for the Union*,
121–23. Puritan theology recognized the authority of the local church as final and
strongly rejected ecclesiastical hierarchy. Church members elected and ordained
their own ministers and lay officials. Thus, these autonomous churches together
formed "the Standing Order" of "the New England Way": "a community of independent churches, each governed solely by the decision of its own members, yet
in fellowship with all other churches so constituted" (see "The Unitarian Controversy and Its Puritan Roots," *The Dictionary of Unitarian & Universalist Biography*, http://www25.uua.org/uuhs/duub/articles/unitariancontroversy.html). Historically speaking, however, the term "Standing Order" is often used to refer more
specifically to Congregational clergy within the context of the controversies that
erupted within the denomination (New Lights / Old Lights) prior to the Revolutionary War, their opposition to the end of state-sponsored religion in Connecticut, and their reaction to the evangelical fervor of the Second Great Awakening.
See Edwin Gaustad and Leigh Schmidt, *The Religious History of America: The
Heart of the American Story from Colonial Times to Today* (New York: Harper-
Collins, 2002).

18. Willingham, "Grass Root Politics in Windham, Connecticut during the
Jeffersonian Era," 128–36.

19. M. Louise Greene, *The Development of Religious Liberty in Connecticut*
(Boston: Houghton, Mifflin, 1905).

20. Willingham, "Grass Root Politics in Windham, Connecticut during the
Jeffersonian Era," 142.

21. Gideon Welles, "Address of the State Convention to the Democrats of Connecticut, 1835," quoted in John Niven, *Gideon Welles: Lincoln's Secretary of the
Navy* (New York: Oxford University Press, 1973), 7.

22. Review of The Development of Religious Liberty in Connecticut, by
M. Louise Greene, *American Historical Review* 11.3 (1906): 687.

23. M. P. Dowe, *Windham County Transcript*, January 24, 1901.

24. In 1850, only 5 percent of Windham County's white population was foreign-
born compared with 15 percent in both Hartford and New Haven. Figures based
on u.s. Census records available through the University of Virginia at http://map
server.lib.virginia.edu.

25. Ellen D. Larned, *History of Windham County, Connecticut*, vol. 2 (self-published, 1874–80), 502.

26. Robert J. Lane, *The Political History of Connecticut during the Civil War* (Washington, DC: Catholic University of America Press, 1941), 121.

27. Register quoted in the *Hartford Courant*, April 7, 1860.

28. Courier quoted in the *Hartford Courant*, April 7, 1860.

29. Niven, *Connecticut for the Union*, 119–20.

30. Bayles, *The History of Windham County*, 5. This configuration of rail lines provided access for all Windham County townships except Eastford, Ashford, Chaplin, Hampton, and Woodstock. Of these, the first three were extremely sparsely populated. Woodstock was well connected to both Massachusetts and the adjoining Windham County towns by very heavily traveled roads. Pomfret and Brooklyn had no rail lines, but their commercial centers were within very short distances of stations.

31. "Train Schedule," *Windham County Transcript*, April 11, 1861.

32. See McPherson, *For Cause and Comrades*; and Ayers, *In the Presence of Mine Enemies*.

33. Bayles, *The History of Windham County*, 83.

34. The infamous Connecticut Path evolved into part of the Post Road system.

35. Bayles, *The History of Windham County*, 61, 65.

36. The now-empty den in Brooklyn is marked by a plaque presented to the Elizabeth-Porter Putnam Chapter of the Daughters of the American Revolution by the Colonel Daniel Putnam Association. It reads, "He dared to lead where others dared to follow." For an account of the wolf story, see, for instance, Fanny Greye Bragg, "Israel Putnam," Connecticut Society for the Sons of the American Revolution, http://www.connecticutsar.org/patriots/putnam_israel.htm.

37. "Boys," said Putnam, to several volunteers of the French war, as he passed them on the field [on Breed's Hill], "do you remember my orders at Ticonderoga?" Promptly came the response, "You told us not to fire till we could see the whites of the enemy's eyes." "Well," said Putnam, "I give the same order now" (Bayles, The History of Windham County, 72).

38. Bayles, *The History of Windham County*, 62.

39. Bayles, *The History of Windham County*, 67–69.

40. *Windham County Transcript*, April 24, 1861.

41. "Windham County Aroused!," *Windham County Transcript*, April 24, 1861.

42. *Windham County Transcript*, April 24, 1861.

43. *Windham County Transcript*, April 24, 1861.

44. *Windham County Transcript*, June 27, 1861. Windham County seemed to have difficulty with native sons who failed to maintain residency. This issue of the *Transcript* also describes Lyon as "an awkward, homely youth, but exceedingly plucky . . . [whose] appearance created little impression . . . among the young ladies of Brooklyn."

45. J.Q.A. Stone, "Editorial," *Windham County Transcript*, December 5, 1861.

46. *Windham County Transcript*, May 4, 1861.

47. Niven, *Connecticut for the Union*, 117–18.

48. David R. Meyer, "The Roots of American Industrialization, 1790–1860," *Economic History Association*, http://eh.net/encyclopedia/article/meyer.indus trialization.

49. Bayles, *The History of Windham County*, 2–3.

50. Niven, *Connecticut for the Union*, 112–13.

51. Jamie H. Eves, "By the Sweat of Their Brows: Mill Workers and Their Lives," Windham Textile and History Museum, http://www.millmuseum.org.

52. Niven's source for this anecdote is D. Hamilton Hurd, *History of New London County* (Philadelphia: J. W. Lewis & Co., 1882), 748–49. The book is available online at www.archive.org/stream/cu31924028841951#page/n3/mode/2up.

53. *Windham County Transcript*, August 21, 1862.

54. Niven, *Connecticut for the Union*, 113. The Eighteenth Connecticut was composed of five companies from New London County and five from Windham County. Niven appears to be referencing the yearlong period following the financial panic of 1857. This revivalism was primarily an urban phenomenon that spawned massive prayer meetings in New York, Philadelphia, and other major metropolitan areas across the country. It is attributed by some scholars to the belief that excessive materialism was heralding the downturn of American society. See, for example, Kathryn Long, *The Revival of 1857–58: Interpreting an American Religious Awakening* (New York: Oxford University Press, 1998). There are multiple problems with Niven's assertion, even as it pertains to Connecticut enlistment in general. First, he cites as an example a "religious revival" in Hartford during the winter of 1851–52—six years prior to the panic of 1857—led by "that rough-hewn old Presbyterian evangelist Charles G. Finney" (see p. 121). Not only had Finney converted to Congregationalism to avoid a heresy trial long before 1851, but he dramatically inflated the success of his 1851 work in Hartford in his 1876 memoirs, upon which Niven ("he converted over 600"; "the new converts [then] conducted the most extensive and successful revival the city had ever witnessed") relies for his account. The *Hartford Courant* paid very little notice to Finney's presence in the city, noting in its "Religious Items" columns only that he was preaching at several different Congregational churches. Upon his departure, it noted only that Finney had been "laboring in Hartford for some time past" (see the *Hartford Courant*, December 27, 1851, and January 3, January 20, and March 13, 1852). On March 11, 1852, however, following Finney's return to New York, a letter from a staunch Finney admirer, purportedly from Hartford but signed only "Tennant," was published in the New York paper *The Independent*. Although the letter spoke glowingly of Finney's efforts in Hartford, it also noted that no attempt had been made to count Finney's conversions (there were "seemingly not a few," "probably many") and also frankly admitted, "It is true that a very large portion of the church members have not been reached." The letter said nothing about the converted conducting their own revival. See "Revival in Hartford," *The Independent*, March 11, 1852, ProQuest Historical Newspaper Database; and *Memoirs of Rev. Charles G. Finney* (New York: A. S. Barnes, 1876), available via http://googlebooks.com. Finney's own friends repeatedly warned him about his conceit and arrogance, which would explain Finney's fabricated account (included by Niven) in which Rev. Joel Dawes

of Hartford's prestigious Center Congregational Church (misidentified by Finney and Niven as "First Congregational Church") seeks out and acts upon Finney's advice. Contemporary scholars have found the memoirs, which were undertaken solely to rebut biographies published by Finney's critics that threatened the continuation of his career, "self-serving" and historically unreliable. See Keith J. Hardman, *Charles Grandison Finney: Revivalist and Reformer* (Grand Rapids, MI: Baker Publishing Group, 1987); and Jerry MacLean, "Review: 'The Memoirs of Charles G. Finney: The Complete Restored Text,'" *Journal of the Early Republic* 11.3 (Autumn 1991): 430–31.

55. Of the two works, Bayles's is the better organized. He addresses the religious and temperance history of each town in its respective chapter.

56. Windham County boasted two local newspapers, the *Willimantic Journal*, which served mainly the towns of Windham, Hampton, Mansfield, and Chaplin, and the *Windham County Transcript*, which was published in Danielsonville and Putnam and was widely distributed throughout the entire county. This chapter is based primarily on the correspondence and editorials that appeared in the *Transcript* from 1861 to 1865.

57. Larned, *History of Windham County, Connecticut*, 556.

58. Larned, *History of Windham County, Connecticut*, 556.

59. Bayles, *The History of Windham County*, 980–81.

60. J. F. Wilkinson, "Civil War Begins," *Windham County Transcript*, April 18, 1861.

61. See, for example, "From the Eleventh Regiment," *Windham County Transcript*, January 16, 1862, which begins, "Mr. Editor—You asked me, as we were about to go Dixie-ward. . . ."

62. Noah Andre, "With Pens and Swords," *Civil War Times* 42.5 (2003): 48–51; Ford Risley, "Bombastic yet Insightful," *Journalism History* 24.3 (1998): 104–12.

63. This is not to suggest that all Windham soldiers were well-educated, but within the county there were ample opportunities for the sons of even middle-class families to extend or expand their education beyond the district schools. By 1850, there were seven private high schools and "academies" in five different Windham townships. This practice was not uncommon for the time period. See J. M. Opal, "Exciting Emulation: Academies and the Transformation of the Rural North, 1780s–1820s," *Journal of American History* 91.2 (September 2004): 445–70.

64. Although there are many collections of personal letters from Connecticut soldiers within the public purview, only a handful are from Windham County soldiers. Of these, however, none reflect sentiment differing from their published correspondence. See, for example, "Caleb Blanchard Civil War Era Letters, 1851–1866" and "George and Fannie Kies Papers, 1854–1900," held at the Connecticut State Historical Society in Hartford. The Transcript contains letters from the following regiments, 1st–8th, 12th, 18th, 21st, 26th, 29th, 30th. For more on Connecticut newspapers, see Warshauer, *Connecticut in the American Civil War*.

65. "The Soldiers and Their Feelings," *Hartford Times*, January 20, 1863.

66. E. S. Simpson, "Editorial," *Willimantic Journal*, April 26, 1861. As quoted

by Robert Wolff in "The Stronghold of Liberty: Civil War Editorials of the Windham County Press, 1861–1865," *Connecticut History* 42.2 (Spring 2003): 132–58.

67. *Windham County Transcript*, June 27, 1861.

68. *Windham County Transcript*, March 6, 1862.

69. Stephen J. Lee, *Windham County Transcript*, December 20, 1862.

70. Lee, *Windham County Transcript*, July 11, 1863.

71. *Windham County Transcript*, August 8, 1861.

72. *Windham County Transcript*, August 27, 1863.

73. For racism in Civil War–era Connecticut, see Warshauer, *Connecticut in the American Civil War*. See also Michael D. Pierson, "'All Southern Society Is Assailed by the Foulest Charges': Charles Sumner's 'The Crime against Kansas' and the Escalation of Republican Anti-Slavery Rhetoric," *New England Quarterly* 68.4 (December 1995): 531–57; Michael E. Woods, "'The Indignation of Freedom-Loving People': The Caning of Charles Sumner and Emotion in Antebellum Politics," *Journal of Social History* (Spring 2011): 689–705; Manisha Sinha, "The Caning of Charles Sumner: Slavery, Race, and Ideology in the Age of the Civil War," *Journal of the Early Republic* 23.2 (Summer 2003): 233–62; William H. Pease and Jane H. Pease, "Antislavery Ambivalence: Immediatism, Expediency, Race," *American Quarterly* 17.4 (Winter 1965): 682–95; Gerda Lerner, "The Grimke Sisters and the Struggle against Race Prejudice," *Journal of Negro History* 48.4 (October 1963): 277–91.

74. Lt. H. H. Brown, "Camp Jottings," *Windham County Transcript*, March 24, 1864.

75. Figures based on u.s. Census records available through the University of Virginia at http://mapserver.lib.virginia.edu.

76. *Windham County Transcript*, June 27, 1861. "H.P." may well be a male relative of a "colored woman of fiery temper" fondly referred to as "Aunt Hannah Phillips" by Henry Vernon Arnold in The Making of Danielson, 162. She lived in the "Sparks bakery building" in Danielsonville during the Civil War.

77. J. F. Wilkinson, "Civil War Begins," *Windham County Transcript*, April 18, 1861.

78. Lt. Col. Warner, "Barbarism of Slavery," *Windham County Transcript*, July 24, 1862.

79. Letter dated June 13, 1861, in *Windham County Transcript*, June 20, 1861.

80. "J.D.L.," *Windham County Transcript*, January 9, 1862.

81. *Windham County Transcript*, June 20, 1861.

82. "F.M.S.," *Windham County Transcript*, January 16, 1862.

83. Ayers, *In the Presence of Mine Enemies*, xix.

84. Larned, *History of Windham County*, Connecticut, 502.

85. Larned, *History of Windham County*, Connecticut, 490–502.

86. Opal, "Exciting Emulation," 445–50.

87. Crandall would have willingly taught both side-by-side. She only discharged her white students after parents threatened to withdraw them and close her school. See Susan Strane, *A Whole-Souled Woman: Prudence Crandall and the Education of Black Women* (New York: W.W. Norton, 1990).

88. William Jay, *Inquiry into the Character and Tendency of the American Colonization, and American Anti-Slavery Societies* (New York: R. G. Williams, 1837), 30–31.

89. Passed in 1834 and repealed in 1838, the hated Black Law prohibited the opening of schools "for the instruction of colored persons belonging to other states and countries" or the admission of out-of-state blacks to existing schools without first obtaining the majority consent of local civil authority. See "Connecticut's 'Black Law' (1833)," http://www.yale.edu/glc/citizens/stories/module4/documents/black_law.html. See also Warshauer, *Connecticut in the American Civil War*; Joanne Pope Melish, *Disowning Slavery: Gradual Emancipation and "Race" in New England, 1780–1860* (Ithaca, NY: Cornell University Press, 1998).

90. "Miss Prudence Crandall," *New Bedford Mercury*, April 19, 1833.

91. "From the Norwich Courier, July 3," *Connecticut Courant*, July 8, 1833.

92. *The Times*, November 29, 1833 (obtained through subscription database: http://archive.timesonline.co.uk).

93. William Yates, *Rights of Colored Men to Suffrage, Citizenship and Trial by Jury: A Book of Facts, Arguments and Authorities, Historical Notices and Sketches of Debates — with Notes* (Philadelphia, 1838), iv (preface).

94. Samuel J. May, *Some Recollections of Our Antislavery Conflict* (Boston: Fields, Osgood & Co., 1869), 39–46.

95. Walter M. Merrill, ed., *The Letters of William Lloyd Garrison: Let the Oppressed Go Free* (Cambridge, MA: Harvard University Press, 1979), 277–84.

96. "Report of the Arguments of Counsel: In the Case of Prudence Crandall, Plff. In Error, vs. State of Connecticut, before the Supreme Court of Errors, at Their Session at Brooklyn, July Term, 1834" (Boston, 1834), Samuel J. May Anti-Slavery Collection, Cornell University, Ithaca, NY.

97. Larned, *History of Windham County, Connecticut*, 502.

98. May, *Some Recollections of Our Antislavery Conflict*, 42–88.

99. William Garrison to George W. Benson, April 10, 1836, in Merrill, *The Letters of William Lloyd Garrison*, 70.

100. There appear to be no surviving copies of this paper.

101. Third Annual Report of the American Anti-Slavery Society (New York, 1836), in Samuel J. May Anti-Slavery Collection, Cornell University, Ithaca, NY.

102. Fourth Annual Report of the American Anti-Slavery Society (New York, 1837), in Samuel J. May Anti-Slavery Collection, Cornell University, Ithaca, NY.

103. See Susan H. Crosbie to Henrietta Buckmaster, St. Petersburg, Florida, December 17, 1939; Wm. W. Cady to W. H. Seibert, Harmon, Illinois, April 10, 1896; Wm. W. Cady to W. H. Seibert, Harmon, Illinois, April 3, 1896; all in the Wilbur H. Siebert Underground Railroad Collection, Ohio Historical Society, Columbus, OH.

104. Fifth Annual Report of the Executive Committee of the American Anti-Slavery Society (New York, 1838), in Samuel J. May Anti-Slavery Collection, Cornell University, Ithaca, NY.

105. Bayles, *The History of Windham County*, 872–73.

106. *Windham County Transcript*, July 3, 1862.

107. *Windham County Transcript*, October 23, 1862.

108. See *Windham County Transcript*, July 18, October 9–30, November 6, and December 25, 1862, and January 29, February 19, April 23, May 14, June 4, and July 9, 1863.

109. Joseph Danielson, "Life among the Contrabands No. 3," *Windham County Transcript*, October 9, 1862.

110. See *Windham County Transcript*, July 3 through October 30, 1862.

111. J. F. Wilkinson, "Life among the Rebels No. 9," *Windham County Transcript*, September 4, 1862.

112. J. F. Wilkinson, "Life among the Rebels No. 8," *Windham County Transcript*, August 28, 1862, and No. 6, August 14, 1862.

113. See, "Life among the Rebels No. 9," *Windham County Transcript*, September 4, 1862, for Wilkinson's observations on southern class, religion, and the press; and "Life among the Rebels No. 15," *Windham County Transcript*, October 23, 1862, for his assessment of the planter-yeoman relationship.

114. Jeremiah S. McGregor, Life and Deeds of Dr. John McGregor (Foster, RI: self-published, 1886), 20–65. Accounts in the *Transcript* confirm those published by McGregor's son following his father's untimely death in a buggy accident.

4 : Untried to Unrivaled

THE FOURTEENTH REGIMENT, CONNECTICUT VOLUNTEER INFANTRY

W hen the men of the Fourteenth Regiment of the Connecticut Volunteer Infantry mustered for duty on August 23, 1862, they could not possibly have imagined that within just a few short weeks they would be thrown into the single deadliest day in American history. The Battle of Antietam, which occurred on September 17 in Sharpsburg, Maryland, was twelve hours of remarkable human destruction. Smoke filled the battlefield as tens of thousands of men, both Union and Confederate, unleashed a torrent of lead upon one another. When the roar of cannon and muskets finally ceased, 23,000 men had lost their lives or been wounded. The approach to Antietam, via South Mountain, was also horrifically bloody. Words could not fully convey what the men witnessed, though Sergeant Benjamin Hirst of Rockville, Fourteenth Regiment, Company D, tried—writing home to his wife that he had awoken on the battlefield and to see "[w]ar without romance, there was dead men lying around everywhere some with their heads shattered to Pieces, others with their bowels protruding while others had lost their legs and Arms. [W]hat my feelings were, I cannot describe, but I hope to God never to see such another sight again."[1]

Additional bloodletting ensued: Fredericksburg, then Chancellorsville. Each time the Fourteenth was battered, bloodied, and demoralized. It was hardly an auspicious start to their Civil War experience. By war's end, however, the men of the Connecticut Fourteenth were the most battle-hardened unit from the state. These men fought in more battles and skirmishes (some thirty-four), among them many of the most imposing and significant of the war, and captured more Confederate battle flags than any other Connecticut regiment. They also, not surprisingly, had the largest percentage of men killed in battle and who died in service. They played a critical role in the Battle of Gettysburg, helping to break Confederate General George Pickett's famous charge, joined General Ulysses

Grant's campaign to hunt down Robert E. Lee's army in the spring and summer of 1864, and stood by as he surrendered at Appomattox Courthouse in April 1865. What had begun as a regiment filled with new, unseasoned men, mustered out on May 31, 1865, as a unit ranked among the greatest heroes Connecticut has ever known, claiming three Congressional Medal of Honor winners and countless achievements that continue to go unrecognized.[2]

Surprisingly, little has been written about the Fourteenth Regiment. In 1906, Charles D. Page published the *History of the Fourteenth Regiment, Connecticut Vol. Infantry* in honor of the war's fiftieth anniversary, noting that it should have been written a generation earlier because "a history written at that time would have been more complete in detail and richer in personal experience." He rightly added that "as time goes on, memory has become weaker, memoranda, diaries, and letters have become scattered and irrecoverably lost." Page specifically addressed the regiment's continued maturation throughout the war, beginning with their awful experience at Antietam, and fully recognized the seeming impossibility that they would ever overcome their demoralizing start: "No one at that time would have ventured the prophecy that this very regiment . . . was destined to play an important part in some of the most sanguinary battles of modern times, and do valiant service in some of the pivotal actions of the great conflict."[3]

William A. Croffut and John Morris's voluminous *A Military and Civil History of Connecticut*, published immediately after the war, in 1869, certainly discussed the Fourteenth's contributions, though they are spread over some eight hundred pages and included as only a small portion of the wider Connecticut war story. More recently, in 1998, anthropologist Robert L. Bee published *The Boys from Rockville: Civil War Narratives of Sgt. Benjamin Hirst, Company D, Fourteenth Connecticut Volunteers*. Utilizing the previously unpublished letters of Hirst, located at the New England Civil War Museum in Rockville, Connecticut, Bee provided a fascinating account of Hirst's war experiences within the context of an anthropological study of immigration and mill workers. In this sense, the work is more limited in scope and not meant to be a wider study of the Fourteenth Regiment. Indeed, the book ends after Gettysburg. Other studies have been written on Connecticut's Civil War experience that include information, but do not focus specifically on the Fourteenth. John Niven's 1965 *Connecticut for the Union: The Role of the State in the Civil War*, and Matthew Warshauer's 2011 *Connecticut in the American Civil*

War: Slavery, Sacrifice, and Survival were published, respectively, for the centennial and sesquicentennial of the war.[4]

Considering the Fourteenth Regiment's remarkable history, it is no less remarkable that a contemporary, dedicated book-length study has not yet been completed. Whereas this chapter certainly does not approach the kind of depth that is needed to record the unit's long engagement in the nation's deadliest conflict, it is an attempt to offer readers a more up-to-date account of the Fourteenth's maturation from untried to unrivaled.

The Fourteenth Regiment developed slowly during the summer months of 1862. Connecticut had already responded with extensive numbers of enlistments after President Lincoln issued not one, but two, calls for 500,000 three-year soldiers. Between the initial formation of the first three-month Connecticut regiments (the First, Second, and Third) following the firing on Fort Sumter, and the formation of seven new regiments, the Sixth through the Twelfth, as well as cavalry and artillery units, the state had put forward some 15,278 men for the Union war effort. It responded with an additional regiment, the Thirteenth, which formed in February 1862, and added yet another 1,480 men.[5] Many within the state hoped that such numbers, combined with the equally devoted response of other northern states would be all that was needed to quell the southern rebellion.

This was not to be. Mounting Confederate victories and General Robert E. Lee's ability to frustrate Union General George B. McClellan resulted in a May 21, 1862, general order from the War Department establishing a contingent of 50,000 men for a "Camp of Instruction" at Annapolis, Maryland. The next day, Connecticut Governor William A. Buckingham directed that "volunteers be received sufficient to form one regiment to be known as the Fourteenth Regiment of Infantry, to serve three years or during the war unless sooner discharged." An encampment was located on the New Haven Turnpike about two miles from Hartford and was designated as Camp Foote, in honor of Connecticut's own Commodore Andrew Hull Foote. Enlistments, however, were slow at the outset. Only some 250 men had volunteered by mid-July.[6] The notion of a camp of instruction was apparently not enough to spur the Union-minded of the state. When yet another call from the government came for volunteers, this time for 300,000 men, a patriotic fervor again swept the state. The *Hartford Courant* announced, "Men of Connecticut! Rally once more at your country's call."[7] Governor Buckingham issued a call to "Citizens of Connecticut," announcing, "You are again called upon to rally to the support of the government. . . . Close your factories and workshops, turn aside

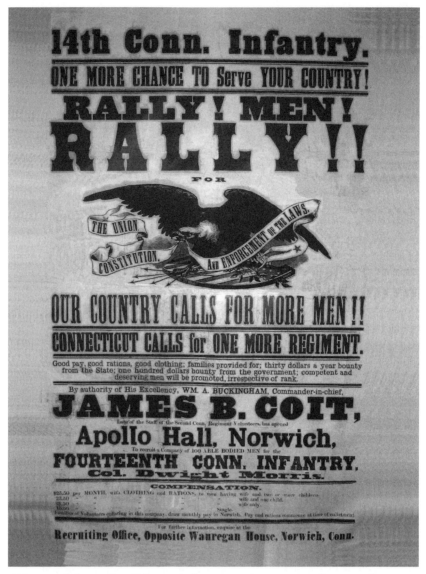

A Fourteenth Connecticut Volunteer Infantry recruitment poster. Courtesy of Tad Sattler, Company G, 14th Connecticut Volunteer Infantry, 1862–65, Inc.

from your farms and your business, leave for awhile your families and homes, meet face to face the enemies of your liberties!"[8]

Young men throughout Connecticut assembled in recruiting offices. Enlistments to the Fourteenth exploded. Historians Croffut and Morris wrote that "the lonely squads that had been drilling for weeks as the nucleus of the Fourteenth were now immediately reinforced." The regiment was the most diverse of any Connecticut unit previously formed, with men from eighty-six different towns.[9] The regiment's assistant surgeon, Dr. Levi Jewett, commented in his diary about the small number of men in early July but noted the first tangible addition toward the end of the month, when Captain Thomas Burpee brought in "a fine company" from Rockville and Vernon, which became the core of Company D. Soon after, a company from Middletown, which eventually formed Company B, entered camp with "a band playing and flags flying and escorted by the firemen of Middletown." Many more companies followed until the last man had enlisted and the last commission was signed on August 22. The men were officially mustered into service on August 23, 1862, with some 1,000 recruits, and two days later departed Hartford aboard the steamer the *City of Hartford* and the *Dudley Buck*, bound for New York where the regiment traveled south via railroad.[10] Dr. Jewitt records in his journal: "We left camp with bands playing and flags flying, marching to the dock in a column of fours. As we moved the crowd increased and when we reached the corner of Main and State Streets, it became so dense that we could hardly make progress. Reaching the dock six companies boarded the steamer 'City of Hartford' and four companies upon the transport 'Dudley Buck. . . . When we reached Middletown, it seemed as if the whole city had turned out to meet us. The dock and all the space about was black with people. Many came to the boats with baskets of fruit and food." Private William B. Hincks, of Bridgeport and in Company A, remarked, "Our progress was a sort of triumphal journey. Steamers salute with their whistles, flags were unfurled and bells were rung. Farmers waved their hands and hats as a hurrah to us as we shot by."[11]

Despite the initial fanfare, the regiment was almost passed over by President Lincoln while on march through Washington. "When the head of B Company," noted regimental historian Charles Page, "reached the stand, President Lincoln was so busy we felt we were not noticed, so with one accord we struck up loudly singing 'We are coming, Father Abraham, three hundred thousand more.'" Lincoln straightened, doffed his

Assistant surgeon, Dr. Levi Jewett, from Charles D. Page, History of the Fourteenth Regiment, Connecticut Vol. Infantry *(Meriden, CT: Horton Printing Co., 1906).*

famous stovepipe hat, and bowed until the entire company passed. After the march, Lincoln allegedly professed that the Fourteenth was "the finest looking body of men that had passed through Washington."[12] The regiment crossed the Potomac River to Arlington Heights, Virginia, then land confiscated from the family of Robert E. Lee and today the site of Arlington National Cemetery.

The three days of travel from Hartford had been exhilarating and exhausting. Lt. Samuel Fiske, a minister from Madison and member of Company K, wrote, "Our boys, on their way to the field, slept on the dirty decks of a steamer, lying together as thick as rows of pins on a paper; were packed in dirty, close cars, like sheep in a pen; marched through dust so thick and fine, that, mixed in proper proportion with the perspiration caused by the intense heat, formed a good plaster cast of every man's face and form. . . . For three days together, in our first week, we had nothing to eat but a few hard crackers, and once a morsel of cheese and once a slice of ham apiece served round." Fiske noted that the life of a soldier is uncertain. "One night the camp is all alive with lights, fires, songs, and shouts of laughter; the next all is silence. . . . The soldier knows least of all men what a day may bring forth."[13]

Fiske's commentary could not have been truer. As September arrived, the men still had received virtually nothing in the way of actual military training. Croffut and Morris note that the regiment "knew nothing about the manual of arms, or company or battalion drill; they received marching-orders to follow the enemy before they had received their muskets. The regiment moved along the heights; halted at Fort Ethan Allen, and found its untried arms awaiting it there." The regiment was soon combined with the 130th Pennsylvania and the 108th New York Volunteers to form the Second Brigade of the Third Division, Second Army Corps of the

Army of the Potomac. Colonel Dwight Morris, the regiment's commander, was placed in charge of the brigade, and Lieutenant Colonel Sanford H. Perkins assumed command of the Fourteenth, which now entered Maryland in pursuit of General Robert E. Lee, who had crossed the Potomac and invaded the North.[14] Antietam was upon them.

The Fourteenth Regiment was ordered to march in the early hours of September 17, 1862, heading toward Antietam Creek in Sharpsburg. After hours on the road, the men forded the creek and formed a line of battle. Page poignantly described the instant before they first tasted war: "The supreme moment of their experience, as there shot through the minds of the men the thought of the loved ones at home: the terrible possibilities of the engagement made vivid by the ghastly scenes through which they had already passed at South Mountain; some indeed would be wounded, some slain outright: there must inevitably be suffering and death: and as they looked at the familiar faces of their comrades, they wondered who it would be."[15]

Colonel Morris, along with a detachment of the 108th New York, was sent to support Major General Israel Richardson's division between Brigadier General John Caldwell's line and the famed Irish Brigade. The Fourteenth was at the division's center, with separate brigades in their front and to the rear. The division arrived at the East Woods and witnessed the horror of the battle that previous Union forces faced only minutes before. Confederate infantry held a position about five hundred yards southwest of the burning Mumma farm buildings, and the Fourteenth was to attack with the rest of Brigadier General William French's division. Croffut and Morris described the regiment at this moment as "little more than a crowd of earnest Connecticut boys."[16]

The order was soon given to advance, and the Fourteenth entered the fray. The moment they moved forward Rebel artillery batteries opened up, forcing the Union men to bypass the burning Mumma farm and head straight toward the farmstead of William Roulette, where enemy skirmishers had taken a strong position for defense. Company B broke away to attack Rebel sharpshooters, as William Roulette shouted encouragement: "Give it to 'em! Drive 'em! Take anything on my place, only drive 'em!"[17] The inexperience of the regiment was immediately apparent. Lt. Fiske wrote, "the battle itself was a scene of indescribable confusion. Troops didn't know what they were expected to do, and sometimes, in the excitement, fired at their own men."[18] Company D, also caught up in the smoke and confusion, rushed into an open field and nearly cost Ben Hirst his life.

Hirst described the scene in a letter dated September 20: "Boys fell on their Bellies, firing indiscrimatley and I am sorry to think wounding some of our own men on the left of our line of Batle. I saw the whole of this at a glance and roard like a mad Bull for our men to cease fireing until they could see the rebs. . . . I fired 13 rounds into their midst seeing our colours falling further back we backed out to our Company."

Following these initial engagements, the Fourteenth was moved through the battlefield to a slope east of Roulette Lane, known as the Sunken Road, later to be renamed Bloody Lane. On their way, Company D was hit by a shell that killed three men and wounded four. Hirst noted the horror and irony of the incident: "While we were lying in the rear of the stone wall . . . W. P. Ramsdell quietly remarked that if he was going to be hit, he would prefer to have the top of his head blown off. When midway between the wall and the position assigned to us, I was about the center of the company, urging the boys to close up, when a rebel shell came whizzing by and struck about two files in my rear. As soon as I could turn I saw about a dozen men lying in a heap and the first man I recognized was W. P. Ramsdell with the top of his head blown off."[19]

The Fourteenth remained just in front of the Sunken Road, where Companies A and B utilized their Sharp's Rifles to hold off enemy sharpshooters. The regimental chaplain, the Reverend Henry S. Stevens recalled that both companies, "ensconced behind perfumed barricades of defunct horses having, as Dr. Jewett used to say, a 'loud smell,' did effective work, tumbling many a Johnny out of trees."[20]

After thirty-six hours in battle with no food or drink besides some hardtack and a little water, the Fourteenth, with many of their brethren killed or wounded, emerged from the single bloodiest day of the entire war. Between 6,300 to 6,500 soldiers from both armies were killed or mortally wounded, and another 17,000 were injured. The Fourteenth counted 123 casualties: 19 killed, 103 wounded, and 1 missing.[21]

Considering their inexperience and lack of training, the regiment performed remarkably well. In his official report of the battle, Lieutenant Colonel Perkins wrote, "Our men, hastily raised and without drill, behaved like veterans, and fully maintained the honor of the Union and our native state." The commander of the brigade, General French, concluded, "There never was better material in any army; and in a month these splendid men will not be excelled," adding, "All glory to the Connecticut Fourteenth."[22] Even without the experience of previous battles, Benjamin Hirst recog-

Regimental chaplain, the Reverend Henry Stevens, from the Antietam Monument Dedication Book, *1894.*

nized the significance of Antietam, writing it was "the greatest Battle ever fought on this Continent." Charles Page recorded it as "one of the most fiercely fought and bloody battles of the war."[23]

The honorable performance of the Fourteenth can be contrasted with other regiments that also saw action for the first time. Connecticut's Sixteenth Regiment, mustered into service at the same time as the Fourteenth, had a very different experience. After Confederate General A. P. Hill attacked Union General Ambrose Burnside's left flank, the Sixteenth fled the battle field in disarray. Private William H. Drake, of Windsor, wrote to his cousin about "some pretty tall running in the 16th and I guess that made myself scarce rather fast."[24] Private William Relyea of Suffield remembered the scene: "I had loaded and was going to fire the third time when, happening to look around, I saw only dead men laying where they fell. I very quickly decided it was no place for me." He ran as quickly as possible back across the field. When the Sixteenth was finally able to ascertain their condition, they counted 44 dead, 1 missing, 159 wounded, and 19 captured. It was a horrific start to their wartime experience, one from which they never fully recovered.[25]

Over the course of the next month, the Fourteenth marched from Antietam to Harper's Ferry, West Virginia. Encamped for a time at Bolivar Heights, they quickly learned that time in camp could be just as deadly as the battlefield. Page notes that "there was much sickness in the camp, many times more than two hundred being under the doctor's care. This was owing to bad water, lack of proper food and no overcoats or blankets, and the nights were cold and frosty." He quoted Albert Hall of Company H, saying that "the water here was so bad and with other conditions caused a great amount of sickness and eventually a large number of deaths."[26] Those who remained relatively healthy dealt with the rigors and routine of camp life. Page described the men up and assembled for roll call by 5:30 a.m., then off to find breakfast; 8 a.m. was guard mounting, when men were chosen to serve as sentries. At 8:30 a.m., the men were drilled for two hours, let go for dinner until 5:30 p.m., then drilled again and released after a dress parade. At 8 p.m. roll call was taken, and the men were then released for the evening. Page added, "The almost universal time killer in camp was cards. Various games were played, but poker was king."[27]

The men departed Bolivar Heights at the end of October and proceeded on their trek south, to Belle Plain, where they continued to suffer. Page wrote that the conditions of the camp were totally miserable: "It rained for nearly a week after the regiment reached there. . . . [T]he camp was situated amid swamps and mud flats, their blankets and clothing were wet through and their fires could not be made to burn."[28] By early December, they were off again, pursuing General Lee's army and headed for the Rappahannock River, opposite Fredericksburg, Virginia. They arrived on December 11, during a heavy Union bombardment and attempted to drive Confederate sharpshooters who were preventing the progress of building pontoon bridges along the river. The Fourteenth eventually crossed on December 12 but temporarily lost its two commanding officers, Colonel Morris and Lieutenant Colonel Perkins, to sickness. Equally as bad, Company D had no commissioned officers present during the day's roll call and suddenly found itself under the command of Orderly Sergeant Frank

Stoughton of Rockville who, along with the only 25 soldiers left in his company, was preparing to attack the city of Fredericksburg.[29]

The Fourteenth was originally to be the only Connecticut regiment engaged in the battle, but the Twenty-Seventh also ended up taking part. After a night's rest in the bullet-riddled houses in the heart of the city on Caroline Street, the regiment formed its lines and prepared for orders to charge atop Marye's Heights, where General Lee's forces surrounded the city in a semicircle on a sloped ridge. The brigade moved from Caroline to Princess Anne Street, then formed on Hanover Street with other regiments. The Fourteenth was positioned on the left of the Fredericksburg Courthouse and moved toward the bullet-pocked Saint George's Episcopal Church. Almost immediately, shot and shell rained down from the surrounding heights as the men marched out of the city and down Princess Anne Street. The Rebel position, coupled with their artillery prowess, quickly and efficiently stopped the Fourteenth's advances. The effectiveness of the enemy shells was compounded by the fact that, according to historian Francis Augustin O'Reilly, the "shells often exploded against the buildings, hurling shrapnel and bricks with equal velocity. Wounded men literally clogged the street." The Fourteenth was under the command of Colonel Oliver H. Palmer, of the 108th New York, and was ordered to fix bayonets, hurry across the exposed intersections of the city, and lead the charge up the heights with the 130th Pennsylvania and 108th New York Regiments to their rear. The Fourteenth's advance quickly degenerated as men of the 130th Pennsylvania "cowered behind the railroad depot," noted O'Reilly, who added, "More men might have fallen had not Lieutenant Colonel Sanford H. Perkins taken the initiative. Perkins, of the Fourteenth Connecticut, told the head of the paralyzed column to follow him. The broken ranks picked through the human debris and sidled to the right, under cover of the millrace depression." Perkins had returned from the sick roll to join his men in battle. Even with such commitment, the Fourteenth got at most to within 150 yards of the Rebel wall before the regiment's line was broken by the withering Confederate fire, and the men were forced to fall back.[30]

Historian James McPherson later described how that Rebel fire "achieved the effect of machine guns," while the regiment's chaplain, Rev. Stevens added, "into a slaughter pen indeed, were the men going, but with brave hearts they pushed forward." Fiske described the battle as a "grand semicircle of death," into which the Fourteenth marched with "rapid and unflinching step." Just as the regiment refused to quit at Antietam, the

Fourteenth pushed on with the charge and, according to Fiske, "behaved splendidly . . . not a man flinched."[31] During the battle the regiment fell, rallied, and fell numerous times, causing a London *Times* reporter who was with Confederate General Robert E. Lee's staff to remark, "no braver men ever lived than those who forced their way up Marye's Heights that day." After the unsuccessful attempt to take the Heights, the total Union casualties numbered 12,321 killed, wounded, and missing, while the Confederate losses were less than half that number. Historian Blaikie Hines stated that the Fourteenth lost almost half of its force, with 124 of 270 men out of action: 23 dead, 96 wounded, 3 missing, and 2 captured. Page questioned, "Who can depict the horrors of that scene? What language can adequately portray the awful carnage of that hour?"[32]

The aftermath of the battle was equally bad. Sam Fiske wrote laconically, "The city is filled with pieces of brave men who went whole into the conflict. Every basement and floor is covered with pools of blood. Limbs, in many houses, lie in heaps; and surgeons are exhausted with their trying labors."[33] Lieutenant Colonel Sanford Perkins gave "notice to the authorities that the Regiment is not fit for duty," then promptly lost his mind. He had been hit in the neck and taken to the hospital, where he suffered from "delusions about his whereabouts" and became certain that he was in a hotel. His service record describes that he was wounded on December 13, then received a disciplinary discharge on April 20, 1863.[34] At some point, he returned to Connecticut and ended up at the Connecticut Hospital for the Insane, created in 1868 in Middletown. Hospital records note his desire to be left alone, a refusal to socialize with others, and an obsession with a fictional character he called "Swino." Perkins drew "Swino" the pig on virtually every piece of available paper, and it was the regular subject of conversation with doctors. Hospital staff recorded multiple symptoms, including paranoia, irrational excitability, violent fits, and withdrawal from social life. Doctors believed that the cause of insanity was the result of his war experience.[35] Fredericksburg, and Antietam before it, had taken a heavy toll on the men of the Fourteenth. It is remarkable they were able to continue.

The regiment wintered at Falmouth, Virginia, under the command of Captain Samuel H. Davis, the highest ranking officer who was left fit for duty. Regimental historian Charles Page wrote, "[W]ho can wonder that the torn and shattered little remnant of the regiment went back to their camp near the dingy old town of Falmouth with bleeding hearts and depressed spirits?"[36] There they remained until spring arrived to offer more slaughter. It came with a march toward Chancellorsville, Virginia, where on the evening of May 2, "Stonewall" Jackson began a surprise attack on the Union's Eleventh Corps and aimed straight toward the Fourteenth. Fiske described the unexpected attack as, "a serious reverse" and a "wild stampede" of men, artillery, wagons, and ambulances, but the Fourteenth stood its ground. After moving south from the battle, the regiment was surrounded by Confederate forces and assaulted on the morning of May 3. Major Theodore G. Ellis, now in command of the Fourteenth, described the situation: "About sunrise on the morning of the 3d instant, the first line of battle having been forced by a terrific assault of the enemy, this regiment became engaged; the enemy appearing on our front and right flank almost simultaneously. We were forced to retire, principally on account of there being no troops on our right to prevent the enemy, who had engaged the front line on our right, from passing through the unoccupied interval, and attaining our rear."[37]

With reverses all around and the Union army in disarray and retreat, the Fourteenth's regimental band did the unthinkable—they held an impromptu concert. Colonel Frederick L. Hitchcock, of the 132nd Pennsylvania Infantry, described the bravery and effect of the Fourteenth's musicians:

> One of the most heroic deeds I ever saw done to help stem the fleeing tide of men and restore courage, was not the work of a battery, nor a charge of cavalry, but the charge of a band of music! The band of the Fourteenth Connecticut went right out into that open space between our new line and the rebels, with shot and shell crashing all about them, and played the "Star Spangled Banner," the "Red, White, and Blue" and "Yankee Doodle," and repeated them for full twenty minutes. They never played better. Did that require nerve? It was undoubtedly the first and only band concert ever given under such conditions. Never was American grit more finely illustrated. Its effect upon the men was magical. Imagine the strains of our grand national hymn, the "Star Spangled Banner," suddenly bursting upon your ears out of that horrible pandemonium of panic-born yells, mingled with the roaring of the musketry, and the crashing of artillery. To what may it be likened? The carol of birds in the midst of the blackest thunderstorm? No simile can be adequate. Its strains were clear and thrill-

ing for a moment, then smothered by that fearful din, an instant later sounding bold and clear again, as if it would fearlessly emphasize the refrain, "Our flag is still there."[38]

Historian John Niven reported that the band played for an astounding twenty-six minutes, while the Second Brigade eventually aided the Fourteenth and reversed the Confederate attack.[39]

Ben Hirst wrote home following the Fourteenth's third harrowing battle, reporting to his wife, "It is with a sad yet thankful heart that I am able once more to assure you that both John [Ben's younger brother, also in the Fourteenth's Company D] and myself have been through one of the greatest (and I fear one of the most disastrous) Battles yet fought without getting a scratch from the thousand destructive misiles, that were showered upon us." The only positive news for the Union after the engagement was the mortal wounding of General Stonewall Jackson.[40]

As the summer marched on, so did the regiment, now ordered to parallel Lee's advance toward Pennsylvania, where he hoped once again to earn a Confederate victory on northern soil. As his gray army marched into the Pennsylvania countryside, news traveled north, hundreds of miles away to Connecticut, where the *Hartford Daily Courant* announced in its June 16, 1863, edition, "Threatened Rebel Invasion in Pennsylvania: Gen. Lee's Army Advancing!" On June 29, the Fourteenth, still numbering only a third of its original size, was ordered to march in its most demanding stretch, more than thirty-two miles in one day, to Uniontown, Pennsylvania.[41]

By July 2, both armies had descended on the little town of Gettysburg, which was now witness to one of the most harrowing battles of the war. For the better part of the day, the men of the Fourteenth occupied a field where, according to the regimental historian, "we could see across the plain the distant spires and houses of Gettysburg." In the afternoon they moved approximately two hundred feet and occupied a position "behind a loosely constructed stone wall. . . . This was the ground occupied by the regiment during the rest of the battle." Little could the soldiers know that it would be the scene of the Confederacy's most desperate charge of the war.[42]

Early the next morning, six companies of the Fourteenth were sent to Bliss Farm, where a building occupied by Confederate sharpshooters was inflicting damage on the Union lines. Sergeant E. B. Tyler of Company B, one of the first companies sent to take the barn at 4 a.m., reported the dangerous accuracy of the sharpshooters as the men crawled toward their objective: "A comrade, I think it was Hiram Fox, next to me on the left, said he had spoken to Corporal Huxam, who was next to him on the left, but obtained no reply. I suggested to him to crawl over to Huxam's position. . . . [H]e did so and reported back that Huxam was dead, shot through the head. He had evidently become tired of lying flat upon the ground and firing through the lower rails, and risen up to a kneeling position. . . . [T]he rebel sharp shooter . . . proved too quick for him and fired the fatal shot." Private Loren Goodrich also recounted a similar story, telling friends in a letter home that "the sharp shooters kept up a continual fire on us from the windows."[43]

As the men of the Fourteenth made their way to the barn, both lieutenants from Company I were shot by Rebels hiding in the building, which prompted orders for the Twelfth New Jersey to aid in the barn's capture. Believing they had successfully driven the Confederates from the position, the Twelfth found themselves trapped in the open and countered by enemy soldiers who had remained in the barn. The New Jersey regiment's failure had come from their approach. They advanced toward the structures in a neat column of companies, described in historian Stephen W. Sears's *Gettysburg* as "rushing in one end while the outnumbered Mississippians escaped out the other. . . . [S]oon enough it was the Jerseymen's turn to scramble back to their lines."[44] Page pronounced that "the men were at the mercy of the enemy, 'in a trap and liable to be exterminated.'" The order then came for the remaining companies of the Fourteenth to burn the buildings. The regiment learned from their comrades' mistake and fanned out for the charge, thereby scattering and making more ineffective the enemy's fire. The attack force consisted of 60 men from the Fourteenth carrying some of the most technologically advanced weapons on the battlefield: breech-loading Sharps rifles that, according to Noah Andre Trudeau's *Gettysburg: A Testing of Courage,* "gave them a firepower out of proportion to their numbers."[45] Page announced somewhat grandly, "It is not to be wondered that such a gallant and perilous deed as capturing and burning these buildings, one of the bravest during the whole progress of war, should be claimed by other regiments and companies, but to the honor and glory of the Fourteenth Regiment must be credited this heroic deed." Reverend Stevens concluded, "This deed was a brilliant and perilous one, as the buildings were nearly one-half mile in front of our line, and the men were exposed, almost from the start, to heavy fire from sharpshooters in the buildings and from skirmishers and reserves."[46] The remaining eight companies of the Fourteenth swiftly and successfully fired the structures and gathered the dead and wounded; the regiment lost only 10 men in the attack, with 52 wounded. Ben Hirst described the end of the events at Bliss Farm by noting, "The Regt held on until they got orders to Burn them down, and the Boys soon had a Fire that effectualy kept the Rebels out for the rest of the Battle."[47]

The men of the Fourteenth then returned to their original position, once again seeking the safety and tactical advantage of the stone wall. Once there, Sergeant Major Hincks reported that the enemy "burst upon us most unexpectedly the heaviest cannonade I had ever witnessed." Fortunately, the Rebel guns fired mostly over the men's heads. Still, the concussion and billowing clouds of smoke, both from the Confederates and the returning fire of Union artillery, was remarkable. Hincks remembered, "I am at a loss to know what they could have seen to fire at, the smoke was so thick. So very thick was it that the sun seemed almost blotted out. One of the guns was directly behind me and at every discharge, the concussion would throw gravel over me and I could not only see and smell the thick cloud of burning powder, but could taste it also." Ben Hirst came to the same conclusion about the intensity of the enemy fire, writing home that it "was the Fiercest Canonading I ever heard, the shot and shell came from Front and Right and Left. It makes my Blood Tingle in my veins now; to think of. Never before did I hear such a roar of Artillery, it seems as if all the Demons in Hell were let loose, and wer Howling through the Air."[48]

When the firing stopped as abruptly as it had begun, the now 100 men of the Fourteenth believed the battle to have ended. Major Ellis immediately formed them in line of battle behind the wall and shouted, "They mean to charge with all their infantry." What came next was, as Ellis put it in his official report, "magnificent," as wave after wave of Confederate soldiers flooded across the field in what became known as Pickett's Charge. Loren Goodrich described the advancing Confederate charge as, "3 battle lines a mile long. . . . Onward they came til within 200 yards when we opened a terrible fire upon them which staggered them for a moment they then rallied and tried to flank us but were repulsed in the same way with great slaughter. They scattered in every direction a great many of them laying down and waving their white handkerchiefs in token of their surrender." Hirst too told of the Rebel tide pouring toward the Fourteenth's line, remarking that they "seemed to march as though upon Parade, and were confident of carrying all before them. But away up that mountain slope in our Rear we knew that (biding their time) as Gallant a body of men as ever Rebels could dare to be were awaiting them. Yes behind that long, low stone Wall is our own Glorious Second Corps so soon to Imortalise themselves by hurling back the Rebelious Crew who brought their Polluting footsteps to our own dear North."[49]

The Fourteenth successfully fortified the wall against the continuous Rebel charges. Fiske insisted, "I don't believe troops ever made a firmer or more persistent charge under such a murderous fire," and added that the Fourteenth, "poured death into the ranks of the advancing foe."[50] Ben Hirst wrote that the Rebel march was turned into lines of surrender, where "a great number of the rebels threw up their hands in token of surrender and we allowed them to come in, disarming them as they reached the wall . . . but opposite the old Fourteenth, none could get over a low rail fence . . . without our permission." Sergeant Edward Wade, of New Britain, explained the determination of the regiment: "By this time the Fourteenth were all excited: they remembered Antietam, Fredericksburg, and Chancellorsville. . . . [N]othing could stop them, and soon they were fighting hand-to-hand with rebels." The men played a critical role in stopping Pickett's Charge at an important spot along the wall at Cemetery Hill, known as "the angle."[51]

The Fourteenth lost 10 killed, 57 wounded, and 4 captured but proved that their road from untried to unrivaled had been fully achieved. Three men from the regiment—Private Elijah W. Bacon, Company F; Corporal Christopher Flynn, Company K; and Sergeant Major William B. Hincks—received the Congressional Medal of Honor for their valor in capturing flags. News of the Union victory at Gettysburg, along with the valor of the Fourteenth, quickly reached Connecticut, where the *Hartford Daily Courant* reported the "Great and Glorious Victory!"[52] *Harper's Weekly* published an article titled "The Fourteenth at Gettysburg," writing triumphantly, "So ended the battle of Gettysburg, and the sun sank to rest that night on a battle-field that had proved that the Army of the Potomac could and would save the people of the North from invasion whenever and wherever they may be assailed."[53] Sam Fiske boasted, "Hurrah for the gallant old Fourteenth! She is getting some pay for Fredericksburg and Chancellorsville." The Fourteenth reversed the misfortunes of previous battles and lifted the spirits of the entire Union Army with their contributions to holding off the enemy forces in what is now regarded as the most significant battle of the war.[54]

John Hirst, Ben's younger brother, also reveled in the successes of the Fourteenth, saying, "[W]e got four colours from they enemy our regm Got

Sergeant Major William B. Hincks, awarded the Congressional Medal of Honor for the capture of Confederate battle flags, from Charles D. Page, History of the Fourteenth Regiment, Connecticut Vol. Infantry *(Meriden, CT: Horton Printing Co., 1906).*

them but they division Got some more." The regimental history of the Fourteenth mentioned six flags captured by the regiment, also confirmed by Sergeant Wade who stated, "We captured six battle-flags and forty prisoners; and over one hundred prisoners came in afterwards. . . . Oh, it was a glorious day for the old Fourteenth!" Ben Hirst's account said, "Out [Our] Corp alone Captured 30 Stands of Colers [colors], our Division taking 13 of them, 6 of which were captured by our own little Regt, besides this we took more Prisoners than we numbered men."[55]

The Fourteenth, though reduced greatly from the heavy toll of battle and the disease of camp, was now a hardened, veteran unit that boasted an unparalleled success among Connecticut regiments. In the aftermath of Gettysburg, the men were consumed by exhausting marches in the Virginia heat, interrupted by a few days of camp here and there. By the end of July, they had marched some four hundred miles since breaking camp at Falmouth and entering Pennsylvania to stop Lee's invasion. The regiment was exhausted and depleted of men. From August 1 to 18, the Fourteenth settled in at Cedar Run, Virginia, where they focused on reorganizing and rebuilding their unit. Colonel Dwight Morris, Lieutenant Colonel Perkins, and Major C. C. Clark had all left the regiment, and Theodore G. Ellis was promoted to colonel.[56] On August 6, the regiment began receiving its first new recruits, substitutes, and conscripts forced into service by the recently imposed draft in Connecticut. Captain Samuel Davis of Company H had been detailed to return home and bring in the new men. Yet he did so with only 42 out of the 117 with which he had begun. As happened with so many such men, they deserted and "skedaddled," as the men called it, at first opportunity. Page noted, "Perhaps no occurrence brought to the minds of the original men of the regiment, now reduced to about 80, the great loss they had sustained by battle and disease since their departure from Connecticut as did the advent of these new recruits." Sam Fiske was far more harsh in his assessment: "Shall our battle-flags, bearing which our best and bravest have gone down on fields of glory, and whose staffs are yet stained with the blood of their dying grasp, be left to the protection of mercenary wretches, who care neither for country nor reputation, who have sold themselves to you only in the hope of deserting to sell over again in endless succession, and who reach the field only because pistols and bayonets have stood between them and flight?"[57]

Late August and well into September saw the Fourteenth once again marching about Virginia. On September 12, the men crossed the Potomac River toward Culpepper, Virginia. John Hirst described the march in a

What was left of the Fourteenth Regiment's national and regimental flags in the aftermath of the war. Many Connecticut regimental battle flags have been restored and are on permanent display at the Connecticut State Capitol Building in Hartford. Courtesy of the Connecticut State Library, Hartford

letter to Ben, writing that "the cavalry was fighting all they way up. they drove they enemy right in front of them and then charged their Battery and captured it 2 three inch rifle pieces and one mountain howitzer."[58] There were also amusing, and filling, times while on the march and in camp. On September 24, a bull strayed into a cornfield directly in front of the Fourteenth's camp and Captain Walter Lucas of Company D ordered a group of soldiers to kill and slaughter the animal. Yet, according to Page, "while the men were skillful in shooting rebels this new object of attack seemed to tax their skill. So many shots were fired in such rapid succession that it was thought that the Confederates had attacked our lines. . . . Some of the boys facetiously called this the 'Third Battle of Bull Run.'" The company did eventually kill the bull, with all members feasting on large portions later that night.[59]

On October 10, the regiment was issued rations for six days and sixty rounds of ammunition, and proceeded to march outside of Culpepper to the Rappahannock River and toward Bristoe Station. The Fourteenth eventually engaged the enemy there, on October 14, and captured five pieces of artillery.[60] Union batteries drove the Confederates back so far that the Fourteenth was eager to follow the retreating units and capture the enemy's battery, but this was forbidden by the officers. One impatient soldier, Sergeant Edwin Stroud of Company B, disobeyed these orders and marched alone into the woods, returning with five prisoners. The regiment was then ordered to withdraw to a point near the railroad tracks and hold its positions. Captain Fiske described the action:

> Our regiment did its share in repulsing the sudden attack of
> the enemy at Bristoe Station. Our loss was twenty-six killed and
> wounded; mostly in the first fifteen minutes of the fight. It would have
> done your heart good to see the steadiness and alacrity with which our
> men, marching by the flank, faced to the front, and advanced in line
> of battle at the double-quick, across the railroad, and into the woods
> whence the fire opened on us, without knowing at all how many rebels
> we should find there; without having had a moment's preparation, or
> thought of being attacked. Scarcely a man faltered . . . the enemy were
> driven out of sight, five-hundred prisoners and a battery captured,
> and the skirmish over.

The regiment quickly lost a large number of men, 12 killed and 18 wounded, but earned yet another victory for the Union by capturing so many prisoners and repelling the Confederate forces.[61]

By November 10, the Fourteenth had marched on toward Stevensburg, Virginia, but before a camp was set up, orders were given to break and travel to Germania Ford on the Rapidan River, where they were instructed not to light fires, owing to the unknown proximity of the enemy. On the morning of November 30, Company D was ordered to construct breastworks and rifle pits, only to be relieved by the First Corps for what was said to be the remainder of the day. Less than an hour into their respite, they were ordered to fix bayonets and charge the enemy, but were deterred when the Confederates flooded a creek that separated the two sides. A new plan of attack was readied, with the Fourteenth taking the left line and set to charge until reaching the enemy's breastworks.[62] Rev. Stevens stated that the regiment "fully expected to engage in one of the most desperate charges the men ever contemplated." Lieutenant William H. Hawley, of Company B, described this tense moment: "The Fourteenth was in the first line of battle where the bullets would strike the thickest in the charge. . . . And now General Warren rides slowly down our lines, his sober face more sober than usual. He evidently dislikes to sacrifice his brave troops in such a desperate undertaking. . . . Whoever is fortunate enough to pass unharmed through the storm of bullets and shell and grape-shot and over the obstructions will find himself confronted by a five foot wall with sharp bayonets behind it."[63]

Nonetheless, the soldiers continued to prepare by removing their knapsacks and other nonessential items. Others wrote their names on paper and pinned them to their coats, not expecting to make it out of the charge alive. John Hirst recalled a conversation with Lieutenant Colonel Moore:

> "Jack, do you see those works?"
> "Yes," I replied.
> "Well, I want to see you plant those colors right upon those works."
> "I shall go just as far as those Johnnies will let me go alive."

The regiment anxiously awaited the word to charge, but mercifully, it never came, as commanding officers realized the low probability of success and disobeyed the orders of a frontal assault. Hirst goes on to say, "It was a good thing for this regiment we did not for we was they first line."[64]

In early December, the regiment returned to its old camp at Stevensburg, where it stayed until the end of the month. The Fourteenth eventually moved to a camp at Stony Mountain, close to the banks of the Rapidan River and within sight of the enemy's pickets. The days here were mostly peaceful compared with the previous encampments of the Fourteenth.

For the first time, relatives were allowed to visit. During these few weeks, a number of Confederate officers and men also came into camp to surrender.[65]

On the morning of February 6, 1864, the Fourteenth was ordered to march out of camp toward the river in an attempt to attract the attention of General Lee's army and distract them from the oncoming attack by Union forces at Richmond. The regiment moved toward the river, watching the Confederates scrambling in front of Morton's Ford. John Hirst describes the movements: "[W]e lay a couple of hours thinking they was laying a bridge. But when we got down their were found out we had to wade it as they pontoons couldn't get up . . . we had to go over they hill on double quick to get out of they shelling. They [Then] we lay with our wet clothes on waiting for night."[66]

Just before night fell, the Rebel forces charged at the entire Second Division in an attempt to push the Union back toward the river, but the Fourteenth instead forced the Confederates nearly a mile backward into a cluster of houses on a hill, and now in total darkness. The men stormed the hill but after sustaining a number of losses were unable to dislodge the Confederates. *The Connecticut War Record* stated that Lieutenant Colonel Moore was "constantly riding up and down the line in the hottest of fire, directing and cheering on his men."[67] The battle quickly became a fierce hand-to-hand fight with bayonets in the darkness. John Hirst wrote, "our regiment taking the blunt of they fight as they number killed wounded and missing . . . they right wing of our reg was fighting them hand to hand . . . it made it bad being dark for you could only see where to fire by the flash of their guns." Men yelled to each other in the blackness and recognized friend or foe by calling out their state or regiment.[68] *The Connecticut War Record* captured the darkened, close-quartered combat: "Men were captured and re-captured and captured over again. Friends were killed by friends' fire. Men fired at each other in rooms of houses not a musket-barrel's length apart, and in a few instances were wounded with thrusts of a bayonet, (and this is the only case to my knowledge where bayonets have been used in this war for any other advantage than to stack arms.)" The Confederates were eventually pushed back, and the Fourteenth left the battle at Morton's Ford. At the end of its article, *The Connecticut War Record*, in a line that essentially described the Fourteenth throughout the entire war, stated, "Such is a brief account of another of the bloody experiences of the old Fourteenth, which seems always to have the luck to be in the advance in every time of danger." After the fierce encounters of

Antietam, Fredericksburg, Chancellorsville, and Gettysburg, and the less-renowned Morton's Ford, no truer word could have been written. The un-rivaled Fourteenth continued to press on.[69]

For John Hirst, the battle was a noteworthy and honorable moment. He proudly wrote that "every reg in they division say it was they 14 Conn that saved them . . . every regiment in they division says that our reg saved them from being took prisoner." Hirst also carried wounded men, including one of the color sergeants, over the river to safety, recounting that it was "they hardest time I ever Put in . . . they closest fighting ever I was in." Charles Page wrote in the official regimental history that "Corporal John Hirst, of Rockville, took the flag after Sergeant Allen fell, and carried it during the remainder of the engagement." After the battle, John sent his brother Ben, still recuperating from wounds suffered at Gettysburg, a small piece of the Connecticut State flag that contained the letter O.[70]

At the beginning of May, General Ulysses Grant, now in charge of all Union forces, launched the largest offensive of the entire war. The goal was to push into the South from multiple directions and crush Lee's army. With reserve after reserve poured into the fighting throughout the spring, the Union casualty toll was striking. Over a seven-week period, noted historian James McPherson, "some 65,000 northern boys were killed, wounded, or missing. . . . This figure amounted to three-fifths of the total number of combat casualties suffered by the Army of the Potomac during the *previous three years*."[71]

The Fourteenth broke camp on May 3. After a night of silent marching and taking great lengths to not be detected by the enemy, the regiment crossed the Rapidan River into enemy territory. There were still visible reminders of the previous Battle of Chancellorsville, where the men of the Fourteenth had fought and bled, with the remains of soldiers still unburied after almost a year.[72] The Fourteenth was the only Connecti-cut regiment to join the Army of the Potomac on its drive south. As they marched onward toward Lee, Sam Fiske wrote that these were to be the "great and terrible battles that are to decide this opening campaign, and probably bring the war to an end." He hoped that "every opportunity may be taken to inspire the patriotism and enthusiasm of our troops, and keep before their minds the great principles which first sent them forth from their peaceful homes to fight for endangered liberty and republican gov-ernment, for God, and freedom throughout the world."[73]

The Battle of the Wilderness was fought amidst a pine forest where tangles and scrub brush were set aflame and men battled not only the enemy, but the rage of nature. The regiment awoke on the morning of May 4 but did not go far before they skirmished with Confederate forces. The eight regiments of the Second Corps formed two lines of battle, the second commanded by Colonel Samuel Carroll of the Eighth Ohio. The Fourteenth was positioned on the left, next to the Tenth New York. Lieutenant Colonel S. A. Moore said of the regiment's actions, "The Fourteenth was in the first line of battle, and behaved nobly; at one time executing a change of front under fire to repel an attack on our left." At one point during the engagement, the regiment scrambled to rally around the company's colors, and was eventually able to gather at a formation of fallen trees. This was a trying time for John Hirst, as he had been carrying the regiment's colors since the beginning of the Wilderness Campaign. The men forced the Rebels back about two miles but later retreated to their rifle pits until reinforcements arrived. The back-and-forth of battle continued over the next several days, and once again the men of the Fourteenth suffered, losing 11 killed and 62 wounded.[74] Among the dead was the prolific and gallant Sam Fiske, who was shot through the collarbone and right lung on May 6 and died sixteen days later, on May 22, in a Fredericksburg hospital. Fiske was joined by his wife and family before passing away. Amherst College professor W. S. Tyler delivered a eulogy in which he noted that Fiske had just been home on furlough and "returned to the field of conflict with a sadness that was unusual, perhaps with a distinct presentiment of what was before him." "When he fell," insisted Tyler, "the whole country, and especially New England felt the blow."[75]

The days of the new push south seemed to blur together for the men of the Fourteenth. The Wilderness Campaign saw them in almost constant movement, and by May 10, the regiment found itself in front of Laurel Hill, where it suffered grievously. At the back of the hill, a Confederate artillery battery fired shells over the men, and as they burst, several of the regiment were wounded. "The advance was over a tangled road which was passed with much difficulty and it was necessary to halt several times to reform the line," wrote Page. "The woods were on fire and the heat and smoke were almost suffocating, but the men moved on till within a few paces of the enemy's works which opened upon them with a galling fire. The men, however, kept up a brisk fire upon the enemy, maintaining their position for several hours when being out of ammunition they regiment was relieved and lay in the second line still in front of the breastworks all that night and during the 11th."[76]

Grant's continuous slog forward, and thus the Fourteenth's, brought them to the next stage of the campaign, Spotsylvania, Virginia, on May 12, with a slow and quiet charge upon the enemy's breastworks, where General Lee rested with his division. The Confederates fired on the charging regiment with eighteen heavy guns but could not hit the Fourteenth because of their poor angle of fire. The regiment quickly came over the enemy's ridge, surprising the Rebels and leading to confusion among the enemy soldiers, who retreated and left their artillery exposed. The Fourteenth captured more prisoners than they had in their own ranks and took control of the artillery.[77] *The Connecticut War Record* reported that the men "turned upon them their own cannon, and worked them with some effect. Lieut. Colonel Moore was particularly active in this, and was ably assisted by our Sergt. Major and Orderly Sergeant Bradley of Madison. Capt. Nickols of Norwhich, with a small guard took back to Corps-Headquarters a large number of the captured rebels."[78] John Hirst attributed the attack's success to the element of surprise, saying, "[W]e caught them getting their breakfast and got amongst them before they new [*sic*] it but some of them fought hard to drive us out again but could not do it. they prisoners say if we had not a made so much noise on they charge we would have got Bobby lee for he was right where we charged talking to they other generals." During the fight, John was undoubtedly involved in close hand-to-hand combat, based on Company G's J. E. Stannard's description that "[t]he colors of both sides were on the works at the same time within a few feet of each other, and bayonets were used freely." Confederate forces attempted to recapture the breastworks, with one charge leading to a hand-to-hand fight within the walls, but were unsuccessful. After keeping control of the works, the Fourteenth marched out to support skirmishers that were advancing further on the enemy and assessing the size and strength of the Confederate Army. Because the enemy was also spread out to evaluate Union forces, there were many small skirmishes.[79] John Hirst described this time of nearly constant conflict: "We have had a rough time of it since we left Stony Mountain. We have thrown away our overcoats and blankets through inability to carry them. The days are warm, but last night was the coldest we have had since breaking camp. We have been marching and fighting nearly every day since I wrote you, but have had no regular battle since Spottsylvania. . . . We are nearer Richmond than I have ever been before and we expect to have more or less fighting every day for some time yet."[80]

John understood that the Fourteenth was chasing Lee and were only steps behind. For weeks, General Grant hammered away at Lee's army all along the crests of Spotsylvania. Croffut and Morris noted that the Four-teenth had a "gallant part" in the campaign. The regiment continued to march, building breastworks along the way, and was heading toward Cold Harbor, Virginia, by the beginning of June. The entire regiment was now armed with Sharp's breech-loading, repeating rifles and had orders to hold the skirmish line while the rest of the Second Corps made a change of base. The Fourteenth reached Cold Harbor under the constant, but un-successful, firing of enemy shells, moving directly to the front of the battle to aid a new Union regiment. John Hirst explained, "[W]e went up to sup-port another regt in they front line as they was afraid of it being their first fight. They rebs bothered us all night."[81]

On the evening of June 2, the Confederates attacked the regiment's wagon train, causing the Fourteenth to withdraw from its position, though it successfully resisted the initial Rebel attack. The regiment then formed a line no more than one hundred yards from the enemy's picket line, ready to charge. Many troops were delayed in forming their lines owing to the surrounding dense woods, which John Hirst described as "heavy woods. Seen some skuls that was not buried since McClellans was here."[82] Dur-ing the attack, many soldiers in the Fourteenth were wounded, especially while negotiating the thick and at times impenetrable brush. The regi-ment eventually succeeded in charging the enemy, only to see them escape toward the larger Rebel regiment waiting in the rear. The firing became so heavy that soldiers of the Fourteenth "fell behind the dead bodies of the Confederate soldiers, using tin plates and pans to throw up earth to cover these dead bodies to serve as protection."[83]

At one point in the Battle of Cold Harbor, a flag of truce was raised so that the dead could be buried. Each side had been fighting for several days, and the bodies of the fallen soldiers quickly covered the fields. Both armies spent an hour collecting their fallen comrades, shaking hands, and conversing along the way. Sergeant E. H. Wade added, "Only one hour be-fore we were but one hundred yards apart, hiding behind trees and breast-works, eagerly watching for a [chance] to shoot each other, and now were together talking and chatting as if the best of friends."[84] John Hirst wrote that the men exchanged goods, such as coffee and tobacco. The heavily wounded and broken Forty-Second North Carolina claimed they would not fire when the battle resumed if the Fourteenth did not fire on them, and even warned the Union regiment to stay low, as their replacement, the Sixth Alabama, would fire at merely the sight of Union soldiers. The Fourteenth continued to hold off charges for the remaining days of Cold

Harbor, as June advanced. The men lost another 5 dead and 9 wounded, which made their losses 45 percent of those who had left Stony Mountain six weeks earlier.[85]

General Grant's orders kept Union forces moving toward Richmond, which successfully set his armies in a position to put Lee's forces on the run. The Fourteenth marched toward Petersburg on the morning of June 16 and received orders to support lines near the enemy's position, which they did under heavy enemy fire. The men advanced on the enemy, forcing them into a retreat, and captured about 50 prisoners. The siege of Petersburg had begun. Over the next few weeks, the regiment constructed breastworks and awaited attack. The constant movement had taken its toll, and the men were satisfied to remain stationary for a time. By July 4, the Fourteenth held its first dress parade in ten weeks and remained within a mile of camp for the next several weeks. Toward the end of July, the regiment crossed the Appomattox and James Rivers, entering Deep Bottom, Virginia. They engaged the enemy, and John Hirst reported, "i believe got they best of them taking 1 Division flag & three regimental flags & a number of prisoners." The Fourteenth twice marched toward Deep Bottom to threaten Richmond, engaging considerable forces along the way.[86]

The worst fighting during this new phase of the hunt came at Ream's Station, where the regiment was ordered to destroy the railroad that supplied the Rebel capital. They moved forward on August 24, with four companies sent out as skirmishers, advancing in a line of battle more than half a mile wide. The enemy attacked the regiment and forced a desperate fight. Sergeant C. G. Blatchley stated, "Our brave men on the railroad held their position against four or five fearful charges by overwhelming numbers and were only driven out when their ammunition was all gone." Six men were killed, 19 were wounded, 1 went missing, and 2 were captured.[87]

For the next few weeks, the Fourteenth remained in a position of observation, stationed at Prince George's Court House, where they remained until September 26. By the end of October, Grant made one last effort to control the southern railroads, and on October 27, the regiment was supplied with four days' rations and ammunition and ordered to the Boydton Plank Road and then to cross Hatcher's Run to command the position.[88] John Hirst described the action:

> We left camp last Tuesday. . . . We went about a couple of miles before we struck the rebel vedettes who fired at us and then ran. Our brigade had the lead and was deployed as skirmished and flankers. A part of

our regiment was out as flankers which left the rest of us at the head of the column. We went along pretty well until between eight and nine o'clock we struck the rebel line, which opened fire upon us, but soon fell back across a creek where they had good works thrown up . . . the rest of us charged and carried the works, taking a few prisoners and losing some men. There was one regiment from Georgia that tried to hold the works, but was broken and scattered through the woods . . . we formed a line of battle and again advanced, while the skirmishing kept up on both flanks . . . when we came to a plank road in possession of the Johnnies who opened upon us with artillery. . . . The rebels were not idle, but hard at work upon our right flank where they drove in our Calvary and making for our battery, which their guns were trying to silence. . . . We charged them and drive them down the road to a mill near a bridge where we captured a few of them. . . . A rifle ball cut the strap of my knapsack clean off my shoulder and went through my rubber blanket.[89]

The Fourteenth did not capture the full battery but kept the enemy from taking the road. Hirst wrote, "If the Johnnies could have got the road our whole brigade would have been captured." After dark, the regiment pulled out of the area, leaving one man from each company on picket, and returned to camp by the next night.[90]

The regiment soon moved to Fort McGilvery, where it remained until November 29, when ordered to move toward Fort Bross. The Rebels made unsuccessful assaults on the fort, sending shells over the walls but failing to engage Union troops. In early December, the men were positioned at Fort Morton on the Petersburg line. Here they set up winter huts, braved the elements, and had a brief respite in the form of witnessing the presentation of the Congressional Medals of Honor awarded for the capture of Confederate battle flags at Gettysburg. This was the only highlight in an otherwise miserable existence. Supplies were low, and wood was scarce. The Confederate mortars and sniper fire were so plentiful that the men "were obliged to live under ground, like a gopher. The shells from the rebels came into our camp too thick to make it healthy to live top of the ground."[91]

As 1865 dawned, the goal of displacing the Confederates at Petersburg continued. In early February, Grant once again hoped to break up the Confederate supply route, and the Fourteenth found itself back at Hatcher's Run. The men skirmished and maintained their lines for several days. Sergeant Charles Blatchley remembered the frigid temperatures: "I had the experience of being frozen in bed; it rained and freezing as it fell, our blanketts were firmly frozen to the earth and we under them in the morning."[92] The regiment remained, back and forth, throughout this region of Virginia, in a constant cat-and-mouse game with Confederate forces, always with the goal of cutting off the besieged city. Blatchley aptly described the men's time during the long campaign:

> The record of these nine months before Petersburg would make a very monotonous story. There are in them intensely stirring incidents; night attacks on both sides; the thrilling experience of creeping noiselessly up with bated breath toward their lines one moment, and the next enveloped in the blinding flash of suffocating smoke of battle. . . . Or lying behind our own works with the ready rifles loaded and capped as they were, even when we slept on them; peering through the darkness into the black space in front of us, to find it suddenly swarming full of the gray and the butternut in the mad attempt to break our lines.[93]

By March 29, under heavy rains, the Fourteenth marched through the "everlasting Virginia mud" out to the now familiar ground of Hatcher's Run. The end of March and the dawning of April, however, offered "a bow of hope that the end was not far off." Page noted that "the resistance of the enemy was visibly more feeble and showed lack of well devised plans of both attack and defense." More and more Confederate deserters appeared with Union lines, and John Hirst wrote, "I never saw men so much demoralized as they was." Sergeant Blatchley recorded the men's final fight of the war, at High Bridge on the Appomattox River. "We came upon them at daylight, setting fire to the bridge; men forgot all rules and discipline in the enthusiasm of the moment."[94] The men took the bridge and drove the enemy back for miles. Rumors of peace soon circulated in the days that followed and were confirmed by April 11.

John Hirst wrote home to his brother, Benjamin: "[W]hen Lees line was broke he had 60 thousand men. When he surrendered he had about 10 thousand muskets. th[e] woods was swarming with them. they day after lee surrendered he had over 10 thousand more come in from they wood that had been fleeing on their own hook. I suppose they had a big time of it north when they got they news for I tell you they boys done some shouting here when old mead [General Meade] come back, our corp took over 400 wagons 16 pieces of artillery & 5 thousand prisoners."[95] The excitement finally came when General Meade returned to camp and passed through the lines of the Fourteenth, congratulating the troops on their victory. Men flung their caps into the air, threw knapsacks down; they danced, laughed, and cried.

On May 2, the Fourteenth left for the march to Washington, and then on to Connecticut. The regiment led the column, with its band playing and flags waving. "Every step of the men grew firmer," wrote Page, "the eye brighter and the musket grasped with more loving grip than ever." Yet there were also moments of stirring remembrance, such as when the men passed over the familiarly haunting ground where they had suffered so grievously at Fredericksburg. "Here they found many tokens of the fight for possession of the city," noted Page. "The men marched on quietly without noise, as if conscious of moving over ground sanctified by the suffering and death of their comrades."[96]

On May 23, the Fourteenth marched in the Grand Review through Washington and remained in the area for a few short days before being mustered out of duty on the 31st. They immediately left for home and arrived in Hartford on June 3, 1865. The *Hartford Daily Courant* readied the city, announcing, "The gallant regiment that left Connecticut over one thousand strong in the autumn of 1862, will arrive here on the steamer Granite State this morning with but about two hundred men all told. . . . Let flags be displayed and other evidences of welcome be given." On the day they arrived, the wharves of the city were packed with crowds, and the men of the Fourteenth marched through the streets to the fanfare as returning heroes. In an article titled "'Johnny Comes Marching Home.' *The Fourteenth Regiment Returned*. Their Reception in Hartford," the *Courant* wrote of the men's bravery and commitment to Union. The paper bemoaned the many who had not come home, reporting, "The story is told. Yet sad as it is, there is glory in it. The nation is saved; freedom has triumphed; and this band of brave men are heroes for all time. . . . It is the only Connecticut regiment which has been constantly identified with the Army of the Potomac, and has participated in all the important battles of Virginia, commencing at Antietam, into the fire of which is was placed almost immediately after its arrival in Washington."[97]

After a horrific beginning at Antietam, only to be followed by the pain and loss at Fredericksburg, then Chancellorsville, the Fourteenth rebounded at Gettysburg, serving in a critical position along the Union line and helping to decimate Pickett's Charge. By war's end, they were the most battle-hardened unit from Connecticut, having fought in some thirty-four

Photograph of the Fourteenth Regiment at the dedication of their Gettysburg monument, July 3, 1884. Courtesy of the Connecticut State Library, Hartford

engagements and suffering the largest percentage of men killed and died in service of any Connecticut regiment. They slogged through the mud in pursuit of Robert E. Lee, manned the lines outside of Petersburg, and rightly claimed the honor of marching through the streets of Washington on their way home. What had begun as a regiment filled with new, unseasoned men mustered out claiming three Congressional Medal of Honor winners. They left Connecticut untried, and they returned unrivaled. Perhaps there is no better way to end their story than with the words of the regiment's official historian, Charles Page, who so aptly captured the unit's sacrifice: "And thus we come to the close of the service of the Fourteenth Regiment. It, indeed, took a heroic and prominent part in what was in many respects the most important and remarkable conflict of arms in modern times. That conflict, [was] so weighty in its import to the destiny of our country. . . . But at what cost? Figures fail to express it, words cannot portray it, a glance through these pages may give but a hint of it."[98]

NOTES

1. Benjamin Hirst, Journal Excerpt #2, Hirst Collection, New England Civil War Museum, Rockville, CT.

2. Blaikie Hines, *Civil War Volunteer Sons of Connecticut* (Thomaston, ME: American Patriot Press, 2002), 169.

3. Charles D. Page, *History of the Fourteenth Regiment, Connecticut Vol. Infantry* (Meriden, CT: Horton, 1906), 11; as the regiment's official history, Page's book is used widely, along with additional materials, to tell the regiment's story.

4. William A. Croffut and John M. Morris, *The Military and Civil History of Connecticut during the War of 1861–65* (New York: Ledyard Bill, 1869), provides detailed accounts of the regiments and batteries from Connecticut. They include personal anecdotes and biographical sketches, along with descriptions of some battles. This book is an excellent source for examining Connecticut's contributions to the war, as compared to Page's regimental history, but still does not specifically emphasize the importance of the Fourteenth. Matthew Warshauer, *Connecticut in the American Civil War: Slavery, Sacrifice, and Survival* (Middletown, CT: Wesleyan University Press, 2011), is by far the most recent examination of Connecticut's role in the war, with Niven's *Connecticut for the Union* (New Haven, CT: Yale University Press, 1965), having been written one hundred years after the war's conclusion. Warshauer focuses more on the political and social effects of the war on Connecticut and, for the most part, does not go into great detail when describing Connecticut regiments' roles in the actual battles. The Fourteenth is mentioned in battles like Fredericksburg and Gettysburg, where Warshauer correctly identifies the significance of their actions by citing the regimental history. See also Kristen Duke, "The Spirit of Citizen Soldiers: The Experiences of the Connecticut Fourteenth Volunteer Regiment in the Civil War" (MA thesis, Central Connecticut State University, 2010); Kevin T. Connelly, "The Fourteenth Regiment, Connecticut Volunteers, Infantry" (Strategy Research Project, U.S. Army War College, Carlisle Barracks, PA, 2000), http://www.dtic.mil/cgi-bin/GetTRDoc?AD=ADA374955.

5. Croffut and Morris, *The Military and Civil History of Connecticut*, 102; Niven, *Connecticut for the Union*, 64; Hines, *Civil War Volunteer Sons of Connecticut*; enlistment figures are tabulated based on Hines.

6. Page, *History of the Fourteenth Regiment*, 14–17; Hines, *Civil War Volunteer Sons of Connecticut*, 165.

7. Niven discusses the difficulties of the spring and summer campaigns and the slowness of filling the Fourteenth. See *Connecticut for the Union*, 76–77. Warshauer notes that patriotism was not the only spur for enlistment. The threats of a draft were also announced, and should a man be drafted, he would not be eligible for the generous enlistment bounties offered by towns and the state. See Warshauer, *Connecticut in the American Civil War*, 90; "Letter to the Editor," *Hartford Daily Courant*, July 12, 1862.

8. Samuel Giles Buckingham, *The Life of William A. Buckingham: The Civil War Governor of Connecticut* (Springfield, MA: W. F. Adams Co., 1894), 249. Buckingham's announcement also appears in Croffut and Morris, *The Military and Civil History of Connecticut*, 225.

9. Hines, *Civil War Volunteer Sons of Connecticut*, provides maps for each regiment that outline the numbers and locations of recruits. For the Fourteenth, see p. 173. Page, *History of the Fourteenth Regiment*, 17–19, provides a complete listing of the towns and numbers, as does Croffut and Morris, *The Military and Civil History of Connecticut*, 225. They are as follows: Company A: Bridgeport, 49 men; Putnam, 8; Stratford, Norwalk, 6 each; Middletown, Trumbull, 4 each; Killingly, 3; Hartford, Brooklyn, Monroe, Berlin, 2 each; Waterbury, Madison, Huntington, Newtown, Litchfield, Plainfield, Wilton, Harrisville, R.I., Thompson, Easton, Sprague, Woodstock, Fairfield, East Haddam, Cornwall, 1 each. Company B: Middletown, 93 men; Durham, 6; Waterbury, 2; Bridgeport, New Haven, Norwich, Vernon, Haddam, 1 each. Company C: Waterbury, 88 men; Bridgeport, Naugatuck, 3 each; Middletown, 2; New Haven, Durham, Thompson, Milford, Ellington, Torrington, Woodbury, Vernon, East Windsor, East Haddam, 1 each. Company D: Vernon, 75 men; Ellington, 10; Waterbury, 5; Coventry, Willington, 4 each; Middletown, 2; Bridgeport, New London, Tolland, South Windsor, Bolton, Rockville, Mansfield, Windsor, Hartford, Westport, 1 each. Company E: Norwich, 21 men; Middletown, 18; Hartford, 15; New Haven, 6; Waterbury, Killingly, 4 each; Griswold, Sprague, 3 each; Windham, East Windsor, Franklin, Putnam, Preston, Coventry, Vernon, 2 each; Bridgeport, New Britain, Lisbon, Marlborough, Hampton, Glastonbury, Chaplin, North Stonington, Madison, Wethersfield, Plainfield, Thompson, Meriden, New London, 1 each. Company F: New Britain, 65 men; Bloomfield, 15; Berlin, 13; Wolcott, 3; Wethersfield, 2; Bridgeport, Hartford, Norwich, New Haven, New London, Barkhamsted, Vernon, 1 each. Company G: Madison, 58 men; Clinton, 12; Old Saybrook, 10; Westbrook, 9; Guilford, 5; Killingworth, 3; New Haven, 2; Bridgeport, Hartford, Norwich, New London, Franklin, East Lyme, Stratford, Vernon, Haddam, 1 each. Company H: New London, 56 men; Waterford, 21; East Lyme, 5; New Haven, 3; Vernon, Waterbury, 2 each; Hartford, Middletown, Durham, Willimantic, Stonington, Ellington, 1 each. Company I: Guilford, 24 men; New Haven, 22; Hartford, 13; Waterbury, 7; Middlebury, 5; Coventry, 3; New London, New Britain, Wethersfield, Farmington, Bloomfield, 2 each; Middletown, Norwich, New Milford, Windham, Avon, Madison, Norwalk, Willington, Vernon, Ellington, Woodbury, Naugatuck, New Fairfield, 1 each. Company K: Norwich, 21 men; Hartford, 18; Chatham, 14, Somers, 6; Middletown, 5; Bridgeport, Ledyard, Griswold, 4 each; Waterbury, Coventry, 3 each; Madison, Stonington, Preston, Sprague, Farmington, 2 each; Suffield, Durham, Winchester, Woodbridge, Andover, Manchester, Stafford, Wallingford, Chaplin, Franklin, Bolton, Windsor, Thompson, East Haddam, Haddam, 1 each.

10. Bee, *The Boys from Rockville: Civil War Narratives of Sgt. Benjamin Hirst, Company D, 14th Connecticut Volunteers* (Knoxville: University of Tennessee Press, 1998), 5–14; Page, *History of the Fourteenth Regiment*, 16–17; Croffut and Morris, *The Military and Civil History of Connecticut*, 225. For total numbers, see Hines, *Civil War Volunteer Sons of Connecticut*.

11. Jewitt and Hincks quoted in Page, *History of the Fourteenth Regiment*, 19.

12. Henry S. Stevens, *Souvenir of Excursion to Battlefield by the Society of the Fourteenth Connecticut Regiment and Reunion at Antietam, September 1891, with*

History and Reminiscences of Battles and Campaigns of the Regiment on the Fields Revisited (Washington, DC: Gibson Brothers, 1893); Page, *History of the Fourteenth Regiment*, 23.

13. Dunn Brown was the pen name for Samuel Wheelock Fiske, a minister from Madison, CT, who sent letters for publication in the Springfield Republican, located in Massachusetts. See Samuel Wheelock Fiske, *Mr. Dunn Browne's Experiences in the Army* (Boston: Nichols and Noyes, 1866), 40–41.

14. Croffut and Morris, *The Military and Civil History of Connecticut*, 260.

15. Page, *History of the Fourteenth Regiment*, 29.

16. Croffut and Morris, *The Military and Civil History of Connecticut*, 260; for details on division movements, see Marion V. Armstrong, *Unfurl Those Colors: McClellan, Sumner, and the Second Army Corps in the Antietam Campaign* (Tuscaloosa: University of Alabama Press, 2008), 207–9; Page, *History of the Fourteenth Regiment*, 36–39.

17. Roulette quoted in Ezra Carman, *The Maryland Campaign of September 1862* (El Dorado Hills, CA: Savas Beatie, 2010), 1, 323; Stevens, *Souvenir of Excursion to Battlefield by the Society of the Fourteenth Connecticut Regiment and Reunion at Antietam*, 51.

18. Fiske, *Mr. Dunn Browne's Experiences in the Army*, 47.

19. Hirst Collection, Letter File #6, New England Civil War Museum, Rockville, CT (hereafter referred to as Hirst Letter File); Page, *History of the Fourteenth Regiment*, 43–44.

20. Croffut and Morris, *The Military and Civil History of Connecticut*, 268–89.

21. James McPherson, *Battle Cry of Freedom* (New York: Oxford University Press, 2003), 544; Hines, *Civil War Volunteer Sons of Connecticut*, 170.

22. Perkins and French quoted in Page, *History of the Fourteenth Regiment*, 57.

23. Hirst quoted in Bee, *The Boys From Rockville*, 58–59; Page, *History of the Fourteenth Regiment*, 29.

24. William H. Drake to Timothy L. Loomis, September 29, 1862, Civil War Collection, Connecticut Historical Society, Hartford.

25. Relyea quoted in John Michael Priest, ed., *16th Connecticut Volunteer Infantry: Sergeant William H. Relyea* (Shippensburg, PA: White Mane Publishing, 2004), 37–38; killed and wounded based on Hines, *Civil War Volunteer Sons of Connecticut*, 183; Leslie Gordon, "The Most Unfortunate Regiment: The 16th Connecticut and the Siege of Plymouth, North Carolina," *Connecticut History* 50.1 (Spring 2011): 37–61.

26. Page, *History of the Fourteenth Regiment*, 62.

27. Page, *History of the Fourteenth*, 65.

28. Page, *History of the Fourteenth*, 71.

29. Francis Augustin O'Reilly, *The Fredericksburg Campaign: Winter on the Rappahannock* (Baton Rouge: Louisiana State University Press, 2006), 264–75; Hirst Letter File #11, #16, #19.

30. O'Reilly, *The Fredericksburg Campaign*, 264–75.

31. McPherson, *Battle Cry of Freedom*, 572–74; for a description of the battle

and Stevens's quote, see Page, *History of the Fourteenth Regiment*, 84; Fiske, *Mr. Dunn Browne's Experiences in the Army*, 106–8; see also Niven, *Connecticut for the Union*, 224.

32. Lee's London *Times* quote: Croffut and Morris, *The Military and Civil History of Connecticut*, 268–89. Hines, *Civil War Volunteer Sons of Connecticut*, 170; Page, *History of the Fourteenth Regiment*, 85.

33. Fiske, *Mr. Dunn Browne's Experiences in the Army*, 106–7.

34. Perkins quoted in O'Reilly, *The Fredericksburg Campaign*, 275.

35. Record of Service of Connecticut Men in the Army and Navy of the United States during the War of Rebellion (Hartford, CT: Case, Lockwood & Brainard, 1889), 552; patient files, Connecticut Hospital for the Insane, vol. 3, pp. 233–34; files currently held at the Connecticut State Library, Hartford, State Archives. For more on psychological trauma produced by war experiences, see Michael Sturges's chapter in this volume.

36. Page, *History of the Fourteenth Regiment*, 104.

37. Fiske, *Mr. Dunn Browne's Experiences in the Army*, 144–45; Ellis quoted in Croffut and Morris, *The Military and Civil History of Connecticut*, 367.

38. Excerpt from *The War from the Inside*, by Colonel Frederick L. Hitchcock, found in the dairy of Nelson L. Stowe, Fourteenth Connecticut, Civil War Collection, Connecticut Historical Society, Hartford.

39. Niven, *Connecticut for the Union*, 229.

40. Hirst quoted in Bee, *The Boys from Rockville*, 123.

41. "Threatened Rebel Invasion," *Hartford Daily Courant*, June 16, 1863; Page, *History of the Fourteenth Regiment*, 132.

42. Page, *History of the Fourteenth Regiment*, 140–41.

43. Tyler quoted in Page, *History of the Fourteenth Regiment*, 143; Loren H. Goodrich to Joseph Wells, July 17, 1863, Civil War Collection, Connecticut Historical Society, Hartford.

44. Stephen W. Sears, *Gettysburg* (New York: Houghton Mifflin, 2003), 390.

45. Page, *History of the Fourteenth Regiment*, 146; Noah Andre Trudeau, *Gettysburg: A Testing of Courage* (New York: Harper Perennial, 2003), 449.

46. Page, *History of the Fourteenth Regiment*, 146–48; Stevens quoted in Croffut and Morris, *The Military and Civil History of Connecticut*, 386.

47. Hirst Letter File #70; see also Charles P. Hamblen, *Connecticut Yankees at Gettysburg* (Kent, OH: Kent State University Press, 1993), 93–103.

48. Hincks quoted in Page, *History of the Fourteenth Regiment*, 149; Hirst quoted in Bee, *The Boys from Rockville*, 149.

49. Ellis quoted in Page, *History of the Fourteenth Regiment*, 155; Loren H. Goodrich to Joseph Wells, July 17, 1863, Civil War Collection, Connecticut Historical Society, Hartford; Hirst quoted in Bee, *The Boys from Rockville*, 149–50.

50. Fiske, *Mr. Dunn Browne's Experiences in the Army*, 188.

51. Bee, *The Boys from Rockville*, 150; Hirst Letter File #70; Wade quoted in Hamblen, *Connecticut Yankees at Gettysburg*, 107.

52. "The Latest News," *Hartford Daily Courant*, July 6, 1863.

53. "The Fourteenth at Gettysburg," *Harper's Weekly*, November 21, 1863.

Medal of Honor recipients: "Bacon, Elijah W. Rank and organization: Private, Company F, 14th Connecticut Infantry. Place and date: At Gettysburg, Pa., 3 July 1863. Entered service at: Berlin, Conn. Birth: Burlington, Conn. Date of issue: 1 December 1864. Citation: Capture of flag of 16th North Carolina regiment (C.S.A.); Flynn, Christopher. Rank and organization: Corporal, Company K, 14th Connecticut Infantry. Place and date: At Gettysburg, Pa., 3 July 1863. Entered service at: Sprague, Conn. Birth: Ireland. Date of issue: 1 December 1864. Citation: Capture of flag of 52d North Carolina Infantry (C.S.A.); Hincks, William B. Rank and organization: Sergeant Major, 14th Connecticut Infantry. Place and date: At Gettysburg, Pa., 3 July 1863. Entered service at: Bridgeport, Conn. Birth: Bucksport, Me. Date of issue: 1 December 1864. Citation: During the high water mark of Pickett's Charge on 3 July 1863 the colors of the 14th Tennessee Infantry C.S.A. were planted 50 yards in front of the center of Sgt. Maj. Hincks' regiment. There were no Confederates standing near it but several were lying down around it. Upon a call for volunteers by Major Ellis to capture this flag, this soldier and two others leaped the wall. One companion was instantly shot. Sgt. Maj. Hincks outran his remaining companion running straight and swift for the colors amid a storm of shot. Swinging his saber over the prostrate Confederates and uttering a terrific yell, he seized the flag and hastily returned to his lines. The 14th Tennessee carried twelve battle honors on its flag. The devotion to duty shown by Sgt. Maj. Hincks gave encouragement to many of his comrades at a crucial moment of the battle" ("Medal of Honor Recipients: Civil War (A–L)," http://www.history.army .mil/html/moh/civwaral.html).

54. Fiske, *Mr. Dunn Browne's Experiences in the Army*, 190.

55. John Hirst quoted in Bee, *The Boys from Rockville*, 144; Wade quoted in Hamblen, *Connecticut Yankees at Gettysburg*, 107; Bee, *The Boys from Rockville*, 152.

56. Bee, *The Boys from Rockville*, 186; Hirst, "War Papers," June 20, 1887, New England Civil War Museum, Rockville, CT.

57. Page, *History of the Fourteenth Regiment*, 175; Fiske, *Mr. Dunn Browne's Experiences in the Army*, 239–40.

58. Hirst Letter File #79.

59. Page, *History of the Fourteenth Regiment*, 182–87.

60. Page, *History of the Fourteenth*, 191–94; Hirst Letter File #83, #84; Croffut and Morris, *The Military and Civil History of Connecticut*, 560–61.

61. The Connecticut War Record, November 1863, Connecticut State Library, Hartford; killed and wounded in Hines, *Civil War Volunteer Sons of Connecticut*, 170.

62. Page, *History of the Fourteenth Regiment*, 199–203, 468; Hirst Letter File #89.

63. The Connecticut War Record, January 1864, 119–20.

64. Hirst Letter File #99, #100, #117; Croffut and Morris, *The Military History of Connecticut*, 564.

65. Page, *History of the Fourteenth Regiment*, 214–16.

66. Hirst Letter File #99, #100, #117.

67. The Connecticut War Record, March 1864, 162–63.

68. Hirst Letter File #99.

69. The Connecticut War Record, March 1864.

70. Hirst Letter File #109; Page, *History of the Fourteenth Regiment*, 224.

71. McPherson, *Battle Cry of Freedom*, 741.

72. Croffut and Morris, *The Military History of Connecticut*, 569; Page, *History of the Fourteenth Regiment*, 233–34.

73. Fiske, *Mr. Dunn Browne's Experiences in the Army*, 390. The Second Connecticut Heavy Artillery were eventually pulled from their defenses outside of Washington, DC, and reassigned as infantry. See Warshauer, *Connecticut in the American Civil War*, 147.

74. Page, *History of the Fourteenth Regiment*, 236–37; Croffut and Morris, *The Military History of Connecticut*, 570; The Connecticut War Record, June 1864; see Hines, *Civil War Volunteer Sons of Connecticut*, 170, for the Fourteenth's casualty figures.

75. "Obituary," *Frank Leslie's Illustrated Newspaper*, June 11, 1864; W. S. Tyler, "Captain Samuel Fiske," *New Haven Daily Palladium*, July 2, 1864; Page, *History of the Fourteenth Regiment*, 275–76; Warshauer, *Connecticut in the American Civil War*, 146.

76. Page, *History of the Fourteenth Regiment*, 246.

77. Page, *History of the Fourteenth Regiment*, 246–51; Hirst Letter File #109.

78. The Connecticut War Record, June 1864, 233.

79. Page, *History of the Fourteenth Regiment*, 246–51; Hirst Letter File #109.

80. Hirst Letter File #114.

81. Page, *History of the Fourteenth Regiment*, 260–63; Croffut and Morris, *The Military and Civil History of Connecticut*, 575; Hirst Letter File #114.

82. Hirst Letter File #114.

83. Page, *History of the Fourteenth Regiment*, 264; Hirst Letter File #114.

84. Wade quoted in Page, *History of the Fourteenth Regiment*, 268–69.

85. Hirst Letter File #114; Croffut and Morris, *The Military History of Connecticut*, 589; Hines, *Civil War Volunteer Sons of Connecticut*, 170.

86. Croffut and Morris, *The Military and Civil History of Connecticut*, 603–9; Page, *History of the Fourteenth Regiment*, 286–87; Hirst Letter File #120, #121.

87. Blatchley quoted in Page, *History of the Fourteenth Regiment*, 303; Hines, *Civil War Volunteer Sons of Connecticut*, 170.

88. Croffut and Morris, *The Military and Civil History of Connecticut*, 664; Page, *History of the Fourteenth Regiment*, 316–18.

89. Hirst Letter File #134; Page, *History of the Fourteenth Regiment*, 317–18.

90. Hirst Letter File #134.

91. Page, *History of the Fourteenth Regiment*, 324–25.

92. Blatchley quoted in Page, *History of the Fourteenth Regiment*, 327.

93. Page, *History of the Fourteenth*, 331.

94. Blatchley quoted in Page, *History of the Fourteenth Regiment*, 333; Hirst Letter File #144.

95. Hirst Letter File #144; Page, *History of the Fourteenth Regiment*, 337.

96. Page, *History of the Fourteenth Regiment*, 338.

97. "The Fourteenth Regiment," *Hartford Daily Courant*, June 3, 1865; "'Johnny Comes Marching Home.' The Fourteenth Regiment Returned. Their Reception in Hartford," *Hartford Daily Courant*, June 5, 1865. Page, *History of the Fourteenth Regiment*, 342, mistakenly reports that the men arrived in Hartford on June 8.

98. Page, *History of the Fourteenth Regiment*, 344.

5 : The Colt Armory Fire

CONNECTICUT AND THE GREAT
CONFEDERATE CONSPIRACY

Connecticut's resolve to fight in the American Civil War was crippled on February 5, 1864. Half of the Patent Firearms Company complex, the symbol of Samuel Colt's Yankee ingenuity and the Connecticut war economy, was destroyed by a leviathan of fire. Infant forensic science produced contagious speculation about the fire's cause. The spirit of the age was one of paranoia and ever-present fear of Confederate invasion and sabotage. Compounded with the caustic presence of southern sympathizers in the state, many filled the void of uncertainty with conspiracy theories. An unproven assumption that the fire was the work of an arsonist captured the imagination of Connecticut and has persisted in lore. The written record, however, lacks a definitive analysis of the reaction to this event. A thorough examination reveals that the armory fire was most likely an ordinary disaster, the cause of which was sensationalized in an extraordinary time. The largely accepted theory of a conspiracy was a symptom of the Civil War. Wicked plots abounded far and wide, but this was not one of them. It is important to understand the creation of the mythology surrounding the Colt Armory Fire and the fire itself as mechanisms for renewing Connecticut's support of continued bloodshed for the sake of the Union. The disaster gave the demoralized Connecticut populace a newfound zeal to win the war for the industrial destiny of the North.

Newspaper accounts of the time provide a sketch of the fire's chronology. Colt Armory workers smelled smoke emanating from the attic in the main building at about 8 in the morning on February 5. Within a matter of minutes, flames spread throughout the east wing. The eyes of Hartford and the surrounding towns turned to Coltsville, as the haunting howl of the factory's steam gong echoed for miles. The fire steamers shuttled to the dike, where the flames now enveloped the five-hundred-foot-long structure. Repeatedly the water hoses burst, making all attempts to extinguish the fire futile. A multitude of spectators gathered at the scene, including Mrs. Elizabeth Colt herself, widow of the factory's namesake,

*Engraving of the calamitous fire and the crowd of spectators at the Coltsville dike,
from* Leslie's Weekly Illustrated Newspaper, *February 21, 1864. Courtesy of the
Museum of Connecticut History, Connecticut State Library, Hartford*

Samuel Colt. Less than two hours after ignition, the blue onion dome, along with the rampant colt atop, collapsed into the flames.[1] The roof fell in, and the armory was left a smoking ruin. Despite the totality of the destruction of the East Armory, most employees walked away with minor injuries, and only one worker, Mr. E. K. Fox was killed in the blaze.

Photographers sold images taken of the charred Portland brownstone and mangled factory works. The *Hartford Daily Courant* acknowledged its incapacity to meet the state's desire for details, requiring extra editions to be "struck off and sold with great rapidity."[2] What echoes throughout the publications is the lack of precedent for a disaster of the size. The *Willimantic Journal* intimated "a grand sight and no pen can describe the sublimity of the scene. Nothing like it has ever occurred in this city before."[3] The *Hartford Daily Courant* was more florid in its description of the ruins: "The student of history will see the standing walls, much to remind him of classic story and song. Historical allusions are frequent among the spectators. Fifteen hundred feet of crumbling masonry forms a scene of confusion which few communities have witnessed. It is a sad

View of the ruins of Colt's Armory after the fire, Delameter and Moore, photographers.
Courtesy of the Museum of Connecticut History, Connecticut State Library, Hartford

sight."[4] This event was the talk of Connecticut's towns, and no amount of information, regardless of its veracity, could satiate the public.

The Colt Armory fire was a disaster that shook Connecticut in the midst the Civil War. Clerics preached on the "moral significance" of the fire, and bards wrote panegyrics to the "Armory of the World."[5] Colt had been a crucial industry at the center of Connecticut's war production, and the calamity struck people as suspicious. Newspapers voiced such concerns with sensation. The definitive cause of the fire could not be determined; it was a mystery.[6] Allegations of Confederate arson and conspiracy ran wild in the heated climate of the times.[7] It appeared the rebels had made an assault on the northern war effort and the renown of a Connecticut hero. Colt's Armory was unlike most local mills and factories, and it was a beautiful embodiment of progress in Hartford. It was the legacy of Sam Colt, the man whose inventions and innovations changed the face of warfare and the world economy. Hartford was proud to have Colt's empire in its backyard; Coltsville was a beacon of a new industrial utopia. The factory

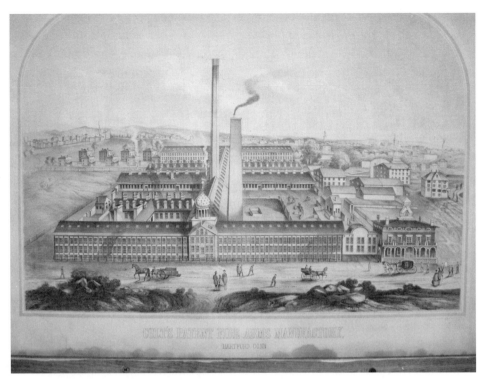

The Colt factory, Hartford, 1862. Courtesy of the Museum of Connecticut History, Connecticut State Library, Hartford

boasted facilities and safety conditions that had not previously been seen in the nineteenth century. Colt built homes for his employees, a library, and great halls for the public's use. His employees formed the Colt Band, and their music delighted Hartford audiences.[8] When Colt died in 1862, all that preserved the empire from oblivion was the armory. Less than two years later, his dream lay in ruin. Seeing the flames devour the blue dome, Mrs. Colt felt as though she were laying her husband to rest all over again.[9] The people of Connecticut were wedded to the idea that Colt represented northern military superiority. The disaster could not simply be an accident; it demanded a scapegoat. A Confederate conspiracy appeared to satisfy this need for closure.

The northern Civil War cause was besieged by myriad obstacles both at home and on the battlefield. Copperheads threatened the political stability of Connecticut's support of the war effort; antiwar and pro-southern groups brought the war to every doorstep. Peace Democrats openly objected to the Lincoln administration, undermining the political legitimacy of the Union platform and discouraging those who had sent their sons to fight in the South. The republic was founded to encourage healthy discourse, yet during wartime, the treasonous agendas of fringe elements ignited irrational responses in Connecticut.[10] Samuel Colt's Armory, the leading private producer of Union weaponry, was compromised; the war-weary people of Connecticut saw the calamity as a victory for the rebels' campaign for peace.

Acts of confirmed Confederate sabotage in the years and months before and after February 1864 emboldened the belief that the armory fire was part of a southern plot to devastate the New England region. The official story of its genesis is cloudy and inconclusive. There is no actual evidence of conspiracy, only conjecture. In writing the history of Hartford and the Colt saga, some authors weigh equally the possibilities of accident and arson, while others definitively claim a conspiracy was to blame. The colorful mosaic of heartfelt reactions to the fire is overlooked in favor of speculation about the fire's cause. This chapter investigates the sabotage thesis and the belief in conspiracy in Connecticut within the context of conspiracies in the North that are documented in the literature.

Getting the facts right is only one aspect of the story—understanding *why* a conspiracy theory took hold is also significant. The "War Between the States" was a struggle over national identity. North and South had long represented divergent social and economic systems; southern agrarian aristocracy was wholly opposed to northern industry and individualism. As the nation expanded westward, these competing regional characters sought to forge new states in their own sectional images. It was clear that the hammer must strike definitively for aristocracy or industry, for slavery or freedom; as Abraham Lincoln said, "It would become all one thing or all the other."[11] Compromise no longer remedied the growing ideological splinter. There was no better representation of the new industrial future of the North than Colt's Armory. This paragon of mass production and wage labor made Hartford its world capital. Coltsville represented the North's adaptation of the plantation of the South, with employees and bosses versus slaves and masters.[12] On February 5, 1864, Connecticut perceived that its culture and way of life were under attack. Grief and anger were redirected into victimization and suspicion. In any other time, logic might have prevailed, but Connecticut's polarized populace and the paranoia of the day gave credence to the conspiracy argument. To this day, however, historians have yet to adequately dissect the validity of this unsubstantiated belief in Confederate fire-starting.

The historical narrative of the fire goes back to the newspapers that reported the event. The debate in history begins a few years later in 1869, when the widow Colt commissioned a memorial publication chronicling the exploits of her late husband and his surviving company. Henry Barnard authored the project, and *Armsmear* adequately addressed the ambiguity of the fire's cause and the public debate on the subject.[13] The fire represents only a brief moment of the Colt saga, and Barnard devoted the remainder of his acclamation to the genius and industry of Sam Colt. The difficulty here is that Colt passed away two years before the fire took place. While there is no shortage of Colt-related literature, biography deals only with the man's life, and other works examine the company's firearms from a technical perspective. R. L. Wilson's *Colt Heritage* is a prime example of a study in Colt weaponry. Wilson supports the idea that Jefferson Davis ordered the armory burned—presenting the conspiracy as a given.[14] The author gives no support for his claim, no evidence, and no secret Confederate diary outlining plans in Hartford. Wilson casually suggests sabotage for dramatic effect, merely an afterthought in his valentine to Colt pistols and muskets. Accepting the irrational claims of the day without criticism does not provide a fair analysis.

Conversely, William Hosley successfully weaves all elements of the Colt story together and has produced one of the most comprehensive works on the fire in Coltsville. His masterwork, *Colt: The Making of an American Legend*, provides the most informed account of the fire gleaned from primary sources. Hosley treats the subject with an even-handed approach, entertaining both sides of the story.[15] Though his account is balanced, Hosley's sources on the fire are limited.[16] Years before, Ellsworth Grant offered a narrative that omits the sabotage thesis in favor of the idea that the fire was simply an unfortunate mishap. The factory floor was soaked in oil grease, and the fire started in the attic, where dry wooden stocks and cotton provided fuel for the smallest spark.[17] This is the most logical explanation, and Grant has little else to say about it: the fire was simply a disaster that scarred Hartford. Similar to Wilson's book, Grant's *The Colt Legacy* is more concerned with the wider story of the man and his company. Because the subjects of Colt and the Civil War are so large, the disaster that in its time was considered unlike any catastrophe previously witnessed in Hartford simply fades into the background.[18]

Overall, there is little historiography on this narrow subject in the public history arena. Only traces remain of the calamity that befell Hartford. A documentary produced for Connecticut Public Television mentions the suspicious fire and the rebirth of the armory under the direction of Elizabeth Colt.[19] There is no museum to Colt other than the furnished rooms of his mansion, Armsmear, and the Colt Collections in the Museum of Connecticut History, the Connecticut State Library, and the Wadsworth Atheneum. The museum's exhibit briefly mentions the 1864 fire, significant only because it halted the production of certain rifles.[20] The story of the fire seems to exist in the ether, fragmented, and lacking a synthesis of opposing viewpoints. Equally important is the mindset of Civil War Connecticut, which intensified confusion.

The zeitgeist of 1863 provides insight into how conspiracy was so quickly associated with the Colt Armory fire. While the historical literature offers the researcher accounts of the national mood, the primary sources provide a fresh glimpse into the events both great and small that influenced the people of Connecticut. On New Year's Day, 1864, the *Hartford Daily Courant* published a war history for the previous year. Looking closely, one may understand how these tumultuous twelve months had crystallized the fear of Confederate subversion on Connecticut soil.

Politically, the Union appeared to be weakening from within. Copperhead senators were elected in New Jersey and Illinois in January, and Democratic candidates for governor threatened Union support in Rhode Island, Ohio, and at home in Connecticut. Proposed peace resolutions suddenly appeared in state legislatures across the North, calling for an end to war and weakening faith in the national government. New Jersey passed its resolutions in March 1863. Despite these events, there were equal wins for Republicans and support for the war. Union officials were elected in New York, Wisconsin, and New Hampshire, and in April, Governors James Smith and William Buckingham were reelected in Rhode Island and Connecticut, respectively. Clement Vallandigham, the exiled Ohio candidate for governor was also beaten. Michigan and Connecticut firmly voted against peace resolutions, and the November elections definitively overcame "the enemy in the rear."[21] The Union persevered, but not without a concerted effort to quell the political and social unrest stirred by the Copperheads. National news only reinforced suspicion that the rebel network was pervasive.

In reality, the third year of the "brothers' war" had been worse for the South than for the North. Yet psychologically, the home front had differing perceptions of the war's progress. Soldiers on the field understood firsthand the success of the Union leadership, who had finally found capable generals and a workable strategy. Northern forces were also better equipped; manpower, infrastructure, and industry were on their side.[22] The average citizens of the North, however, were detached from the scenes of battle and the disparities between the armies. Instead they witnessed the war of opinions, immersed in the political wrath of the antiwar groups.

At the onset of the Civil War, the South had capable friends in northern secret societies. Calling themselves the Knights of the Golden Circle, Order of the American Knights, and the Sons of Liberty, they encouraged collaboration with southern principles. Ultimately their purpose was to wear down the steadfastness of Union support. If a counterrebellion was manifested in the North, the Lincoln administration could be forced to end its campaign of coercion.[23]

Connecticut looked promising to Jefferson Davis initially, where he had won support in some Democratic publications. In 1861, he commissioned one of his most capable operators, Parker French, with the task of organizing chapters of the Knights of the Golden Circle in the state. The agent drummed up support in Bridgeport, New Haven, Fairfield, and other centers of Confederate accord, but he was quickly found out. Connecticut responded adroitly to the threat of rebel collusion, passing a stern espionage act months later. The General Assembly levied a heavy $1,000 fine and imprisonment if one were found guilty of "direct or indirect written or verbal contact with a rebel, or selling or transport of war goods."[24] This fervent opposition to treason provided a great disincentive to commit acts of sabotage in Connecticut.

Given that there are no accounts of witnesses to suspicious activity before the blaze, it is unlikely a group of conspirators was responsible for the conflagration. As part of the antiespionage legislation, "unionist prudential committees" had been founded to watch closely for dubious characters and activities. The federal government had eyes all over the state, aiding the countermovement defending Connecticut from subversion.[25] No reports of spying or of plotting this alleged mission to reduce the armory to ashes have ever surfaced, which is extraordinary, given the vigilant record keeping and reporting of antisubversion groups. As it happens, these committees were possibly overly vigilant. In June 1863, a group of innocent surveyors working in Goshen found themselves accused of scheming on a secret project for Jefferson Davis.[26] This example of another baseless conspiracy theory further displays the rash paranoia rampant in the Civil War era. Connecticut protected itself from internal disintegration, costing some measure of good sense in the process.

Dissenters in the North were dealt their greatest blow in July 1863. The

Battle of Gettysburg was a great Union victory that pushed the Confederacy into retreat. Public faith was renewed, and the elections that followed indicated political cohesion. In Connecticut, the likelihood of a Confederate sympathetic takeover receded after these events.[27] Without the benefit of foresight, the terror of Connecticut's populace did not fade away so quickly. As national news poured in, conspiracy survived in rumor and gossip. In 1863, Confederate spies were arrested in New York and Ohio, and plots originating in Canada were discovered. Angry mobs raged against the draft in Boston and New York; Connecticut seemed to be at the heart of a maelstrom of discontent and treason.[28] Governor Buckingham dispensed arms to preempt a violent reaction to Connecticut's own draft.[29] The governor could not, however, shield his constituents from the injurious rhetoric of extremists.

Clement Vallandigham, the rogue candidate for governor in Ohio, displayed brazen confidence in the southern cause, addressing devotees in Canada: "I warn the men in power, that there is a vast multitude, bound together by the strongest and holiest of ties, to defend by whatever means, their natural and constitutional rights as free men, at all hazards, to the last extremity."[30] Vallandigham was speaking in 1863 of the eternal ethos of the defenders of revolution, the southern secessionists and Copperheads. In their hearts, the people of Hartford felt that the flames soaring into the February morning light were a message sent by this multitude. The pervading influence of southern sympathy by 1864 was, however, only superficial at best. Yet rebel advances were perceived everywhere in the Nutmeg State. It is little wonder that several months later a factory fire, an otherwise common catastrophe, was grouped in league with these events.

Regardless of peace or war, disastrous factory fires were common in this era. The *Courant*'s summary of 1863 lists the explosions of two powder mills and the burning of one shoddy mill in Connecticut.[31] Although newspaper accounts continually described the Colt Amory disaster as unlike any ever seen in the state in terms of scale, calamities of that nature were quite usual if not routine. On February 6, 1864, the same day most of the greater state was reading the story of the fire, the *Willimantic Journal* reported the burning of a rubber mill in Colchester, caused by a broken watchman's lamp.[32] Five months later, a fire almost identical to the Coltsville inferno destroyed part of the U.S. Armory in Springfield, Massachusetts. According to the *Courant*, the fire started in the attic, caused by the ignition of dry wood close to the hot chimney.[33]

Numerous parallels between these events and the Colt Armory fire vitalize the rejection of the conspiracy thesis. Sam Colt employed watchmen to guard against sabotage, and that system was still in place in February 1864.[34] The fire's cause and trajectory mirrors that of the Springfield Armory, right down to the oil-soaked floors. In the face of these similarities, neither the *Courant* nor any other source in this canvass revisited or revised the story of the Colt Armory fire as a potential exaggeration. All of these other above-mentioned incidents were reported simply as accidents. Perhaps it was more desirable to forget about the fire and the ensuing hysteria altogether. That the fire in Hartford was believed by many to be a conspiracy was largely due to a public desire to give the tragedy some meaning. As rebel plots were part of the Civil War experience, the idea of southern treachery provided the perfect milieu.

In a time long before the twenty-four-hour news cycle, before film and television, newspapers were the sole arbiters of news. No other sources were available to common citizens, and the news they consumed was a function of the newswriter's point of view. Entrenched in political dogma, newspapers were the organizing tools for parties and war committees. Democrats read papers with Democratic agendas; likewise Republicans sought out sources that catered to their own perspective. Events of the Civil War were framed from the ideological standpoint of the publication; there was little objective journalistic integrity in this era.[35] Newspapers during the Civil War battled one another, and Colt Armory fire story was rife with conflicting angles.

The account provided by the *Hartford Courant* was impartial, conceding that "perhaps the mystery will never be explained." The fire started in the attic, where a driving pulley was situated near cotton waste and drying gunstocks, the wooden skeletons of pistols and rifles. While the *Courant* acknowledged the theories surrounding the fire's cause, the arson hypothesis quickly gained influence: "Many believed that it was the work of an incendiary, and among them were some of the most prominent contractors in the concern."[36] The emotional appeal of conspiracy was most attractive to those whose millions of dollars powered the machines that now lay in a smoking pile in the South Meadow. The culture of the Colt Patent Firearms Company was rife with the paranoid spirit of Sam Colt himself, who was obsessed with protecting his ideas from the intrigues of competitors.[37] Overwhelming demand for the story and details of the "great conflagration" ensured that the *Courant*'s coverage was certainly the most circulated throughout Connecticut, and the *New York Times* ran its story.[38] Accounts like this inadvertently bred a belief that the defenders of slavery had attacked Union commerce and industry. Harmless gossip was overshadowed by more biased retellings of the fire.

Unlike the *Courant*, the *Hartford Press* had no qualms in promoting the conspiracy theory. The *Press* took great editorial liberty, declaring "an emissary of Jeff. Davis did this deed." The flammable attic thesis is thrown out completely, replaced by a secret maneuver of "rebel sympathizers and disloyal men" in the employ of the Patent Firearms Company.[39] This mythical report gained much attention throughout Connecticut, and it was carried by the *Norwich Morning Bulletin*, the *Bridgeport Standard*, *New Haven Palladium*, and others.[40] Readers across the state no doubt slept poorly that night, terrorized by the invisible rebel network sensationalized by the *Hartford Press*. Flight of the imagination misled the public from the reasonable, albeit less exciting, truth.

The Democratic *Hartford Times* also provided an unbiased story, with slightly greater clarity than that which appeared in the *Courant*, and the most logical argument *against* conspiracy. On February 5, the *Hartford Times* echoed the particular details of the fire: the dry wood, the flammable nature of the oil-slicked floors, and the like. Further on, the article dwells on the material loss of the factory, the hundreds of men now unemployed, and the unprecedented nature of the disaster in Connecticut history.[41] Whereas the fire might potentially have been framed as a victory for peace, and a calamity welcomed by Democrats, the *Hartford Times* felt the sting along with the rest of the community. Republican or Democrat, the burning of the armory was a harrowing experience. For some, conspiracy balanced the weight of the tragic and inexplicable. Others saw past whimsical fancies and political attitudes and sought to quell the fear spread by conspiracy theories.

On February 6, after hearing the murmurs of sabotage, the *Hartford Times* delivered a definitive response to nip all rumors in the bud. Calling the claim of deliberately incendiary origins "absurd," the denial insisted that the fire was only to be attributed to misfortune. Moreover, the paper poked holes in the assertion of the *Hartford Press*, citing the improbability of a secret fire set by the light of day when hundreds of witnesses could have spotted the alleged saboteurs.[42] No other publication brought such a rousing reply to the claim of conspiracy. The veil of intrigue and mystery might have faded had the *Hartford Times* article been carried in larger newspapers, as were those of the *Courant* or the *Press*, or if it had been cited more often in the historical literature. It is startling to uncover such a lucid report from the time period, especially from an expectedly biased source.

Certainly, if the Colt Armory fire was a conspiracy, the Confederate press could shed some light on the subject. The *Richmond Daily Dispatch* contains no such acknowledgment of southern participation in the event. In the hope of preventing the friction and excitement caused by opinion, rumor, and hearsay, the South founded a Press Association in the spring of 1863. The chief conduit for all reporting, the association was able to provide reliable information for all Confederate newspapers. The *Richmond Daily Dispatch* also professed no political creed and was impartial in its analysis of events.[43] Following the fire in Hartford, the *Dispatch* provided the facts, nothing more.[44] Conversely, the paper acknowledged Confederate espionage and the Union's readiness for the planned arson attacks in New York City.[45] Had any information about Confederate intrigues in Hartford been known by the Press Association, it should have appeared in the southern press. The fact that the *Dispatch* contains no recognition of rebel involvement is a great blow to the conspiracy thesis. Ironically, the South appeared to have more journalistic integrity than the North in the Civil War. The rebels had greater union of purpose and less dissent than the North, and they took action to prevent hysterical rhetoric from confusing that resolve. Still, national periodicals cultivated the capricious rumors around the fire. *Scientific American* persisted that a "deserter from the rebels" employed at the factory was to blame, for "no one but a rebel sympathizer could have ordered its destruction."[46] This line of thinking was impervious to argument. Those who desired to see conspiracy saw it everywhere. Allusions to fires set by the rebels were immediately associated with the burning of the armory. The fact that the steamer hoses repeatedly burst meant that someone had rigged the system of piping to ensure the blaze from being extinguished.[47] Newspapers and periodicals needed only the existence of Connecticut opponents to the war to substantiate the claim that the unfortunate fire was intentional. Beneath the surface, the details belie the invention of conspiracy.

Near the end of his life, Sam Colt commissioned an identical wing built off the original armory, ensuring capacity for the coming tide of manufacturing to supply the Union armies.[48] This new west wing was built for the sole purpose of producing weapons for government contracts, a point astutely furnished to the public by the *Hartford Times* and the *Hartford Daily Courant*.[49] Concerned employees sequestered the fire to the east wing, where work on orders for the public was being conducted. Operations continued undaunted in the west wing, and the supply of Union guns was unaffected.[50] In this way, though devastating to the Hartford economy and public psyche, the so-called rebel plot failed to inflict any substantial damage to the northern war machine. Because the Colt factory was producing more than six hundred thousand rifles and four hundred thousand revolvers, more than any other gun making concern in the North, the Confederacy had a logical motive for eliminating the largest supplier of Union arms.[51] Yet the fact that the fire started in the civilian wing disproves that the "attack" was a success.

As the embers cooled in Coltsville, Confederate conspiracies *did* become more far-reaching. The fighting spirit of the South began to fade as the Union found a footing at Gettysburg. General Ulysses S. Grant's iron will induced Jefferson Davis to seek drastic new strategies. To that end he mobilized a radical contingent of spies in Canada. From Toronto these agents harnessed Confederate support in the hopes of fostering a "Northwest Confederacy."[52] This group of extremists believed that if the North could be divided, the cause of peace and southern independence might be realized.

What followed was a torrent of failed ventures—desperate maneuvers to end the war through terrorism and disruption. A kidnapping of Andrew Johnson was orchestrated, only to fail after his travel plans were changed at the last minute. A plot to rob a bank in Maine was foiled by turncoats, and local authorities arrested the perpetrators.[53] Designs to release Confederate prisoners from an Ohio prison were never realized.[54] The Toronto organization even contaminated blankets and clothing on a Washington train in the hope of transmitting yellow fever to the president and members of his cabinet.[55] Federal infiltration, internal defection, and sloppy organization plagued these exploits. After several months, the force mobilized in April 1864 had been whittled down to a few embittered fundamentalists. Northerners heard more of impotent Confederate conspiracies than successful schemes, thanks to the preparedness of state and federal law enforcement. Minor successes bolstered the fear of sabotage and contributed to the misattribution of conspiracy to the Colt Armory fire.

Armsmear described this causal connection: "Regarding the origin of the fire, opinions will perhaps never coincide. Some traced it to rebel emissaries, such as burned western steamers and New York Hotels."[56] Indeed, a prevailing theme in these conspiracies was arson. The Confederates sought to set fire to passenger and military steamboats and other targets to incite civil unrest and fear. Primitive grenades, bottles filled with liquid phosphorus, were used to ignite the blazes. "Greek fire," as it was known, was highly combustible and equally unreliable. For instance, the plot to burn Union ferries in St. Louis was a partial success at best, inflicting minimal damage.[57] In late November 1864, a group of agents set out to burn hotels in New York City in the hope of creating a chaotic situation in which the city could be taken over and reestablished a Confederate capital. More than a dozen hotels were targeted. The Confederates were successful in organizing and executing the plot, starting fires from individual rented rooms. The problem, again, was the accelerant. The Greek fire required oxygen to ignite. Once the arsonists closed the rooms' doors upon fleeing, all the fires did was smoke.[58] Despite the organization, the New York City plan was a failure in that it did not create the revolution that Confederates envisioned.

The fire in Hartford does not fit with the modus operandi of the known conspirators. If Greek fire was used, it was certainly the most successful such application. After the repeated failures, the Toronto group resolved to abandon phosphorus in its operations.[59] In 1864, the strategy of the South was to create civil unrest and fear—there is no evidence that the Confederacy was interested in seizing Union weapons. Money was of greater concern to the spies and saboteurs. More than $1 million was spent on futile enterprises, and raids in Maine and Vermont illustrated this frenzied need for capital.[60] The adjoining office building of the armory that was compromised contained a safe that held priceless plans and diagrams of new Colt products, as well as a great deal of money. The safe was recovered without a scratch.[61] Had a party of Copperheads, Confederate spies, and other enemies sought to torch the armory, they had not only succeeded in burning the wrong side of the complex, but they also failed to steal anything.

The Colt Armory is never spoken of in the literature as a target or an example of Confederate arson. Even if the Confederacy was not responsible, they might have feigned a victory in this fortunate calamity. There is no evidence to support this claim. Further, if the conflagration was a conspiracy, it represented an unparalleled triumph of southern subversion. The Canadian agency did not have the means to accomplish an act of this magnitude. Those who believed Hartford had experienced an act of treachery had given the South far too much credit. Connecticut did not factor into the strategy of the Northwest Confederacy. The South had greater support in the Midwest and directed most of its attention outside of New England.[62]

To foster an insurrection, the Confederates sought to undermine public opinion and the legitimacy of the government through physical sabotage. Failing to stop the North on the battlefield, they hoped to damage the hearts and minds of the people. The reelection of Abraham Lincoln menaced the South's will to keep fighting. In the hope of derailing the electoral process, Jefferson Davis and his fanatics sought to instigate uprisings on Election Day in major northern cities. Despite their best efforts, Cincinnati, Boston, Chicago, and New York experienced no acrimony or violence. Canadian officials seized Confederate correspondences, and local authorities were on the alert.[63] Lincoln and the Republicans carried the day; the groundswell of Union support was strong. Northern political momentum was undeniable, secured by intelligence gathering and rigorous counterinsurgent initiatives. Notwithstanding all that was done to protect the North, fear and fantasy still flourished in Connecticut.

The question remains, why has the history of the fire been fraught with so much debate? Because the fire has never been proven to have been a Confederate attack, it has drifted out of memory and the historical literature. The fact that the work of the company did continue and the factory was rebuilt makes the fire an unfortunate footnote in the Colt saga. Yet when the fire is mentioned today, murmurs of conspiracy linger. The narrative is couched as an act of arson for which the evidence has simply never surfaced. There is no doubt in the sound mind that the great conflagration was simply a catastrophe whose cause was hyperbolized by a public seized with fear. The Civil War had produced a confirmation bias that made the conspiracy theory plausible. Despite the ineffectual ability of the South to coordinate sabotage, Connecticut's lack of appeal in southern strategy, and the vigilance of law enforcement, many people endorsed the claim that Confederate conspiracy had come to Connecticut. Fingers were continually pointed at subversive Democrats, yet Colt himself was an ardent Democratic political operator who opposed Abraham Lincoln's candidacy in 1860.[64] Factories burned with great frequency in the Civil War era, and such misfortunes were deemed accidents, but Colt's Armory had a special meaning to Connecticut's people, and its destruction required an extraordinary explanation.

In the final analysis, the cause of the fire is irrelevant, for its unifying effect was universal. Connecticut's reverence for Colt and his mission refused to die so easily. Mrs. Colt insisted that the factory was to be rebuilt, and the public exulted in this.[65] Newspapers, regardless of political bias, expressed a sorrow for the loss of the armory and delight for its reconstruction. Conspiracy notions were put forth only in a few disparate editorial opinions that unfortunately echoed throughout the state and have received more attention in the historical literature than coherent descriptions of the fire and its cause. Just as the *Hartford Press* inadvertently advanced the campaign of fear spread by the Confederacy, those who supported the armory stood in solidarity with the Union. The work was judged as right and good—one and the same with the war effort. In the conscience of the common citizen, rebuilding the factory was an affirmation of the North's industry and a denial of the Confederacy.

Two years later, the factory with the blue onion dome rose from the ashes in Hartford, as though the fire that confronted the population with the specter of conspiracy had never happened. In the heat of the times, the fire was framed as an attack, a plot to burn the city into submission. The logical rejections of this theory and a great outpouring of grief were drowned out by the fantastic explanations that appealed to the mind's eye. The enormity of the tragedy required a rationalization that measured up to the horror it produced. Conspiracies were *everywhere* in this time— foremost among them, the multiple plots to assassinate President Lincoln. Whether or not the armory fire was a conspiracy will never be known for sure. The emotional response of the people of Connecticut is unquestioned, and it testifies to the deep feelings attached to the armory and that for which it stood. The North was defending the political idea of Union and the new American identity characterized by Sam Colt's individualism, tenacity, and respect for the common people. No amount of burning rhetoric or smoldering brownstone permanently dismantled the prevalence of these ideals or the nation founded for their pursuit.

NOTES

1. "A Terrible Fire in Hartford," *Hartford Times*, February 5, 1864.

2. "City Intelligence: Our Report of the Fire," *Hartford Daily Courant*, February 9, 1864.

3. *Willimantic Journal*, February 6, 1864.

4. *Hartford Daily Courant*, February 8, 1864.

5. *Hartford Times*, February 8, 1864.

6. *Hartford Times*, February 5, 1864.

7. William N. Hosley, *Colt: The Making of an American Legend* (Amherst: University of Massachusetts Press, 1996), 198.

8. John Niven, *Connecticut for the Union: The Role of the State in the Civil War* (New Haven, CT: Yale University Press, 1965), 355.

9. Hosley, *Colt*, 198.

10. Joanna D. Cowden, "The Politics of Dissent: Civil War Democrats in Con-

necticut," *New England Quarterly* 56.4 (December 1983): 538–54; Joanna D. Cowden, "Sovereignty and Secession: Peace Democrats and Antislavery Republicans in Connecticut during the Civil War Years," *Connecticut History* 30 (1989): 41–47; John E. Talmadge, "A Peace Movement in Civil War Connecticut," *New England Quarterly* 28.3 (September 1964): 306–21; Matthew Warshauer, *Connecticut in the American Civil War: Slavery, Sacrifice, and Survival* (Middletown, CT: Wesleyan University Press, 2011).

11. Robert W. Johannsen, ed., *Lincoln-Douglas Debates of 1858* (New York: Oxford University Press, 1965), 14.

12. Hosley, *Colt*, 125.

13. Henry Barnard, *Armsmear: The Home, the Arm, and the Armory of Samuel Colt. A Memorial* (New York: Alvord, 1866), 254.

14. R. L. Wilson, *The Colt Heritage: The Official Story of Colt Firearms from 1836 to the Present* (New York: Simon and Schuster, 1979), 123.

15. Hosley, *Colt*, 196–99.

16. William Hosley cites only two articles, one from the *Hartford Daily Courant* and one from *Scientific American*.

17. Ellsworth S. Grant, *The Colt Legacy: The Colt Armory in Hartford, 1855–1980* (Providence, RI: Mowbray Co., 1982), 20.

18. "Fire in Hartford," *Willimantic Journal*, February 6, 1864.

19. Kenneth A. Simon, *Colt: Legend & Legacy* (Connecticut Public Television, 1997), online transcript, "Faithful Affection & Memory," SimonPure Productions, http://www.simonpure.com/colt06.htm (accessed October 20, 2010).

20. Colt Firearms Collection, Connecticut State Library, Hartford.

21. "Chronological Table of the principle battles, skirmishes, and events of the year 1863," *Hartford Daily Courant*, January 1, 1863.

22. Niven, *Connecticut for the Union*, 166.

23. Historians have debated the reality of a northern conspiracy. See Wood Grey, *The Hidden Civil War: The Story of the Copperheads* (New York: Viking Press, 1942); George Fort Milton, *Abraham Lincoln and the Fifth Column* (New York: Vanguard Press, 1942); Frank L. Klement, *The Copperheads in the Middle West* (Chicago: University of Chicago Press, 1960); Donald E. Markle, *Spies and Spymasters of the Civil War* (New York: Hippocrene Books, 1992); Frank L. Klement, *The Limits of Dissent: Clement L. Vallandigham and the Civil War* (New York: Fordham University Press, 1998); Frank L. Klement, *Lincoln's Critics: The Copperheads of the North*, edited and introduced by Steven K. Rogstad (Shippensburg, PA: White Mane Publishing, 1999); Jennifer L. Weber, *Copperheads: The Rise and Fall of Lincoln's Opponents in the North* (New York: Oxford University Press, 2008).

24. Niven, *Connecticut for the Union*, 298–99.

25. Niven, *Connecticut for the Union*, 299.

26. *Hartford Daily Courant*, January 1, 1864.

27. Niven, *Connecticut for the Union*, 290.

28. *Hartford Daily Courant*, January 1, 1864.

29. William A. Croffut and John M. Morris, *The Military and Civil History of Connecticut during the War of 1861–65* (New York: L. Bill, 1868), 459.

30. Vallandigham quoted in James D. Horan, *Confederate Agent: A Discovery in History* (New York: Crown Publishers, 1954), 90.

31. *Hartford Daily Courant*, January 1, 1864.

32. *Willimantic Journal*, February 6, 1864.

33. "Fire in Springfield," *Hartford Daily Courant*, July 4, 1864.

34. Hosley, *Colt*, 198.

35. For more on the partisanship, and usefulness, of Civil War–era newspapers, see Mark E. Neely Jr., *The Union Divided: Party Conflict in the Civil War North* (Cambridge, MA: Harvard University Press, 2002).

36. "Great Fire at Colt's Armory!," *Hartford Daily Courant*, February 6, 1864.

37. James L. Mitchell, *Colt: The Man, the Arms, the Company* (Harrisburg, PA: Stackpole, 1959), 265.

38. "City Intelligence," *Hartford Daily Courant*, February 9, 1864; "The Fire at Colt's Armory," *New York Times*, February 7, 1864.

39. *Hartford Press*, February 5, 1864.

40. *Norwich Morning Bulletin*, February 6, 1864; *Bridgeport Standard*, February 6, 1864; *New Haven Palladium*, February 6, 1864.

41. "A Terrible Fire in Hartford. Colt's Armory Destroyed!," *Hartford Times*, February 5, 1864.

42. "Origin of the Fire," *Hartford Times*, February 6, 1864.

43. Clement Eaton, *A History of the Southern Confederacy* (New York: Free Press, 1954), 221.

44. "Later from the North," *Richmond Daily Dispatch*, February 15, 1864, http://imls.richmond.edu/d/ddr (accessed November 11, 2010).

45. *Richmond Daily Dispatch*, December 1, 1864.

46. "Colt's Armory," *Scientific American*, March 12, 1864, American Periodical Series Database, http://o-proquest.umi.com.www.consuls.org/pqdweb?index=17&did=164256801&SrchMode=3&sid=1&Fmt=10&VInst=PROD&VType=PQD&RQT=309&VName=HNP&TS=1292264144&clientId=13942&aid=2 (accessed October 30, 2010).

47. *Hartford Press*, February 5, 1864.

48. *Hartford Times*, February 7, 1864.

49. *Hartford Times*, February 6, 1864; *Hartford Daily Courant*, February 6, 1864.

50. *Hartford Times*, February 6, 1864.

51. Niven, *Connecticut for the Union*, 357.

52. Markle, *Spies and Spymasters of the Civil War*, 51.

53. Markle, *Spies and Spymasters of the Civil War*, 53.

54. Horan, *Confederate Agent*, 61.

55. Markle, *Spies and Spymasters of the Civil War*, 69.

56. Barnard, *Armsmear*, 254.

57. Markle, *Spies and Spymasters of the Civil War*, 54.

58. Nat Brandt, *The Man Who Tried to Burn New York* (Syracuse, NY: Syracuse University Press, 1986), 120.

59. Brandt, *The Man Who Tried to Burn New York*, 140.

60. Markle, *Spies and Spymasters of the Civil War*, 55.

61. *Hartford Times*, February 6, 1864.

62. Brandt, *The Man Who Tried to Burn New York*, 140.

63. Brandt, *The Man Who Tried to Burn New York*, 91.

64. Herbert G. Houze, *Samuel Colt: Arms, Art, and Invention* (New Haven, CT: Yale University Press, 2006), 13.

65. *Hartford Times*, February 8, 1864.

6 : Post-Traumatic Stress Disorder in the Civil War

CONNECTICUT CASUALTIES AND A LOOK INTO THE MIND ?

The Battle of Fredericksburg was a bloody affair. Confederate General Robert E. Lee positioned troops atop Marye's Heights, a steep ridge that extended upward from 150 to 200 feet, forming a half-circle around the town.[1] Rebel cannons pointed from multiple directions and gray-clad soldiers filled trenches, awaiting the doomed onslaught of northern soldiers. Seven Connecticut regiments joined Union General Ambrose Burnside at Fredericksburg in December 1862, although only two, the Fourteenth and the Twenty-Seventh Connecticut Volunteer Infantry Regiments, took part in the ghastly assault. "Who can depict the horrors of that scene?" asked the Fourteenth's regimental historian. "The belching of two hundred pieces of artillery seemed to lift the earth from its foundation, shells screeched and burst in the air among the men as if possessed by demons and were seeking revenge, the shot from tens of thousands of musketry fell like rain drops in a summer shower." Samuel Fiske, a member of the Fourteenth from Madison, Connecticut, wrote painfully, "Oh! My heart is sick and sad. Blood and wounds and death are before my eyes; of those who are my friends, comrades, brothers. . . . The city is filled with pieces of brave men who went whole into the conflict. Every basement and floor is covered with pools of blood. Limbs, in many houses, lie in heaps; and surgeons are exhausted with their trying labors."[2]

Shortly after the battle, the Fourteenth's Lieutenant Colonel Sanford H. Perkins of Torrington suffered a psychotic break. Records reveal he had "delusions about his whereabouts" and, while recovering in a hospital from a glancing neck wound, was convinced that he was in a hotel, even treating nurses and doctors as hotel staff. Perkins ultimately ended up at the Connecticut Hospital for the Insane, created in 1868 in Middletown, Connecticut. He was the subject of many entries in patient log books. Staff noted his desire to be left alone, his refusal to socialize with other patients or staff, and his obsession with a fictional character he called "Swino."

S. H. Perkins, 14th Conn. Courtesy of the Civil War Photographs Collection,
Prints & Photographs Division, Library of Congress, LC-DIG-cwpb-04959

Perkins drew "Swino" the pig on virtually every piece of available paper, and it was the regular subject of conversation with doctors. His hospital records reveal a variety of symptoms and multiple addenda over his stay in the asylum. Entries included paranoia, irrational excitability, violent fits, and withdrawal from social life. Staff consistently noted that the cause of insanity was rooted in his war experience, theorizing that it was perhaps in part a side effect from his neck wound, or the result of intemperate behavior picked up in camp.[3]

In the twenty-first century, it is rather easy to conclude that Sanford Perkins suffered from post-traumatic stress disorder (PTSD), an illness first officially recognized in the 1980 *Diagnostic and Statistical Manual of Mental Disorders III* and most commonly associated with Vietnam veterans. Researchers theorized that the especially atrocious nature of the Vietnam War exposed soldiers to scenes of surreal horror, an atmosphere of relentless pressure, and crushing fear. This, combined with the war's failure and the absence of a grateful, cathartic homecoming, produced a predisposition to psychological pathology.[4] Consequently, PTSD was considered to be a phenomenon unique to Vietnam veterans.

Clearly, this theory of PTSD's origins is false. Historians and clinicians have since looked backward and found in America's many conflicts some of the essential psychological ailments of war trauma. Whether it was termed "combat fatigue," as in the Korean War, "battle exhaustion" in World War II, "shell shock" in World War I, or "soldier's heart" in the Civil War, American soldiers across the centuries have suffered a wide range of symptoms of varying severity from their wartime experiences.[5]

Nor is PTSD a phenomenon that has been lessened in our modern wars. In 2008, the RAND Corporation conducted a study to assess PTSD among Iraq and Afghanistan war veterans. Finding that one in five veterans suffered from PTSD-related symptoms, the study suggested that the rate of psychological wounds was very likely disproportionately higher than physical injuries. Nonetheless, PTSD sufferers underreported their symptoms, and a majority of soldiers were not treated or were undertreated. Concerns over the potential impact on future employment and social stigma among peers were the primary reasons for underreporting. The study insisted, "Unless they receive appropriate and effective care for these mental health conditions, there will be long-term consequences for them and for the nation. Unfortunately, we found there are many barriers preventing them from getting the high-quality treatment they need."[6]

In the 150 years since the Civil War, physicians have come a long way in their understanding of the mind. Unlike in the nineteenth century, few today would conclude that mental disorder is a moral failure, or that related substance abuse is a personal flaw rather than a self-medicated treatment for underlying symptoms. Still, the stigma associated with mental health problems remains rather doggedly attached. This can be seen in the attitudes of returning soldiers and their concern over being labeled, as outlined in the RAND study, and in the refusal of the Connecticut Department of Mental Health and Addiction Services (the organization that today operates the Connecticut Valley Hospital—formerly the Connecticut Hospital for the Insane) to aid in the release and research of records related to Civil War soldiers.[7] And there is most certainly an important confluence between understanding the stories and needs of soldiers in twenty-first-century America and those of the Civil War era—namely, that the psychological trauma of war has always been with us. It is the product of brutal experience, and revealing its historical origins can offer reflections on how far we have come in understanding what war can do to the human mind, and in letting today's soldiers know that they have never been alone in their experiences.

The focus of this chapter, then, is threefold: first, to explain how those in the nineteenth century perceived the workings of the mind and body, and then to translate PTSD within that context—no easy task, as the language and diagnostic understanding of the period were quite different from what we know today; second, to explain how the records of Civil War soldiers who suffered from PTSD-related symptoms were found; third, to tell some of the Connecticut stories that have been uncovered.

Insanity in early America was a condition that had serious negative social consequences. It was most often explained in terms of physical or moral deficiency. In many cases, physicians assiduously avoided the label "insanity" because of the severe social stigma attached to it and the fact that it was assumed to be hereditary.[8] Indeed, records of facilities such as the Connecticut Hospital for the Insane noted family history immediately after the name, age, and gender of a patient.[9] This belief that insanity was a stain on the family bloodline led many patients and their families to downplay the severity of symptoms or avoid care altogether. Rather than "insanity," milder terms were utilized. Patients suffered from "nerves" or "nervous hysteria," which was considered temporary and the result of a variety of socially acceptable causes. This less severe language also implied a highly curable outcome, even if symptoms recurred regularly. In studying Civil War soldiers, such terms are particularly noteworthy, be-

The Hartford Retreat for the Insane, founded in 1823. Today it is the Institute of Living at Hartford Hospital. Courtesy of the Connecticut Historical Society, Hartford

cause so many veterans were diagnosed with a plethora of nervous disorders. Within a modern understanding of PTSD, today's clinicians note that sufferers often display irrational fears and excitability only when exposed to certain stimuli, such as loud noises or the sight of violence, which may trigger memories and bring on symptoms for a limited time. To the nineteenth-century observer, this might have appeared to be a mild or intermittent fit or a flare-up of a previous nervous disorder.[10]

Like medicine in general, psychiatry (the modern distinction between psychology and psychiatry was not yet developed) was in a premodern state when the Civil War began. Indeed, it was not until the 1840s that a truly separate branch of medicine concerned with the mind was even recognized. In 1825, there existed in the nation a mere nine institutions for the mentally ill, which rose to sixty-two by 1865.[11] The Hartford Retreat for the Insane (today the Institute of Living at Hartford Hospital), founded in 1823, is a prime example of the innovations of the era. The primary focus of psychiatric reformers like Eli Todd, the first superintendent of the Hartford Retreat, was on finding more effective treatments for mental disorder, not on gaining a better understanding of what caused mental illness or of how the mind worked. Todd was a pioneer of the "moral cure," which conceived of mental illness as stemming from an overstimulated brain, the best treatment for which was a carefully structured regimen of rest, exercise, and kindness. Todd represented a departure from an ancient system of treatment that had remained virtually unchanged since the Middle Ages.[12]

Todd, however, was at the front of a movement. Most doctors lagged far behind, believing that all mental illness was somatic, meaning that psychological disorders were caused by a physical problem within the body, such as too much blood pressure, or a blockage of the intestines that threw off the body's four "humors," which the Greeks related to the four seasons and four elements. The most famous physician of early America, Benjamin Rush, prescribed the same treatments for mental illness that he did for virtually all other illnesses: bloodletting and purgatives. This concept of humors, or interdependent systems within the body, caused many physicians up through the end of the nineteenth century to believe that an injury in one part of the body could have consequences in the mind.[13] For instance, a pinched nerve in the foot could cause an imbalance of the body's nerves and thus insanity. They failed to conceive of the idea that a traumatic experience, or fear of repeating that experience, could impact the brain in a nonphysical way. This attitude—that the seat of insanity was in the organ of the brain instead of the concept of the mind—was the dominant paradigm of the entire nineteenth century, until the time of Freud in the 1890s.[14]

One of the other factors that influenced how physicians conceived of mental illness was rooted in early America's religious underpinnings. From the antebellum period well through the Civil War, doctors were heavily influenced by tenets of religious morality, often viewing sin and intemperance as the causes of insanity. In fact, conscious efforts were made in medicine, and in other sciences of the time, to make findings and theories conform to religious doctrine.[15] Behaviors like excessive drinking, hypersexuality, masturbation, and impure, "immoral" thoughts were considered the cause of insanity rather than the symptoms. Religious morality became something like a "fifth humor," which asylum physicians, like Eli Todd in Hartford, sought to rebalance. Because the widespread acceptance of the idea of psychogenic insanity was still decades away, the possibility that experiences could cause insanity independent of any physical damage or moral imbalance was not even considered when explaining mental illness. This is particularly important to keep in mind when considering substance abuse, one of the primary indicators of PTSD, which would have been seen as a cause of mental disorder rather than a disease in its own right or a coping strategy for dealing with past trauma.

At its core, the concept of insanity was essentially the same as that of the ancient Greeks, and it included three core ideas—mania, dementia, and melancholia.[16] Those trying to explain mental illness had been modifying and reorganizing these three archetypes for millennia. By the mid-nineteenth century, the various terms revolving around these core ideas included "neurasthenia" (dissociation, depression), "nostalgia" (flashbacks and potentially depression), "inebriation" (substance abuse), and various nervous disorders (such as "nervous hysteria," "nervous irritability," "nervous disease," "nervous exhaustion," or "nervous agitation," among others).[17] The outcome of these disorders often manifested themselves in the form of mental paralysis, imbecility, suicide, alcoholism, and violent outbursts. It is worth noting here, that today's PTSD and psychological combat disorders include dissociation, irritability, hyperarousal, hallucinations or "flashbacks," substance abuse, suicide, violent outbursts, paranoia, and depression.[18]

One of the great challenges for contemporary researchers is to try to understand the concepts and language of the nineteenth century and thereby to attempt the translation of earlier diagnoses within modern descriptions of PTSD. In many ways, this is a newly emerging field. Only one detailed study, Eric T. Dean's *Shook over Hell: Post-Traumatic Stress, Vietnam, and the Civil War*, currently exists, and it was published in 1997. Dean concluded that significant numbers of Civil War veterans suffered from psychological trauma as a result of their war experiences. His study group included the records of 291 Civil War veterans housed at the Indiana Hospital for the Insane (unlike Connecticut, Indiana has no restrictions on Civil War–era records), and he made observations based on the definitional outlines of PTSD.[19] It should be noted that the understanding and definition of PTSD has grown considerably since Dean's work and continues to evolve. Moreover, some researchers utilize the term "psychological combat disorder," which allows for the incorporation of more symptoms, all associated with PTSD, but not necessarily a part of the actual diagnosis. This is especially important when measuring substance abuse, which was the most common disorder noted in the nineteenth century and one that remains an important associated symptom of PTSD today.[20] The primary point here is that defining PTSD and related combat-associated problems is a moving target. Owing in part to the Afghanistan and Iraq wars, the military's and physicians' understanding, and thus their definitions and diagnoses, are ever changing.

With a fairly limited, premodern understanding of the mind, physicians in the midst of the Civil War would have first attempted to categorize a soldier or veteran within the terms of "mania," "dementia," "melancholia," or perhaps some type of "nervous disease." The next logical step was to connect some sort of physical trauma that had disturbed the body's natural balance in one system or another. Hence the notes in Sanford Perkins's patient file that theorized a relationship between his disturbed mental state and his neck injury. Especially for the veterans diagnosed after the war, a common conclusion was that the use of substances, either alcohol or opium, negatively impacted their mental state. Again, Perkins was listed as potentially having learned "intemperate" habits while in camp.[21]

It is extremely difficult to fully embrace how nineteenth-century physicians, even in the midst of the Civil War, managed to overlook the links between cause and effect. With men literally blowing up all around them, battlefields that could be traversed by walking from body to body without ever touching the ground, and battles like that at Antietam Creek, where more men were killed and wounded in a single day than in all previous American wars combined, it is virtually inconceivable that physicians would fail to make connections. Surely the bloodletting at Fredericksburg and quick onset of symptoms experienced by Perkins should have been an eye-opener. Yet the "science" of the time predominated.[22] Physicians for the most part either conformed to the existing categories or ignored the problem.

Of the huge, six-volume *Surgical and Medical History of the War of the Rebellion*, only a few pages are devoted to a discussion of mental or nervous disease.[23] This is particularly surprising, because those very same volumes reveal that out of twenty-two causes of disease in northern troops, nervous disease ranked tenth, and insanity accounted for six out of every one thousand soldiers discharged.[24] Moreover, "nostalgia," described as debilitating melancholy and homesickness that could lead to nervous paralysis if left unchecked, was responsible for 5,213 cases of disease among northern troops.[25] Clearly psychiatric conditions accounted for a significant portion of lost manpower for the Union Army during the war, yet it garnered little attention in medical records of the war or in professional journals of the day, such as the *American Journal of Insanity*.[26]

What attention psychological ailments did get from military doctors was unsympathetic. Civil War military physicians had a very different set of priorities and a different population of patients from that of civilian doctors. Here was no Eli Todd, making sure that rest and kindness were in abundance. War doctors were concerned with getting men back into active duty and getting unfit men removed from the field. Most soldiers who exhibited psychiatric ailments like nostalgia or nervous disease were assumed to be malingerers, trying to shirk duty out of laziness or cowardice.[27] One had to display "manifest" insanity to gain a discharge, and after September 1863, field surgeons lost the authority to discharge soldiers for reasons of insanity. Such discharges could be approved only by the administration at the Government Hospital for the Insane in Washington, D.C. During the entire war, only 1,231 discharges for insanity were granted.[28] Such miniscule numbers hardly represent the reality of PTSD-related symptoms suffered by Civil War soldiers generally, or Connecticut men in particular. Identifying Connecticut veterans who suffered from psychological ailments stemming from their service in the Civil War requires a careful reading of both state and federal census data, as well as pension records.

One of the first postwar sources is the 1880 census of "Defective, Dependent, and Delinquent Classes" in the state of Connecticut, which counted the insane, mentally challenged, and incarcerated, as well as orphans throughout the state, and organized them by town of origin in most cases or location of institutionalization in other cases. This census was carried out by many different agents, and the report varies widely in terms of detail. Another source is a census of pensioners commissioned by the state of Connecticut in 1883, which listed the pensioners not only by name but also by injury and pension level. An interesting group among them are the men identified as being driven insane by their war experiences, whose injuries were entirely psychological.[29] What is of particular note comes not specifically from these censuses themselves but rather from cross-referencing them. Of some ten men listed as "insane" in the 1880 census, eight also appeared in the 1883 census. In 1883, five of these men were patients at the Connecticut Hospital for the Insane, one was a patient at the Hartford Retreat for the Insane, and two were listed as residing in their town of origin. The nature of disability was recorded only for the five men at the Connecticut Hospital for the Insane. Three were listed as suffering from mania, and two from dementia.[30]

The 1883 census of disabled veteran pensioners collected veterans' names, date of injury, the disability that caused the pension to be awarded, and the monthly payment each man received. The records reveal that there

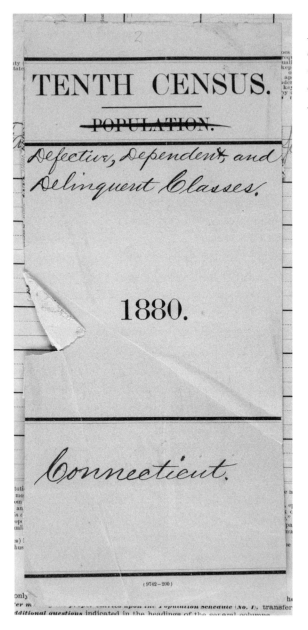

TENTH CENSUS.

POPULATION.

Defective, Dependent, and Delinquent Classes.

1880.

Connecticut.

(9742—200)

LIST

OF

PENSIONERS ON THE ROLL

JANUARY 1, 1883;

GIVING

THE NAME OF EACH PENSIONER, THE CAUSE FOR WHICH
PENSIONED, THE POST-OFFICE ADDRESS, THE RATE
OF PENSION PER MONTH, AND THE DATE OF
ORIGINAL ALLOWANCE,

AS CALLED FOR BY

SENATE RESOLUTION OF DECEMBER 8, 1882.

VOLUME I.

WASHINGTON:
GOVERNMENT PRINTING OFFICE.
1883.

List of Pensioners on the Roll, January 1, 1883, *part of the 1883 special census.*
This federal publication is reprinted from United States Pensions in Connecticut,
January 1, 1883 *(Hartford, 1883). Courtesy of the Connecticut State Library, Hartford*

were between ten and sixty-five Connecticut veterans receiving pensions for conditions that today would be associated with PTSD. A broader interpretation (one that includes the wide range of PTSD symptoms) would find that all sixty-five veterans suffered varying degrees of psychological combat-related trauma. This includes a host of "nervous diseases," such as nervous agitation, nervous exhaustion, neurasthenia, or simply nervous disorder. This diagnosis affected fifty-five of the soldiers listed. Even the most limited reading of the census data concludes that at least ten of the veterans suffered from severe psychological disorders caused by their war experiences. Six of the men had "insanity" specifically listed as their sole disability, a noteworthy factor considering the avoidance of such a diagnosis by the medical establishment of the time.[31]

This determination of insanity is important for two very particular reasons: first, the U.S. government recognized that these ten men became disabled directly as a result of their war experiences; second, their disability was permanent, as per the Pension Act of 1862. Also important is that the ten men received generous pensions, another recognition of their serious disability. Of the six men whose insanity was recognized as their sole disability, five received $50 a month, the same pension given to men who had lost both legs or their dominant arm. The remaining man received $72 a month, the amount given to a soldier who had lost both eyes and both arms.[32]

Although the 1883 census is extremely useful in offering some basic information on Connecticut Civil War veterans and also allows for some level of conjecture about the total numbers who could be considered psychological casualties of the war, it fails to provide detailed information on diagnosis and the conditions of patients. Turning to the actual pension files helps to fill out the story. Veterans receiving pensions were required to jump through several levels of government hoops. Requirements included testimonials of those familiar with the applicant, testimony from family, and a doctor's deposition. This information was meant to establish that the applicant was in fact disabled and unable to fully support himself; that the debility did not exist before the war; and that the injury was the result of military service. These records provide excellent information on Civil War veterans who suffered from psychological problems connected to the war.

Ithamar Butler, from New Britain, served in the Sixteenth Connecticut Volunteer Infantry as a hospital steward during the war.[33] There is no indication of his having been wounded, though the pressures on the Sixteenth were particularly brutal. They were arguably Connecticut's most unlucky regiment, receiving their baptism of fire at Antietam and later being captured en masse in North Carolina and sent to Andersonville Prison in Georgia.[34] Butler's is one of those tricky stories: he was unwounded; he does not appear to have been among the men who were captured; and he seems to have blended normally into civilian life for about ten years after the war. Then began "congestion of the brain" and fits of "nervous prostration." One such episode left him bedridden for six months. In terms of psychological diagnoses of the time, it is significant that Butler insisted in his pension statement that he was not an alcoholic or someone of intemperate behavior, which would have disqualified him for a pension.[35] His physician's affidavit to the pension board listed him as "½ insane" and unable to support himself through his own labors. Even Butler's relationship to the war is, at best, dissociative. One neighbor's affidavit stated that on multiple occasions Butler had claimed that he never served in the war. Yet with that same neighbor, sometimes in the same conversation, Butler recalled his service in vivid detail.[36] His is one of those cases that is so hard to determine today, and the same would have been true for doctors in the postwar era. With no outward trauma, and especially because the onset of symptoms came well after the war's end, Butler's later difficulties of the mind cannot be readily connected to the war. There is, however, no doubt that he suffered from some form of dementia.

The fullest and most fascinating story of Connecticut Civil War veterans suffering in the aftermath of the war comes from the patient files of Connecticut Hospital for the Insane (CHI), and the closely related records of Fitch's Soldiers' Home in Darien, Connecticut. As noted previously, CHI was opened a mere three years after the end of the war, in 1868, and housed a large number of veterans. It was the primary destination for soldiers who were either not admitted into dedicated soldiers' homes, were removed from homes, lacked the financial wherewithal to be admitted into more expensive private institutions like the Hartford Retreat, or were institutionalized by law enforcement. Fitch's was founded in 1863 by Benjamin Fitch, a local resident who promised to look after the families of soldiers while they were away at war, and later became a home for indigent veterans. This was the first such home in the United States, after which was modeled the modern Veterans' Administration (VA) homes. Indeed, Fitch's was moved in 1940 from Darien to Rocky Hill, where the state's main VA site continues to operate.

The first indication (during the course of this study) of veterans being treated at CHI came as a result of a document located at the Connecticut State Library. Titled "Fitch's Home for the Soldier Beneficiaries Transferred to the Connecticut Hospital for the Insane, 1891," the document listed forty-one veterans who were moved to CHI.[37] The records related to the deaths of these men were subsequently returned to Fitch's Home, and they include information about their stay in the hospital. It is clear that every one of the men suffered from PTSD-related conditions in varying degrees: eleven from alcoholism, five from inebriety (a term used for intoxication apart from alcohol, most likely opium), five from mental paralysis, four from dementia, eight from mania, seven from neurasthenia and one from intemperance (likely extreme irritability, given the presence of alcoholism and inebriety as separate categories). Most were single, though some were married. Roughly 60 percent were foreign born, mostly Irish. Only two of the forty-one were listed as being illiterate, and only six were listed as laborers, the others being tradesmen of various types. Of the forty-one men who made up this group of transferees, thirty-seven died in the asylum.[38]

The hospital records themselves, though incomplete in terms of chronology (many files are missing or partial), provide comments from doctors, many of whom recognized that a given patient's disturbances were caused directly by his wartime experiences. Second Lieutenant Charles W. Gleason of Bridgeport, for example, was consumed by his involvement in war—not just the Civil War, but the American Revolution as well.[39] CHI staff noted in the patient book that Gleason regularly made delusional claims and seemed to have very sincerely believed them. Among his most frequent and emphatic assertions was that he was a reincarnated Revolutionary War general who had served in many battles, most often at Bunker Hill. He claimed to "own England" and to have buried treasure or vast stashes of valuable property, which was constantly at risk of theft, throughout the world. Doctors most frequently commented on his paranoia and distrust of staff. Gleason had originally been committed to CHI in 1871, after he went on a "spree" of violent behavior and attacked his brother and mother. Previously, he gone on several alcoholic binges in Bridgeport and was arrested multiple times for vagrancy, public immodesty, and eventually burglary.[40]

Hospital staff noted that Gleason suffered frequent, sometimes violent breaks from reality in which he was incoherent, then very abruptly returned to normal behavior. These attacks seemed to have been preceded by military delusions in which he was an officer of great rank and responsibility. He apparently never decided exactly what rank he was, as his ranting continually increased his rank until in 1876, just before his death, he had reached the level of major general. Doctors noted that he had no prior history of psychological pathology or a family history of insanity.

Other CHI patients displayed similarly troubling behavior as a result of their war experiences. Allen Chalker, of the Fourteenth Connecticut Volunteers, suffered from severe paranoia and delusions.[41] Doctors noted in the patient log that Chalker "[r]etains his old delusions of his head having been destroyed by a cannon ball," and included that he was belligerent and untrusting toward staff, maintained a state of nearly constant "high irritability," and distanced himself from fellow patients. At one point he jumped out of a window and injured himself in an attempt to flee imaginary pursuers. Records indicate that he had been transferred to CHI from the Hartford Retreat for the Insane in August 1871. Chalker had been previously admitted at the Hartford Retreat in 1862 after being discharged from the army, for reasons not included in his files. He was not, according to his doctors, injured during the war and received no pension based on wounds.[42] Chalker's "high irritability" would, today, surely coincide with hypervigilance and dissociation, or perhaps even hallucinations, all of which are prime symptoms of psychological combat disorders and PTSD.

Other cases included Samuel Perry and Jacob Hall, both of Middletown. Perry served in the First Connecticut Cavalry and Hall in the First Connecticut Light Artillery. Both suffered from depression and unresolved feelings of guilt. Perry enlisted on December 21, 1863, and was captured while fighting at Ream's Station, Virginia, on June 29, 1864. He was paroled by the Confederates several months later, in December, and received a disciplinary discharge shortly after the war ended, on July 3, 1865. Hall was listed as having been discharged in December 1864, owing to disability, though there is no indication that he ever suffered from a physical wound.[43] Perry's hospital records reveal that he showed a debilitating "obsession with past sins," which caused him to be institutionalized several times during the 1870s. Hall demonstrated "morbid manifestations of a disordered imagination," which was often preoccupied with the horrors of war. After episodes of "animated excitement," he would retreat into periods of intense, self-imposed isolation. Doctors at CHI diagnosed Hall with chronic mania, as did doctors at his previous institution, Butler Hospital in Providence, from which he escaped.[44]

A final example of Civil War veterans housed at Connecticut Hospital for the Insane and who clearly suffered psychological trauma as a result of their war experience was George Hazen, a private from Derby who enlisted in the Thirteenth Connecticut Infantry on January 18, 1862, and was discharged toward the end of the war on January 6, 1865. Hazen spent nearly half his postwar life in one Connecticut asylum or another. More than one of his institutional stays was at the CHI, where a doctor noted that Hazen's intemperance was "a result of his enlistment," when he apparently fell in with low company during his military service. This was a common conclusion many observers in the postwar period made about veterans: that the army had harmed their moral fiber. Such a conclusion was in keeping with the medical tradition of blaming psychosis on a failure of moral rectitude. Yet intemperance was hardly the chief problem suffered by Hazen. He compulsively picked his nose to the point of bleeding because he believed "there was frost in it." He refused to eat, was considered a severe hypochondriac, and was cited for frequent masturbation (considered a serious moral and psychological problem in the 1870s). Perhaps the most troubling of Hazen's compulsions was his head rubbing. He rubbed constantly, to the extent of making himself bald.[45] It is hard to conclude that Hazen's later life experiences were somehow unrelated to his military service.

Other institutions that provide information on Connecticut Civil War veterans suffering from PTSD-related symptoms can be found in the records of the state's two major soldiers' homes, Fitch's Home (discussed previously) and the Connecticut Veterans' Home in Rocky Hill. These facilities served disabled and destitute veterans who had no other place to turn. From the records of these institutions several factors emerge that show the impact of psychological trauma attributable to the war.

The most commonly displayed symptom of PTSD, substance abuse, was rampant in the homes. Although alcoholism and opium abuse were by no means evidence of PTSD on their own, it is not unreasonable to assert some correlation between substance abuse and war-related psychological trauma in a population made up entirely of veterans who lacked other means of support besides the soldiers' home. This likelihood becomes even more apparent when the substance abuse was severe enough to result in a veteran's removal from what many considered their home and what was certainly a last refuge from complete poverty. In the case of Fitch's Home, discharge records reveal that between 1870 and 1900, sixty veterans were discharged involuntarily for either possession of alcohol (23), drunkenness (16), alcoholism (15), or possession of opium (6).[46] These were men who had been warned repeatedly and had multiple transgressions for substance abuse.

Similar evidence appears in the Historical Register of the Connecticut Veterans' Home, which includes the records of 493 residents, lists their infirmities, and for many includes physicians' notes about special requirements. Twenty-nine residents were listed as suffering from PTSD-related symptoms, including (in order of frequency) alcoholism, inebriety, imbecility, mania, dementia, neurasthenia, and insanity (unspecified nature). The trend established in the Fitch's Home records regarding the nation of origin also appears in the Connecticut Home as well: eighteen of the twenty-nine veterans in this grouping were foreign born.[47]

A third facility housing Connecticut veterans was the National Home for Disabled Volunteer Soldiers, Central Branch, in Dayton, Ohio. Available records are consistent with the two Connecticut homes regarding the incidence of substance abuse. Of the 128 soldiers from Connecticut living in the Dayton facility, 10 were involuntarily discharged for substance abuse issues, and 4 of those were also cited for violent behavior.[48] Based on the overall number of veterans housed at these facilities, and given the comments in records and discharge paperwork, it can be reasonably concluded that between 5 and 15 percent of veterans exhibited PTSD-related symptoms, and that most prevalent among these was substance abuse.

There is a remarkably fragmented component to studying war-related psychological trauma in a conflict that occurred 150 years ago. This is due in part to the limited availability and/or incomplete nature of the records. In many ways they are like an unfinished jigsaw puzzle, pieced together in a disjointed way—with one record leading to another, other records that are often fragmentary, and some records made off limits by organizations that should be most interested in understanding the history of mental illness. An equal, if not larger, challenge is that the field of medicine was hardly what we today would consider modern. Diagnosis by the medical establishment was still steeped in ancient understandings that had hardly changed in centuries. The very terminology that practitioners used was far too general in nature, often falling back on nervousness, or some form of it, to explain many different pathological behaviors. Quite simply, there existed a different understanding of the mind—one that did not fully recognize that post-traumatic stress (trauma that occurred either shortly or long after a horrifying experience and that had nothing to do with any sort of physical trauma) could be debilitating in and of itself.

This failure of understanding was further compounded by severe social stigma that inhibited people from seeking care, as well as the attendant shame brought on one's family by being institutionalized. In this sense, as the RAND study discussed at the start of this chapter indicates, soldiers returning from war today remain concerned about what the impact may be if they admit to the psychological damage of war and thus seek treatment. "Insanity" continues to have a distinctly negative connotation. Yet war is in and of itself insane. One can hardly read about the experiences of soldiers on Civil War battlefields and not be struck by the fact that many, many more of them should have been institutionalized based on what they experienced. The death toll in the war was 750,000 men, more than any war in American history—more than all American wars combined. Perhaps what is most important for a study like this one is for current veterans to understand that they have never been alone in experiencing the brutality of war and suffering in one form or another from that experience.

NOTES

1. James K. Bryant, *The Battle of Fredericksburg: We Cannot Escape History* (Charleston, SC: History Press, 2010).

2. Charles D. Page, *History of the Fourteenth Regiment* (Meriden, CT: Horton Printing, 1906), 85; Samuel Fiske, *Mr. Dunn Browne's Experiences in the Army* (Boston: Nichols and Noyes, 1866), 106–7; the Connecticut regiments presents at Fredericksburg were the Eighth, Eleventh, Fourteenth, Fifteenth, Sixteenth, Seventeenth, and Twenty-Seventh. See Blaikie Hines, *Civil War Volunteer Sons of Connecticut* (Thomaston, ME: American Patriot Press, 2002).

3. Perkins is listed as Lt. Colonel of the Fourteenth Regiment in Record of Service of Connecticut Men in the Army and Navy of the United States during the War of Rebellion (Hartford: Case, Lockwood & Brainard, 1889), 552. His records from the Connecticut Hospital for the Insane are from Connecticut Hospital for the Insane, Connecticut State Library, State Archives, RG 021:001, Connecticut Valley Hospital, case history books, vol. 3, October 1, 1873, to September 1, 1874, pp. 233–34.

4. Eric T. Dean, *Shook over Hell: Post-Traumatic Stress, Vietnam, and the Civil War* (Cambridge, MA: Harvard University Press, 1997), 17–21. For the DSM-III-R, see American Psychiatric Association, *Diagnostic and Statistical Manual of Mental Disorders*, 3rd ed. (Washington, DC: American Psychiatric Association, 1987), 247–51.

5. PTSD is hardly a uniquely American phenomenon. See Edgar Jones, "Historical Approaches to Post-combat Disorders," *Philosophical Transactions of the Royal Society* 361 (April 2006): 533–42, http://www.pubmedcentral.nih.gov/articlerender.fcgi?artid=1569621.

6. RAND Corporation, "One in Five Iraq and Afghanistan Veterans Suffer from

PTSD or Major Depression," April 17, 2008, http://www.rand.org/news/press/2008/04/17.html.

7. The story of the Department of Mental Health and Addiction Services (DMHAS) fight against the release and research of records is beyond the scope of this paper. The basic outline is that Connecticut Valley Hospital, via DMHAS, was requested to allow historical researchers see patient records, and the request was refused. The case was brought before the Connecticut Freedom of Information Commission, where DMHAS lost its attempt to restrict records. All patient books were turned over the Connecticut State Library. DMHAS, with the help of some in the General Assembly, has subsequently done an end run around the Commission decision by adding new legislative language to expand the scope of what records are protected. See Jesse Leavenworth, "Researchers Gain Access to Mental Health Records of Civil War Veterans," *Hartford Courant*, February 27, 2010; Thomas Scheffey, "A Legal Skirmish over Civil War Records," *Connecticut Law Tribune*, April 26, 2010; Thomas Scheffey, "FOI Exemption a 'Victory' No One Claims," *Connecticut Law Tribune*, November 14, 2011. For a full discussion of this issue, see Matthew Warshauer and Michael Sturges, "Difficult Hunting: Accessing Connecticut Patient Records to Learn about Post Traumatic Stress Disorder during the Civil War," *Civil War History* (forthcoming, fall 2013).

8. Lawrence B. Goodheart, *Mad Yankees: The Hartford Retreat for the Insane and Nineteenth-Century Psychiatry* (Amherst: University of Massachusetts Press, 2003), 75. Also see Leonard K. Eaton, "Eli Todd and the Hartford Retreat," *New England Quarterly* 26.4 (December 1953): 435–53.

9. Each entry contains at least one reference to known family history of insanity in the registration documents. This was usually a simple yes or no marked on registration documents, though in some cases additional notes are present. For an example, see Connecticut Hospital for the Insane, Connecticut State Library, State Archives, RG 021:001, Connecticut Valley Hospital, case history books.

10. Dean, *Shook over Hell*, 79–81.

11. Norman Dain, *Concepts of Insanity in the United States, 1789–1865* (New Brunswick, NJ: Rutgers University Press, 1964), 55. Further general histories of psychology in the United States in the nineteenth century include John A. Popplestone, *An Illustrated History of American Psychology* (Akron, OH: University of Akron Press, 1999); Cherie Goodenow O'Boyle, *History of Psychology: A Cultural Perspective* (Mahwah, NJ: L. Erlbaum Associates, 2006), 191–201. For sources specifically on the institutionalization of the insane in the nineteenth century, see Roy Porter and David Wright, eds., *The Confinement of the Insane: International Perspectives, 1800–1965* (Cambridge: Cambridge University Press, 2003).

12. Goodheart, *Mad Yankees*, 36–60.

13. Edward Shorter, *A History of Psychiatry: From the Era of the Asylum to the Age of Prozac* (New York: John Wiley and Sons, 1997), 15.

14. John C. Nemiah, "Early Concepts of Trauma, Dissociation, and the Unconscious: Their History and Current Implications," in *Trauma, Memory, and Dissociation*, ed. J. Douglas Bremner (Washington, DC: American Psychiatric Press, 1998), 11.

15. Shorter, *History of Psychiatry*, 59.

16. Dean, *Shook over Hell*, 116.

17. Dean, *Shook over Hell*, 132–33.

18. Jones, "Historical Approaches," 540.

19. Dean's work in the mid-1990s operated under a different definition from the DSM III-R, published in 1987, which included a narrower, more quantitative definition involving how many types of dissociative, arousal-based, or hallucinatory symptoms a patient has. I base this contention on the fact that Dean's work on the subject comes from a series of works beginning in 1987 and culminating in his 1997 book. For that definition, see American Psychiatric Association, *Diagnostic and Statistical Manual of Mental Disorders, 3rd ed.* (Washington, DC, 1987), 247–51. The DSM IV-TR, in which the definition used first appears, was published in 2000. It is important to note that another revision (DSM-V) is planned for 2013; see http://www.ptsd.va.gov/professional/pages/diagnostic_criteria_dsm-5.asp.

20. The extent of substance abuse among returning veterans from the wars in Iraq and Afghanistan is reported in "Substance Abuse among the Military, Veterans, and Their Families: A Research Update from the National Institute on Drug Abuse," National Institute on Drug Abuse (Washington, DC, 2011), http://www.drugabuse.gov/sites/default/files/veterans.pdf. This study finds that more than 25 percent of veterans suffer from alcoholism, more than 40 percent require mental health services, and that prescription drug abuse has been growing faster than any other form of substance abuse among the veteran population. A particularly troubling finding is that drug and alcohol abuse are "involved in 30 percent of the Army's suicide deaths from 2003 to 2009 and in more than 45 percent of non-fatal suicide attempts from 2005 to 2009."

21. Connecticut Hospital for the Insane, Connecticut State Library, State Archives, RG 021:001, Connecticut Valley Hospital, case history books, vol. 3, October 1, 1873 to September 1, 1874, pp. 233–34.

22. It is worth noting that even before the clear connection, via PTSD, with psychological trauma as an outcome of war, the military realized that quicker access to mental help in the field was warranted. See Edward A. Strecker, "Military Psychiatry: World War I, 1917–1918," in *One Hundred Years of American Psychiatry 1844-1944* (New York: Columbia University Press for the American Psychiatric Association, 1944), 385.

23. Albert Deutsch, "Military Psychiatry: The Civil War, 1861–1865," in *One Hundred Years of American Psychiatry 1844-1944*, 377.

24. U.S. Surgeon General's Office, *Surgical and Medical History of the War of the Rebellion* (Washington, DC, 1870), http://www.archive.org/details/MSHWR Medical1 (accessed November 15, 2008).

25. For instances of nostalgia, see Deutsch, "Military Psychiatry," 376. For the definition of nostalgia, see Dean, *Shook over Hell*, 116.

26. Deutsch, "Military Psychiatry," 377.

27. Deutsch, "Military Psychiatry," 379.

28. Dean, *Shook over Hell*, 117–21.

29. State of Connecticut, "Census: Defective, Dependent, and Delinquent Classes" (Hartford, 1880); United States Pensions in Connecticut, January 1, 1883 (Hartford, 1883), Connecticut State Library (ultimately reprinted in a federal publication) includes pensioners identified as being driven insane by their war experiences. The names and certificate numbers of these men are Edward Quigley (#91,876), George P. Langdon (#93,645), William Blodgett (#162,636), Cornelius Dayton (#111,949), Charles Atkins (#119,284), Charles Pendleton (#21,316), William Bronson (#186,557), and David Mallory (#157,615).

30. State of Connecticut, "Census: Defective, Dependent, and Delinquent Classes."

31. United States Pensions in Connecticut, January 1, 1883.

32. United States Pensions in Connecticut, January 1, 1883. If the number of soldiers in this record is expanded to include all soldiers suffering from some form of mental disability that we now associate with PTSD, then nearly 10 percent of all veterans listed (roughly 215) qualify. This is consistent with what Eric Dean discovered in his Indiana sample, where he found roughly 10 percent of Civil War veterans suffered from symptoms we would today associate with PTSD.

33. Butler in *Record of Service of Connecticut Men in the Army and Navy of the United States during the War of Rebellion*, 619.

34. Lesley J. Gordon, "'The Most Unfortunate Regiment': The 16th Connecticut and the Siege of Plymouth, NC," *Connecticut History* 50.1 (Spring 2011): 37–61.

35. However, this may be attributable to the liberalizing of pension requirements in 1890. In the an act of June 27, 1890, pensions were awarded to all veterans who were honorably discharged and invalid. Butler was in his early fifties when the documentation of his debility begins; therefore senility is unlikely.

36. Surgeon's certificate for Ithamar Butler, November 16, 1892; pension application of Ithamar Butler, Pension Application files, National Archives, Washington, DC.

37. "Fitch's Home for the Soldier Beneficiaries Transferred to the Connecticut Hospital for the Insane, 1891," Connecticut State Library, State Archives, RG 73, box 174.

38. Collected final papers of residents from Fitch's Home, Connecticut State Library, State Archives, RG 73, box 81.

39. Gleason in Record of Service of Connecticut Men in the Army and Navy of the United States during the War of Rebellion, 168. This record reveals that Gleason resigned his commission on June 4, 1862. There is no indication of why.

40. Connecticut Hospital for the Insane, Connecticut State Library, State Archives, RG 021:001, Connecticut Valley Hospital, case history books, vol. 3, p. 58.

41. Chalker has been difficult to identify. He does not appear in the Record of Service of Connecticut Men, nor in records specifically related to the Fourteenth. His identification as part of that regiment comes from doctors' notes, which may have been in error, or Chalker could possibly have lied about his service. Connecticut Hospital for the Insane, Connecticut State Library, State Archives, RG 021:001, Connecticut Valley Hospital, case history books files, vol. 3, p. 58.

42. Connecticut Hospital for the Insane, Connecticut State Library, State Archives, RG 021:001, Connecticut Valley Hospital, case history books, vol. 3, pp. 121–22.

43. Perry in *Record of Service of Connecticut Men in the Army and Navy of the United States during the War of Rebellion*, 88; and Hall in the same source, 102.

44. Records for both Perry and Hall can be found in Connecticut Hospital for the Insane, Connecticut State Library, State Archives, RG 021:001, Connecticut Valley Hospital, case history books, vol. 4.

45. Hazen in *Record of Service of Connecticut Men in the Army and Navy of the United States during the War of Rebellion*, 531; the hospital records refer to him as Hagen. See Connecticut Hospital for the Insane, Connecticut State Library, State Archives, RG 021:001, Connecticut Valley Hospital, case history books, vol. 4.

46. Discharge papers of Fitch's Home for the Soldier Beneficiaries, 1870–1919, Records of Fitch's Home, Connecticut State Library, State Archives, RG73, box 174.

47. Connecticut Veteran's Home, "Historical Register of the Connecticut Veteran's Home, 1880–1889 Rocky Hill" (1890), Connecticut State Library, State Archives, RG 73, item #1.

48. The National Home for Disabled Volunteer Soldiers, Central Branch, "Muster Roll of Connecticut Soldiers Admitted" (Dayton, OH, 1880), Connecticut State Library, State Archives, RG13, box 160.

7 : Patriot, Soldier, Statesman

GENERAL JOSEPH R. HAWLEY AND
CIVIL WAR COMMEMORATION IN
CONNECTICUT

Factories, schools, and stores sat closed and motionless. At 9:30 a.m., church bells rang across the city on cue, prompting twenty thousand citizens to gather alongside downtown streets in anticipation of a parade of patriots. On this day, thirty-five years after the Civil War, six hundred veterans marched in ordered lines through New Britain, Connecticut, receiving thunderous applause from grateful and awed residents as the procession slowly passed. On their way to Central Park, the veterans knew they were the stars of the day: the day the city dedicated its Soldiers' Monument. In the streets, on rooftops, and occupying nearly every open window, viewers gazed at a platform adjacent to the memorial. Prayers were preached; patriotic songs sung. Roaring cheers, from veterans and citizens alike, greeted the day's orator as he rose to speak.[1]

At seventy-four years old, General Joseph R. Hawley took the platform just as he had at dozens of other Dedication Days. His speeches at such events tended to cover the same ideas, often with the very same words. Pleased with the opportunity to speak, the general announced that he "could not resist a whisper from New Britain, which to me is equal to the loudest command." He mentioned how the new monument would teach the city's youth strength and patriotism, and he recalled memories from the war years. In a favorite line, the general cried: "War is not an unmixed evil. It develops the noblest qualities, it gives terrible but necessary lessons."[2] War is hell, and Hawley knew it, but he also wanted people to know that war creates the most patriotic and respected of all Americans: soldiers. Citizen, republican soldiers won the great war, and later became statesmen and leaders of a united nation. For some reason on this day, the aging Hawley chose not to end as he customarily did, by reading Abraham Lincoln's Gettysburg Address. Yet, no doubt as he stepped down, the general noticed the young children in the crowd and surely hoped they had been inspired by his tales of patriots, soldiers, and statesmen.

Connecticut's Joseph Roswell Hawley was a U.S. senator, general in the Union Army, captain in the First Regiment of the Connecticut Volunteer Infantry, and lieutenant colonel of the Seventh Regiment. Courtesy of the Civil War Photographs Collection, Prints & Photographs Division, Library of Congress, LC-DIG-cwpbh-04725

Claiming well over half a million lives, the Civil War was America's bloodiest and arguably most significant war. Many in the generation that lived during this great trial became active patriots and dutiful soldiers. After the ordeal, they continued to battle for the nation through civic rather than military leadership. Hawley was surely one of these men. As the century crept on, though, veterans became worried that their deeds would either become forgotten, or worse, undone in the future. Monuments and other forms of commemoration became a medium through which veterans could remind those who followed about what the Civil War generation had accomplished and to hold up their actions as models of character for the nation's inevitable future struggles. With the words eternally emblazoned on both his gravestone in Hartford's Cedar Hill Cemetery and a memorial on the north steps of the State Capitol Building, Joseph R. Hawley proudly considered himself a "patriot, soldier, and statesman"; and, as seen through the many speeches he gave at commemorative events, the general clearly wanted all Americans to live by the virtues of those characteristics, in the present, but especially in the future.[3]

The history of Connecticut's Civil War monuments and of Dedication Days has rarely been studied with adequate depth. Nor has Hawley received the attention he deserves for a man who was a prominent force in late-nineteenth-century Connecticut society and politics. No biography exists, and thus individual facets of his life, such as his role in commemorations, have been sparsely addressed.[4] Civil War remembrance was an important aspect of nineteenth-century American life, as evidenced by the sheer number of monuments that were built both nationally and locally. There are literally thousands of monuments dotted over every state that took part in the war, at national battlefields, and in cities that suffered the disaster of war. In Connecticut, there are at least 150 monuments, and the state boasts the oldest permanent monument in the entire country.[5] This was a generation subsumed by the experience and trauma of war. The monuments were a panacea to the heartache of a people who had survived the destruction but still had to make sense of the slaughter. To fully understand Connecticut in this period, one must look at the monuments. To fully understand the monuments, one must look at Joseph R. Hawley.

Born in 1826 to Yankee parents, ironically, in North Carolina, Joseph Roswell Hawley moved to Connecticut by age ten. Living in the Nook Farm neighborhood of Hartford, he later became a founder of the state Republican Party and editor of the *Hartford Courant*. A staunch abolitionist, Hawley once partnered with another prominent Hartford citizen to purchase an escaped slave his freedom, earning the general much respect from the city's African American community. After the Confederate firing on Fort Sumter, Hawley became the city's first volunteer, as a captain in the First Connecticut Regiment. Later, along with General Alfred H. Terry, Hawley helped form the Seventh Connecticut Regiment. Eventually rising to the rank of brevet major general, Hawley had an illus-

trious war record. After Appomattox, the general served a year as governor, headed the 1868 Republican National Convention in Chicago, and became president of the U.S. Centennial Commission in Philadelphia, where he successfully headed the national exhibition there in 1876. Considered a potential Republican presidential nominee in 1884, Hawley enjoyed a prominent national political career, serving three terms in the U.S. House of Representatives, and spending the last twenty-four years of his life in the Senate. General Joseph R. Hawley died in Washington, D.C., on March 17, 1905, after a long illness.[6]

Throughout his postwar life, General Hawley took a decidedly active role in veterans' affairs. After his death, veterans of the Seventh Connecticut fondly remembered Hawley's frequent attendance at reunions, and veterans from a Grand Army of the Republic (GAR) post in Meriden recalled how the general "was no stranger" and noted that "his genial

presence will be missed at Department and National G.A.R. meetings."[7] ~~G.A.R.~~
Hawley himself belonged to Hartford's Nathaniel Lyon GAR Post No. 2,
and was junior vice commander in chief at the organization's national level
in 1868.[8] He was also president of an 1874 Army of the James reunion in
New York, and he was appointed to a committee in charge of preparing for
General Ulysses Grant's 1880 visit to Hartford.[9]

Also closely involved in the monument building process Hawley helped
place the cornerstone of the Bridgeport Soldiers' Monument in the late
1860s.[10] In 1879, he was on one of the first committees organized to form
Hartford's Soldiers' and Sailors' Memorial Arch, and it was later alleged
that Hawley's actions were instrumental in the decision to erect an arch
instead of a memorial library.[11] The general also personally wrote the inscription that appeared on the Soldiers' Monument in Brooklyn, Connecticut, in 1888: "Erected to the memory of all the brave men of Brooklyn who fought on land and on sea for the preservation of the union."[12]
Historian Sarah Denver Beetham notes that a monument's inscription
was one of the most important ways through which the meaning and message of the memorial was demonstrated. In regard to Civil War causation,
Beetham says that earlier inscriptions tended to emphasize slavery, while
later ones, such as Hawley's, stressed preservation of the Union.[13] According to historian Thomas J. Brown, monuments built after the 1880s, such
as Brooklyn's, were rarely dedicated exclusively to the dead, but rather to
all who served the Union cause.[14]

In 1895, a Southington man wrote to Hawley for assistance "about that
monument business," hoping to make a monument in Hartford's Bushnell Park for the Sixth, Seventh, and Tenth Connecticut Regiments, and
the First Connecticut Light Battery. He made clear to the experienced
Hawley: "I am not much on art and such things, but I have an immense capacity for drudgery, and for any of that which is involved please command
me." Busy in Washington at the time, the senator could offer only limited help. The monument to these regiments was ultimately built in New
Haven in 1905 and dedicated about three months after Hawley's death.[15]
Clearly, though, Hawley was a man to turn to when veterans wanted to
construct a monument.

Ever present in commemoration, Hawley acted as grand marshal during the famous Battle Flag Day Parade on September 17, 1879, when Connecticut's eighty war banners were transported from the State Arsenal to
the newly completed Hall of Flags at the State Capitol in Hartford.[16] Later,

as a U.S. senator in 1900, in a true example of reconciliation, Hawley the statesman even appropriated money to bury some Confederate soldiers in a special section of Arlington National Cemetery.[17]

Hawley's voice, though, proved his greatest asset in commemoration, and he used it often. Historian Ellsworth S. Grant writes that "almost a Hawley cult existed" in the state, and his speaking at commemorative events was basically a requirement.[18] In 1886, the *Hartford Courant* announced, "No civic rite since the war has been thought complete unless the people were addressed by Senator Hawley." In 1905, the *Courant* added that "General Hawley was in demand as an orator, and particularly for Grand Army reunions and occasions of patriotic interest."[19] His popular public-speaking skills guaranteed that oratory was Hawley's greatest contribution to Civil War commemoration, and he spoke often at veterans' gatherings, Memorial Day ceremonies, and especially at monument dedications. Through these speeches, one can fully extract the general's passion for the virtues of patriots, soldiers, and statesmen, and his keen interest in seeing those characteristics adopted by future generations.

Excessively patriotic, Hawley once, almost religiously, stated, "I believe in the Fourth of July all over, from the crown of my head to the sole of my feet. . . . I believe in the flag."[20] His enthusiastic devotion also included his home state, about which he claimed, "I have no sovereign but Connecticut and Uncle Sam," and insisted that "Connecticut had the proudest history in the world."[21] In Dedication Day speeches, such as at Manchester, Connecticut, in 1872, Hawley told the crowd how Europeans claimed the United States "had no history," but that the Civil War changed all that and provided an even "nobler history" than that of the Old World.[22] The nostalgic storyteller loved to talk about the patriotic past. At Hartford's Memo-

---

(Opposite) *View of parade through the Soldiers' and Sailors' Memorial Arch, Bushnell Park, Hartford, September 17, 1886. Crowds of spectators line Trinity Street as military units march through the arch, with its round gothic towers and sculptured frieze, then across the Ford Street bridge. In the foreground is the Park River, bordered by a stone retaining wall and an embankment. Commercial and industrial buildings and the steeples of two churches are in the distance. A building at the left has a sign that reads: "Monuments." A large tent and a fountain are in the park in the background. Several trees appear to be elms. Inscribed on the back: "Parade through Memorial Arch Bushnell / Park / Sept. 17, 1886. / Dedication of Arch." (Description provided by the Connecticut Historical Society.) Courtesy of the Connecticut Historical Society, Hartford*

Halt of the veterans, Battle Flag Day parade, Main Street, Hartford. Crowds line both sides of a city street. Commercial buildings are draped with American flags and bunting. Ranks of men stand in the street and beneath a temporary arch. A sign at the left reads: "Wilson & Toms." (Description provided by the Connecticut Historical Society.) Courtesy of the Connecticut Historical Society, Hartford

rial Arch dedication in 1886, Hawley went all the way back to Thomas Hooker and the Fundamental Orders, which he saw as Connecticut's great contribution to free government.[23]

Hawley's patriotism centered on American democracy and what he called "the grand experiment of government by the people." At a dedication in Springfield, Massachusetts, in 1885, he announced that victory in the Civil War validated the American experiment and had immeasurable influence on all nations of the world.[24] At Mystic, Connecticut's Dedication Day in 1883, he trumpeted the noble meaning of the war, insisting that "failure of the republic would have put the world back a century," adding, "some day this is to be the form of government for the world."[25] He told audiences that European despots, acting as "enemies of republican government filled the air with prophecies of our downfall." Rulers felt happiness and relief with the possibility that the American experiment might fail.[26] Yet the Union prevailed and saved freedom, not just for the United States, but for the entire world, as Hawley exclaimed in Greenwich in 1890: "We were fighting the battle of the centuries and the world . . . it was *for* the North, *for* the South, *for* the slave, *for* the master, for the whole people and *all* people. It was the battle of the World and of Humanity."[27]

In addition to love of country, Hawley also had extreme love for God. He was a good friend of his pastor and fellow veteran, Rev. Joseph H. Twichell of Hartford's Asylum Hill Congregational Church, who after the general's death gave a long sermon on Hawley the Christian. Twichell noted that Hawley was a true Puritan in his beliefs, and had even fought to have the 1876 Centennial Exposition in Philadelphia, for which he served as president, remain closed on Sundays.[28] At commemorative speeches, the general commonly quoted scripture and always made multiple references to God. He often called the Civil War a "holy struggle" or "holy war."[29] Hawley took pride in how the Union, "a Christian civilization," fought the war with restraint and discipline, unlike the way in which wars were fought in Europe. Except for General William Sherman's crushing March across Georgia, which Hawley insisted "was demanded by military policy," he commended the godly work of Union soldiers who gave food to civilians, and the moral accomplishments of the Freedmen's Bureau, Sanitary Commission, and Christian Commission.[30] Through Hawley's patriotic lens, the fight to save the Union was more than just a war, it was a crusade.

That crusade was ultimately won, according to the senator, by noble soldiers who "laid down the implements of peaceful industry and went forth in the uniform of war . . . doing their duty."[31] In Meriden, Connecticut, in 1873, Hawley told the crowd how citizen soldiers "had been taught that next to our duty to God was duty to our country, and went to battle with that idea."[32] Yet Hawley did not revel in the mere notion of killing. Rather, in his eyes a soldier's duty was to be more than a battlefield ruffian. Soldierly nobility evinced a cause worthy of the fight. Hawley explained at a dedication in Torrington, Connecticut, in 1879: "The true soldier is not one who kills, but one who preserves law and order."[33] The duty of a democratic army was to uphold the Constitution against such treasonous ideas as secession.

All Union soldiers of the Constitution-saving crusade were brave of course, but Hawley often set apart those from Yankee New England and Connecticut. He insisted that "roughs or men of the lowest dregs of society . . . never made real soldiers." Not the streets and back alleys, but "churches, Sunday schools, and academies," created the brave soldiers of the Union. He also attributed the moral courage and ideals of the soldiers to "the virtue of New England mothers." He wanted to clear up the misconception that Yankees were somehow militarily inferior to "fiery" Confederates.[34] And though he was most complimentary to those of Yankee, Anglo-Saxon heritage, the general noted that the people must recognize "the black man" and "our comrades of foreign birth" who fought nobly.[35]

Hawley's limited mention of blacks was something of an anomaly, considering his forthright abolitionist, antislavery outlook both prior to and throughout the war. Such views placed him in the minority for much of Connecticut. For most, the war was not fought to end the peculiar institution or to grant greater rights to blacks.[36] To be sure, Hawley always noted that the war was fought for freedom, but he meant it in the larger democratic sense of the term. At Mystic, Connecticut, in 1883, he announced that the Union cause was "the dear land we love, the flag, the declaration of independence." He listed five issues that the United States was entrusted to "work out" for the world: "self government, free government, education, liberty, [and] equal rights."[37] Such ideas were in keeping with his divinely nationalistic view of the war and its impact on the world. In an exceptionally long address at Springfield, Massachusetts, in 1885, Hawley did mention slavery as "the underlying cause" of the nation's "calamities" and claimed that "universal liberty was established" with the end of slavery in 1865. Yet this was a decidedly passing reference in a speech primarily dedicated to lauding the success of loyal soldiers in preserving the American experiment.[38] One might have expected that Hawley, a resident of Hartford's progressive Nook Farm neighborhood, and a former editor of the *Charter Oak* abolitionist paper in the 1850s, would have delved more deeply into the "cause" of a war that he saw as a moral crusade.[39] Perhaps it was the politician in Hawley, who undoubtedly understood the underlying racism of white Connecticut society, which muted his otherwise laudable personal views of slavery's immorality.

Hawley did not focus on the heroic deeds of men alone. In New Britain, he insisted that "we must not forget on these occasions the women of the Union, who prayed, wept, worked for their absent boys, and were sorely affected by the death of so many."[40] In Greenwich, he remembered "the little army of nurses who gave many lives, with a courage not surpassed on the field."[41] The work of women in the war was just as important for victory, and just as patriotic, as the work of men. Hawley, like all soldiers, was grateful for the care received from women, and he made sure not to forget them on Dedication Days. The General's late first wife, Harriet Foote Hawley, had been heavily involved on the home front. After she died in 1887, Hawley's old Seventh Connecticut Regiment created a special memorial for her in Hartford's Asylum Hill Congregational Church. It commemorated "the bravery, patriotism and humanity of Mrs. Hawley" and called her a "Soldier and servant of Jesus Christ."[42]

Hawley's many appearances were almost always driven by the dedication or remembrance of specific monuments. In this sense, the old veteran provided the words to the stone sentinels that were meant to honor one generation and inspire others. The stoic, noble image of the brave Civil War soldier was an eternal reminder, and Americans in the North and South built thousands of them after 1865. Historian Kirk Savage writes that veterans fully understood the importance monuments had, which is why the source of funds, design, and location of the memorials often created so much controversy. Monuments were permanent and lasting, representing a community and its ideals for all time.[43] Monuments also told stories of patriotism, and the massive stone statues had authority and respect beyond the reach of comparatively temporary and isolated forms of commemoration, such as veterans' reunions.

Monuments were also an effective medium through which to influence collective memory. David W. Blight, one of the nation's foremost scholars on Civil War memory, notes that collective memory has a way of shaping a group or nation's consciousness. Memory creates heritage, and it is usually considered more sanctified, even tangible when compared to the traditional historian's craft.[44] Anthropologist Paul A. Shackel has written that memory is often shaped more by contemporary events than actual events of the past.[45] Memorials, according to James M. Mayo, through their design and perceived meaning, occupy a synthetic location on the public landscape, representing what a society chooses to remember and in what context.

The monuments' designs provided the imagery of duty and sacrifice. They tended to take on a fairly common architectural theme. Many included the physical image of a soldier: always male, always white, and always in uniform. These models were the embodiment of what nineteenth-century Americans viewed as manliness.[46] According to Sarah Beetham, statues of soldiers, through the very act of bearing stone weapons, served as perfect representations of manhood and masculinity.[47] Almost universally, local and community monuments on town greens did not feature a general on the pedestal but instead bore the common, citizen soldier that Hawley had so often described and commended.[48]

In Connecticut, monuments were constructed in nearly every community. As a result of the strong demand, a national monument industry grew, and some of the best-known companies were based in Connecticut, such as James G. Batterson's, which built many of the state's local monuments. The statues standing sentry over the greens of the Constitution State became symbols of local pride, which is why every town wanted one.[49] Civil War monuments were literally everywhere in late-nineteenth-century America, which greatly pleased veterans, who wanted the nation to remember the great deeds and ideals of 1861–1865.[50] The monuments guided public memory and heritage. They had power. Hawley understood this and sought at every dedication, every Memorial Day rally, to infuse the stark stone imagery with the magic of the spoken word.

In many ways, the monuments were Hawley's muse. His speeches always included their value in teaching young children and future generations the virtues that characterized the patriots, soldiers, and statesmen of his own generation. At Bridgeport's Dedication Day, Hawley told the crowd that "honoring the dead soldiers teaches patriotism to the young, who will for centuries be asking what this monument means, and it guards the future of the country by educating young men to be ready to fight for it if need be."[51] At Mystic he said, "It is a good thing to build these monuments and perpetuate the memories of the men who fell. . . . Let us erect monuments to the fallen heroes and bring our children to them to learn the lesson which they so frequently teach."[52] In September 1879, during Torrington's Dedication Day, the General cried, "Let monuments be raised in every town," and "bring children to see" them.[53] At the dedi-

The Torrington Soldiers' Monument, Coe Memorial Park, erected in September 1879. Created by New England Granite Works, James G. Batterson, owner. Courtesy of Matthew Warshauer

cation of New London's Soldiers' and Sailors' Monument in 1896, Hawley singled out the children of the crowd, specifically explaining to them, "if ever your country should be compelled to summon you to a righteous war, remember that you have seen many an old, halting, weakened, and disabled soldier who would not exchange his badge and honorable discharge for the wealth of the Vanderbilts."[54] Regarding the "badge," Hawley may have been referring to Stephen Crane's *Red Badge of Courage* (published the year before), or more likely to the yellow badges that veterans commonly wore. At Greenwich, Connecticut, the general summarized what he so often said at Dedication Days, telling those assembled that "wisdom for future trials requires" us to build monuments and that "they teach and comfort us." He made it clear that "monuments are not for the dead alone," that they tell future generations "this and more too, shall be done for all who so love their flag and country."[55]

The monuments alone did not guide the nation forward. The generation that erected them made their way from the battlefields to the halls of government. This, of course, was the route that Hawley had followed, from general, to governor, congressional representative, and finally senator. Other generals went even further, with Ulysses Grant, Rutherford B. Hayes, James Garfield, Chester A. Arthur, and Benjamin Harrison entering the White House. Yet veterans did not have to enter politics to influence government. According to historian Larry M. Logue, former soldiers in the late nineteenth century were considered "a special class" by the American people and were the recipients of billions of dollars in federal pension money as a result.[56] Soldiers, under the influence of groups such as the Grand Army of the Republic, preferred to vote for other veterans and always supported the candidate who would most expand their pensions. Politicians understood this and coveted the massive "soldier vote." In fact, by the 1890s, more than 40 percent of the federal budget involved pensions; more than $5 billion was spent.[57] It was said that the soldier vote both *for* veteran Benjamin Harrison and *against* Grover Cleveland (who had hired a substitute in the war and then vetoed a massive pension bill as president), had determined the presidential election of 1888.[58]

As a loyal Republican and a distinctly political man, Joseph Hawley undoubtedly coveted his many Dedication Day and monument events as a way to offer himself before the veterans, who were his greatest supporters. His electoral pragmatism, however, did not diminish the belief in his message. Hawley was a devout patriot forged in the fire of battle, as were many of his Civil War comrades. As such, the seemingly never-ending reunions, monument dedications, and Memorial Days carried forward messages of sacrifice and duty. Their belief was that war had made them truer citizens. Hawley once announced that "[m]ultitudes to-day are better citizens for having been soldiers" and that they had "learned lessons of duty, obedience and respect to law which they carry with them. They came back with higher ideas of law and government."[59] In 1876, he highlighted a result of this, saying "there is much less of the element of rowdyism in all our large cities than there was twenty years ago."[60]

Yet, or perhaps because of, their experiences, Hawley and his fellow veterans worried for the nation's future. During a flag-raising event at Trinity College in 1894, Hawley spoke to a crowd of students who had not likely seen battle, commenting, "It is difficult for you to comprehend that we of the passing generation, as we look upon you and other like congregations of those to whom the Republic will soon be committed . . . [ask,] what shall be your part in the work of the next century?"[61] The senator continued, offering wisdom from the Civil War generation: "The future is waiting to reveal wonders greater than the world has yet seen. . . . [T]he flag has not altogether passed all its troubles. They may not come in battle; they may be more dangerous. Fight the stupidities and demagoguism, and national dishonor, all shames and crimes that would make the flag ashamed."[62] These concerns had made their way into earlier speeches as well. In his Memorial Day speech in Hartford in 1886, Hawley noted with uncertainty, "Young men who were born after Lee's surrender are this year putting their first votes into the ballot box," while so many of his generation were "in their graves."[63] In most of his speeches, Hawley made mention of "the ballot box" and how a free people's defense of liberty lay with voting.[64] Yet he worried that voters who did not feel and understand true patriotism and duty might have their electoral judgment impaired.

As much as Hawley counseled the nation's youth, he consoled its elderly veterans, assuring them in statue and word that their sacrifice would not go unremembered. In 1895, a confident and hopeful Hawley reassuringly told a crowd of veterans at Bridgeport's Army and Navy Club meeting, "Do not feel discouraged. . . . [H]ave no fears that the future will ever forget you or your ideas."[65]

Hawley, of course, was not alone in preaching the virtues of Civil War veterans or the examples that they provided to the nation. Throughout the United States, in the North and South, remembrances and dedications engrossed the people.[66] Orators hit upon many of the themes that the ubiquitous Hawley engaged, and most events hosted multiple speakers. Connecticut Governor George Lounsbury spoke at the monument dedication in New Britain in 1900 just prior to Hawley's address at the same event. The governor told veterans that "the state today salutes you and your comrades as men that shall never die," insisting that the monument will "stand forever . . . to remind the citizen of duty."[67] Preceding General Hawley at Greenwich, Colonel Heusted W. R. Hoyt noted how New England soldiers in particular "had faith in God, believing He intended this Republic to be the most enlightened, the most advanced, the freest and greatest nation of the earth."[68] In a famous Memorial Day address at Harvard University in 1895, veteran Oliver Wendell Holmes Jr. asked, "What kind of world do you want? The ideals of the past for men have been drawn from war," and war, although horrible in nature, is a "teacher of the kind we all need."[69] In 1883, Confederate veteran John W. Daniel gave a speech about the South's ideal patriot, soldier, and statesman, Robert E. Lee, at the dedication of a memorial for that general in Virginia. Flowing in the Lost Cause mythology that lionized the southern struggle as a noble one that cherished the values of home and states' rights idealism, which so often characterized southern monument dedications, Daniel's address portrayed Lee as the ultimate model citizen, "the strong, honest, fearless, upright man."[70] In addition, just as Hawley had similarly told audiences to be ready for future struggles, Booker T. Washington, at the dedication of the Robert Gould Shaw Memorial in Boston in 1897 (Shaw had achieved fame by leading the Massachusetts 54th Colored Regiment), spoke of the need to continue the war's unfinished work for African Americans: "What these heroic souls of the 54th Regiment began, we must complete," and until then, "this monument will stand for effort, not victory complete."[71]

As the nineteenth century closed, the drums of war once again could be heard echoing in the distance. This time on foreign soil, in Cuba, but it once again rallied many Civil War veterans to remember their own sacrifices and wonder what the future held for the youth of America. Hawley was certainly one of those who expressed concern and patriotism. In 1898, the United States entered war with Spain. Hawley had often said that war defined men and nations, and he announced to a group of Spanish-American War troops that going to war stirs patriotism, and "carries you outside and beyond yourself. You make sacrifices for a great idea."[72] The Spanish-American War (1898), though, likely provided a glimpse of hope for many veterans, because it demonstrated the moral courage and patriotism of a new generation. Senator Hawley fully supported the venture, emphasizing in New Britain, Connecticut, that "the necessity of war came upon us. The necessity, I say."[73] It is even likely that the very speeches and forms of commemoration performed by veterans, such as those by Hawley, actually contributed to the cause of that war. Historian John Pettegrew, in his article "'The Soldier's Faith:' Turn-of-the-Century Memory of the Civil War and the Emergence of Modern American Nationalism," discusses the importance of Memorial Day addresses in teaching Americans about patriotism and of the duty of soldiers, "through the ritualized invocation of the sacrifice of the dead."[74] He notes that during the late nineteenth and early twentieth centuries the image of the Civil War soldier became the standard for American manhood, patriotism, and citizenship. Through speeches, people such as Hawley used the Civil War as an example of what a nation could and must do in a struggle. According to Pettegrew, in the 1890s, America was characterized by an atmosphere of national aggressiveness, which helped cause the Spanish-American War, and that atmosphere could trace its own existence to the themes of patriotism, duty, and war perpetuated through Memorial and Dedication Day speeches. The war with Spain, Pettegrew says, "became a national expression of masculinity," as a new generation of Americans, raised on an heroic idolization of Civil War soldiers from contemporary literature and popular culture, attempted to duplicate the patriotism and duty that their fathers had spoken, even bragged, of for so long.[75] This was their time: 1898 was their 1861.

Hawley's Civil War experience unalterably defined the lens through which he saw America, both its past and present. His role extended beyond Connecticut. He spoke at Civil War monument dedications in Dayton, Ohio, Cleveland, Ohio, and Utica, New York. Nor did his commitment stop with championing his fellow veterans or lauding the actions of young military men who continued to define America's place in the world. Hawley engaged himself in commemorating virtually every aspect of America's military past. He spoke at the dedication of a Revolutionary War monument in Stony Point, New York,[76] and gave addresses at the centennials of the Battle of Groton Heights and the founding of Cleveland, Ohio, and attended another for the Battle of Bunker Hill.[77] He was also a member of the Society of Colonial Wars, as well as the American Institute of Civics.[78] His entire postwar life seemed dedicated to spreading the ideals of patriots, soldiers, and statesmen.

When Hawley died in March 1905, veterans wrote words that echoed the general's own Dedication Day speeches. Veterans in Hartford "revere[d] his name as a synonym for Courage, Loyalty and Devotion," and

The Joseph R. Hawley Medallion, located on the north steps of the Connecticut
State Capitol Building, notes that Hawley was "The First Volunteer in Connecticut
1861" and "Brevet Major General 1865." On the right-hand side, it lists the following
positions and dates: "Governor," 1866–1867; "Representative in Congress," 1873–1875,
1879–1881; and "United States Senator," 1881–1905. The medallion was commissioned
under the supervision of the Connecticut State Commission on Sculpture and
dedicated October 18, 1912. It was designed by Herbert Adams, a founder of the
National Sculpture Society. Courtesy of Matthew Warshauer

said, "in his career as a citizen, as an advocate of right and freedom, as a
loyal and brave soldier, and as a trusted and honored statesman, he ex-
emplified to an exalted degree the true character of a loyal, patriotic and
faithful American."[79] Men from his old Seventh Regiment said the senator's "words have often guided our thought and held us firm to the purpose to make the Union we had saved worth saving."[80] Hawley's body lay
in state at the Capitol rotunda in Hartford, and the *New York Times* reported that his funeral "brought together the most notable gathering of

men prominent in public and business life that has been seen here for more than a generation." Governor Henry Roberts addressed the General Assembly and suggested "the erection of a substantial memorial on the Capitol grounds." Hawley's body was then removed from the building and escorted by the First Regiment Connecticut National Guard and veterans of the Grand Army of the Republic to the Asylum Hill Congregational Church where his longtime friend Dr. Joseph Twichell performed the funeral service.[81] Hawley was interred at Cedar Hill Cemetery, where Hartford Mayor W. F. Henney championed the old general as a "soldier, citizen, statesman."[82] A more fitting epithet could not have been written, and thus these words were used to adorn the bronze medallion placed on the north steps of the State Capitol Building, as Governor Roberts had advocated.

Ultimately, the general wanted to see future generations embrace the best of what the Civil War generation had to offer. He also wanted the nation's youth to become patriots, soldiers, and statesmen when freedom was again challenged. As during the Civil War and Spanish-American War, a generation of Americans mobilized and rose to the occasion during the First World War. Among the many women who traveled overseas in 1917 and 1918 with the Red Cross to help with war relief was Roswell Hawley, the general's daughter.[83] No doubt he would have approved, not only of his daughter's actions, but of the patriotic virtues exhibited by her entire generation; for that was what he had wanted all along.

NOTES

1. "New Britain's Heroes," *Hartford Courant*, September 20, 1900, 13.

2. "Services in Dedication of the Soldiers' Monument, September 19, 1900," Parks-Central-Soldiers' Monument (Civil War) folder, Local History Room, New Britain Public Library, New Britain, CT.

3. "At General Hawley's Grave," *Hartford Courant*, November 2, 1905, 12; Hawley's grave is in Section A of Cedar Hill Cemetery, and the plaque is on the exterior north portico of the Connecticut State Capitol, opposite a similar one for Senator Orville Platt, who died not long after Senator Hawley.

4. John Niven's landmark book, *Connecticut for the Union: The Role of the State in the Civil War* (New Haven, CT: Yale University Press, 1965), mentions Hawley quite often, but only as a Republican politician and Civil War officer. Niven fails to mention anything about Connecticut's many Civil War monuments. General histories of Connecticut, such as David M. Roth, *Connecticut: A History* (New York: W.W. Norton, 1979); and Albert E. Van Dusen, *Connecticut* (New York: Random House, 1961), also reference Hawley only briefly, and only in regard to his political and military careers. The best national-scale studies on monuments are Kirk Sav-

age, *Standing Soldiers, Kneeling Slaves: Race, War, and Monument in Nineteenth-Century America* (Princeton, NJ: Princeton University Press, 1997); and Michael Panhorst, "Lest We Forget: Monuments and Memorial Sculpture in National Military Parks on Civil War Battlefields, 1861–1917" (PhD diss., University of Delaware, 1988). Both mention nothing on Hawley and little regarding Connecticut. The most comprehensive resource on Connecticut's Civil War monuments is an online database provided by the Connecticut Historical Society: David Ransom, *Civil War Monuments of Connecticut*, online database by the Connecticut Historical Society, http://www.chs.org/ransom/default.htm. It lists town memorials but also provides historic details on designs, locations, and dedications. Ransom briefly mentions Hawley in connection with Dedication Day ceremonies but does not go into nearly as much detail as might be expected for a man so heavily involved in local commemoration. Matthew Warshauer, *Connecticut in the American Civil War: Slavery, Sacrifice, and Survival* (Middletown, CT: Wesleyan University Press, 2011) briefly discusses the importance and meaning of Connecticut monuments and Hawley's role as the state's principal dedication speaker.

5. Ransom, *Civil War Monuments of Connecticut*, lists 139, but since the study was done in 1993, several towns have erected monuments, and since sesquicentennial commemoration has begun, a number of additional monuments, missed by the original Ransom study, have been identified. For information on the nation's oldest monument, located at the Kensington Congregational Church, see Warshauer, *Connecticut in the American Civil War*, 189–91.

6. Alfred D. Putnam, ed., *Major General Joseph R. Hawley, Soldier and Editor (1826–1905), Civil War Military Letters* (Hartford: Connecticut Civil War Centennial Commission, 1964), 3–5; Ellsworth S. Grant, *The Miracle of Connecticut* (Hartford: Connecticut Historical Society, 1992), 103–6; "Our Greatest Soldier," Hartford Scrapbook Vol. 13, Hartford History Center, Hartford Public Library, Hartford, CT; "Biography of Hawley," in The Papers of Joseph R. Hawley, Biographical Sketches, 1875–December 2, 1899, and undated, container 35, reel 20, Connecticut State Library, Hartford (hereafter referred to as Hawley Papers).

7. "Memorial Record," March 23, 1905, in Hawley Papers, Correspondence, container 23, reel 12; James R. Sloane to Mrs. Joseph R. Hawley, March 30, 1905, Hawley Papers, Correspondence, container 23, reel 12.

8. Grand Army of the Republic, Department of Connecticut, Roster of the Department of Connecticut, Grand Army of the Republic, 1914–1915, Organized April 11, 1867 (Meriden: Headquarters, 1914), 4; Robert Burns Beath, *History of the Grand Army of the Republic* (New York: Bryon, Taylor & Co., 1889), 87 and 102.

9. "Society of the Army of the James, Third Triennial Reunion, New York City, October 21, 1874, Union League Theater," Program, Memorabilia Folder, Joseph R. Hawley Manuscript Collection, Connecticut Historical Society, Hartford (hereafter referred to as Hawley Manuscript Collection); "The Hartford Union Veterans," Hartford Courant, October 7, 1880, 3.

10. "Our Tribute to the Dead," *Bridgeport Daily Standard*, August 18, 1876, 2.

11. Committee on the Soldiers' and Sailors' Memorial, Records, 1874–1890,

Manuscript Collection, Connecticut Historical Society, Hartford; S. H. Barber, "For General Hawley," Letter to the Editor, *Hartford Courant*, May 31, 1917, 8.

12. "At Brooklyn, Conn.," *Christian Union*, June 21, 1888, 792; a copy of Brooklyn's Dedication Day program found in a scrapbook made by Morgan Bulkeley shows that Hawley's name was listed as the day's main orator, but Bulkeley crossed out the name and wrote his own above it. This evidently shows that Hawley was invited to speak, and intended to go, but for some reason had to drop out at the last minute, possibly asking his close friend to serve in his stead. See "Dedication of the Soldiers' Monument at Brooklyn, Conn., Thursday, June 14, 1888," in Scrapbook 1881–1889 of Morgan Bulkeley, 68, Manuscript Collection, Connecticut Historical Society, Hartford.

13. Sarah Denver Beetham, "Soldiers' and Sailors' Monuments and the Rhetoric of Reunion" (PhD diss., University of Delaware, 2008), 45. Warshauer, *Connecticut in the American Civil War*, 198, notes that this is not the case for Connecticut, where out of some 150 monuments, very few engaged the issues of slavery or emancipation.

14. Thomas J. Brown, *The Public Art of Civil War Commemoration: A Brief History with Documents* (Boston: Bedford/St. Martin's, 2004), 35–36.

15. Stephen Walkley to Joseph R. Hawley, October 12, 1895, Hawley Papers, Correspondence, container 22, reel 11; "The Seventh Regiment," *Hartford Courant*, August 25, 1898, 3; First Connecticut Light Battery and the Sixth, Seventh and Tenth Connecticut Volunteers Monument Association, Program of Exercises at the Dedication of a Soldiers Monument Erected by the First Connecticut Light Battery, the Sixth, Seventh, and Tenth Connecticut Volunteers Monument Association, at the Broadway Park, New Haven, June 16, 1905 (New Haven: The Price, Lee & Adkins Co., 1905), 11.

16. "Battle Flag Parade, at Hartford, Wednesday, September 17, 1879," 1879, Broadsides Collection, Connecticut Historical Society, Hartford; *History of Battle Flag Day, September 17, 1879* (Hartford: Lockwood & Merritt, 1879), 57–58.

17. United States Senate, Senate Reports Vol. 9, Nos. 1114–1872 Except No. 1243, Miscellaneous, 56th Congress, 1st Session 1899–1900, Report No. 127; United States Congress, Congressional Record, Vol. 33, Part 5, 56th Congress, 1st Session, 1900, April 11, 1900, 4000; Hilary A. Herbert, *History of the Arlington Confederate Monument* (Washington, DC: United Daughters of the Confederacy, 1914), 7.

18. Grant, *The Miracle of Connecticut*, 104.

19. "Senator Hawley," *Hartford Courant*, September 30, 1886, 1 (originally quoted from the *New York Mail* and *Express*); "What the State and the Country Thought of General Joseph R. Hawley," *Hartford Courant*, March 21, 1905, 12 (the *Courant* quoted the passage from the *Springfield Republican*).

20. Hawley, "General Hawley Talks Fourth of July," date unknown, Hawley Papers, Correspondence, container 24, reel 12.

21. Connecticut Army and Navy Club, Reports Nos. 1–17, 1879–1895, "Report from 1891," Connecticut State Library, Hartford, 11; Hawley, "Speech on Connecti-

cut History, 1890s," Hawley Papers, Speeches & Statements, 1880–October 1, 1894, container 32, reel 19.

22. "Manchester's Dead Heroes," *Hartford Courant*, August 19, 1890, 2.

23. "The Memorial Arch," *Hartford Courant*, September 18, 1886, 1.

24. "The Memorial Arch," *Hartford Courant*, September 18, 1886, 1.

25. "Honor to the Heroes, Dedication of the Soldiers' Monument at Mystic Bridge," *The Day* (New London), June 14, 1883, 1.

26. "The Memorial Arch," *Hartford Courant*, September 18, 1886, 1.

27. "Honors to the Dead! The Monument Unveiled!," *Greenwich Graphic*, October 25, 1890, 1. Italics are Hawley's.

28. "Tributes to Hawley from the Pulpit," *Hartford Courant*, March 20, 1905, 12.

29. "Torrington Soldiers' Monument," *Hartford Courant*, September 11, 1879, 3; "Manchester's Dead Heroes," *Hartford Courant*, September 18, 1877, 3.

30. Hawley, "Dedication of the Soldiers' Monument, Springfield, Mass., Sept. 28th, 1885."

31. Hawley, "Oration Delivered at Arlington, May 30, 1874 by General Joseph R. Hawley," Hawley Papers, Notes, container 34, reel 20.

32. "Dedication Day," *Riggs' Meriden Literary Recorder*, June 21, 1873, 6.

33. "Torrington Soldiers' Monument," *Hartford Courant*, September 11, 1879, 3.

34. "Dedication Day," *Riggs' Meriden Literary Recorder*, June 21, 1873, 6.

35. "Honors to the Dead! The Monument Unveiled!," *Greenwich Graphic*, October 25, 1890, 3.

36. See Warshauer, *Connecticut in the American Civil War*, introduction, and one of the primary theses of the book.

37. "Honor to the Heroes, Dedication of the Soldiers' Monument at Mystic Bridge," *The Day* (New London), June 14, 1883, 1.

38. Hawley, "Dedication of the Soldiers' Monument, Springfield, Mass., Sept. 28th, 1885."

39. Samuel Hart, *Encyclopedia of Connecticut Biography* (New York: American Historical Society, 1917), 20.

40. "Services in Dedication of the Soldiers' Monument, September 19, 1900," Parks-Central-Soldiers' Monument (Civil War) folder, Local History Room, New Britain Public Library, New Britain, CT.

41. "Honors to the Dead! The Monument Unveiled!," *Greenwich Graphic*, October 25, 1890, 3.

42. "Memorial to Mrs. Hawley," *Hartford Courant*, November 9, 1887, 8.

43. Savage, *Standing Soldiers, Kneeling Slaves*, 7.

44. David W. Blight, *Beyond the Battlefield: Race, Memory, and the American Civil War* (Amherst: University of Massachusetts Press, 2002), 1–4.

45. Paul A. Shackel, "Public Memory and the Search for Power in American Historical Archaeology," *American Anthropologist* 103.3 (September 2001): 656.

46. Savage, *Standing Soldiers, Kneeling Slaves*, 8.

47. Beetham, "Soldiers' and Sailors' Monuments and the Rhetoric of Reunion," 48.

48. Savage, *Standing Soldiers, Kneeling Slaves*, 162; David W. Blight, *Race and*

Reunion: The Civil War in American Memory (Cambridge, MA: Belknap Press of Harvard University Press, 2001), 197–98.

49. Ransom, *Civil War Monuments of Connecticut*, see pages on "Purpose of Monuments" and "Suppliers and Materials."

50. James M. Mayo, "War Memorials as Political Memory," *Geographical Review* 78.1 (January 1988): 75.

51. "Our Tribute to the Dead," *Bridgeport Daily Standard*, August 18, 1876, 2; see also "Southington's Great Day," *Hartford Courant*, August 19, 1880, 2.

52. "Honor to the Heroes, Dedication of the Soldiers' Monument at Mystic Bridge," The Day, June 14, 1883, 1.

53. "Torrington Soldiers' Monument," *Hartford Courant*, September 11, 1879, 3.

54. Hawley, "Gen. Hawley at the New London Celebration and Dedication, Wednesday, May 6, 1896," Hawley Papers, Speeches & Statements, Printed, September 28, 1886–July 26, 1896, container 32, reel 19.

55. "Honors to the Dead! The Monument Unveiled!," *Greenwich Graphic*, October 25, 1890, 3.

56. Larry M. Logue, "Union Veterans and Their Government: The Effect of Public Policies on Private Lives," *Journal of Interdisciplinary History* 22.3 (Winter 1992): 412.

57. Logue, "Union Veterans and Their Government," 424–25; Thomas J. Schlereth, *Victorian America: Transformations in Everyday Life* (New York: Harper Perennial, 1991), 282–83.

58. Logue, "Union Veterans and Their Government," 426.

59. "Honors to the Dead! The Monument Unveiled!," *Greenwich Graphic*, October 25, 1890, 2.

60. "Our Tribute to the Dead," *Bridgeport Daily Standard*, August 18, 1876, 2.

61. Hawley, "Address of the Hon. Joseph R. Hawley at the Flag-Raising at Trinity College, Hartford, Connecticut, Wednesday, June 27, 1894," Hawley Papers, Speeches & Statements, Printed, September 28, 1886–July 26, 1896, container 32, reel 19.

62. Hawley, "Address of the Hon. Joseph R. Hawley at the Flag-Raising at Trinity College, Hartford, Connecticut, Wednesday, June 27, 1894."

63. "Memorial Day," *Hartford Courant*, June 1, 1886, 1.

64. "Madison's Memorial," *Shoreline Times* (Guilford), June 4, 1897, 1; Ransom, *Civil War Monuments of Connecticut*, see page on "Dedication Ceremonies."

65. Hawley, "Speech at Army and Navy Club, Bridgeport, July 1895," Hawley Papers, Speeches & Statements, July 11, 1895–1900, container 32, reel 19.

66. Blight, *Race and Reunion*, 74; Blight noted that thousands of soldiers spoke at both Memorial Day and Dedication Day events across the nation.

67. "Services in Dedication of the Soldiers' Monument, September 19, 1900," Parks-Central-Soldiers' Monument (Civil War) folder, Local History Room, New Britain Public Library, New Britain, CT.

68. "Honors to the Dead! The Monument Unveiled!," *Greenwich Graphic*, October 25, 1890, 3.

69. Oliver Wendell Holmes Jr., "The Soldier's Faith, May 30, 1895," in Thomas J.

Brown, ed., *The Public Art of Civil War Commemoration: A Brief History with Documents* (New York: Bedford/St. Martin's, 2004), 47 and 48.

70. John W. Daniel, "Oration at the Dedication of the Lee Memorial in Lexington, June 28, 1883," in Brown, *The Public Art of Civil War Commemoration*, 92–96.

71. Booker T. Washington, "Address at Dedication of the Shaw Memorial, May 31, 1897," in Brown, *The Public Art of Civil War Commemoration*, 128.

72. "The Passing Regiment," *Hartford Courant*, October 31, 1898, 7.

73. "Services in Dedication of the Soldiers' Monument, September 19, 1900," Parks-Central-Soldiers' Monument (Civil War) folder, Local History Room, New Britain Public Library, New Britain, CT.

74. John Pettegrew, "'The Soldier's Faith': Turn-of-the-Century Memory of the Civil War and the Emergence of Modern American Nationalism," *Journal of Contemporary History* 31.1 (January 1996): 50.

75. Pettegrew, "'The Soldier's Faith,'" 61.

76. "The Soldiers at Dayton," *Hartford Courant*, August 2, 1884, 2; J. J. Elwell to Joseph R. Hawley, July 22, 1896, Hawley Papers, Correspondence, container 22, reel 11; Fred N. Bassett to Joseph R. Hawley, October 9, 1891, Hawley Papers, Correspondence, container 21, reel 10; Hawley, "Speech at Stony Point by Gen. J. R. Hawley," Hawley Papers, Speeches & Statements, Printed, September 28, 1886–July 26, 1896, container 32, reel 19.

77. Untitled newspaper clipping, January 28, 1881, Springfield Republic, Newspaper clippings folder, Hawley Manuscript Collection; "Cleveland's Fete Day," *Hartford Courant*, July 23, 1896, 8; Bunker Hill Monument Association, "Invitation to Attend First Centennial of the Battle of Bunker Hill," June 17, 1875, Hawley Manuscript Collection.

78. "Application for Membership, Society of Colonial Wars," November 21, 1893, Hawley Papers, Correspondence, container 27, reel 11; Henry Rendall Waite to Joseph R. Hawley, May 9, 1895, Hawley Papers, Correspondence, container 22, reel 11.

79. Henry W. Burrill to Mrs. Joseph R. Hawley, April 6, 1905, Hawley Papers, Correspondence, container 23, reel 12. The letter by Burrill was written on behalf of all the veterans of Robert O. Tyler Post No. 50, GAR, Hartford.

80. The Seventh Connecticut Regiment Association, "Memorial Record," March 23, 1905, Hawley Papers, Correspondence, container 23, reel 12.

81. "Gen. Hawley's Funeral, New York Times, March 21, 1905.

82. "Church Service; Military Burial," *Hartford Courant*, March 22, 1905, 2. Memorial services were also held at numerous schools throughout Hartford. At West Middle School, a speaker told the students of Hawley's patriotism and bravery, saying he was a model gentleman and citizen whom the students should emulate, even when there was not a war to fight. "Hawley Exercises," *Hartford Courant*, March 23, 1905, 5.

83. "Miss Hawley Back from War Relief," *Hartford Courant*, December 10, 1917, 14; "Miss Roswell Hawley on Way to French Port," *Hartford Courant*, May 10, 1918, 7.

8 : From Decoration Day to the Centennial Commission
CIVIL WAR COMMEMORATION IN
CONNECTICUT, 1868–1965

T he Civil War, even a century and a half since its start, continues to loom large in the American imagination. Novels,
movies, television "miniseries events," and ongoing public
arguments over emblems such as the Confederate flag are
all strong indications that, as a nation, the United States is
not about to forget the Civil War. Since the conflict ended, the nation has
also commemorated the war through a variety of formal means of observance, and Connecticut has participated in most of those commemorative
modes. While the main focus of this chapter is the work the Connecticut
Civil War Centennial Commission (ccwcc) undertook in commemorating Connecticut's role in the Civil War at its hundredth anniversary, it is
also worthwhile to review older commemorative exercises in Connecticut in order to understand how effective they have been. Additionally, as
the sesquicentennial observances approached, it was logical and useful
to compare the state's centennial commemoration to the national commemoration. This review contributes to an overall understanding of how
past remembrances of the war succeeded in, and sometimes fell short of,
fulfilling their goals.

Although there had been organized public remembrances of the Civil
War dead from the time that the first deaths were reported back to soldiers' hometowns, 1868 marked the last broad, nationwide, and in Connecticut, statewide, attempt to adopt a formal, annual ritual of recognition and remembrance. Variously known as Memorial Day or Decoration
Day, on May 30, 1868, towns and cities across the Union (even including,
on a drastically more limited scale, those states that had lately been of the
Confederacy) honored their lost warriors by decorating their graves with
flowers.

In 1868, the veterans' group Grand Army of the Republic (GAR) was
determined to make sure that "the loyal people of twenty-seven states
thronged to the heroes' graves and . . . vied with the surviving veterans in

rendering homage to the beloved dead." According to a compilation volume published by the GAR, that group had organized observances in nineteen of the larger towns and cities in Connecticut.[1] The *Hartford Courant*, which had largely supported the Civil War, unsurprisingly heartily endorsed the observance, commenting in an editorial, that "[w]e hope to see general observance on the part of our citizens of 'decoration day,'" and emphasizing that "[a]ll returned soldiers and sailors, the ladies, and citizens generally, are invited to join."[2]

The *Hartford Times*, which had been opposed to the war, still feeling the sting of defeat, offered a dissenting opinion, decrying the "bands of music, military escorts, speeches, poems, &c" that would accompany decorating the soldiers' graves, and editorializing that "we cannot but think that the ceremony would be much more impressive, if the comrades of the deceased would go quietly and alone, in the early morning, and lay their offerings on the graves." As much as the *Hartford Times* would have preferred a day "leaving out all the pomp and martial display, speeches, and music," the editorial writer nevertheless concluded by giving the information about where the GAR was going to assemble in Hartford.[3]

Eventually, of course, Decoration Day became the strongest annual reminder of the Civil War, though it shifted to the last Monday of May and its name was finalized as Memorial Day. Additionally, it became a day for honoring those who had died in subsequent American wars. Monuments, the other most immediate post–Civil War commemoration, were specifically meant to honor those who had died in that war.

Unlike Memorial Day, which was celebrated on the same day every year, monuments were largely divorced from a specific day or anniversary. Individual communities generally unveiled and dedicated their monuments after an often protracted process of raising funds, commissioning and executing a design, and receiving the monument for installation. The first Civil War monument in Middletown, for example, known simply as Soldiers' Monument, was first suggested in 1865, but the town did not begin to organize for its purchase until 1870. In 1872, one Middletown editorial suggested that there had been some question as to whether or not a monument was even needed; the editorial advocated for the monument, acknowledging that at a projected cost of $12,000, it would have to be paid for by additional taxes, but that it was worth the price.[4]

The public agreed; the monument was eventually dedicated on June 17, 1874, with a parade and exercises including a prayer, a hymn, the unveiling of the monument, and two speeches. The first, by the Honorable Benjamin

Douglas, was largely a narrative about how the monument came to be built, including stories of committee meetings and lists of members. The second, by the Reverend Dr. Joseph Cummings, addressed not only the necessity of building the monument, but was also a meditation on the Civil War itself, not yet ten years in the past. Cummings spoke of the need not to view the monument as an excuse to "promote sectional feeling and give occasion for strife and bitterness. . . . This monument was erected to fulfillment of the pledge given to those who went from us to the war. We promised to honor them, to perpetuate their memories and to cherish the children they left behind."[5] David Ransom's work on Civil War monuments throughout Connecticut suggests that the overall pattern that Middletown followed in erecting its first Civil War monument (three more were to follow) was fairly standard throughout the state.[6]

While it was largely up to individual Connecticut towns to erect and dedicate Civil War monuments according to their own civic needs and fiscal realities, and Memorial Day continued to be observed annually, Battle Flag Day proved to be a highly successful one-time event that simultaneously commemorated the war and honored its veterans. The Connecticut legislature passed a resolution in March 1879 that various regimental and other battle flags should be prominently displayed in the State Capitol. On September 17, 1879, tens of thousands of citizens thronged Hartford to watch approximately ten thousand veterans march, while bands played and children formed living pyramids to add to the festive air of the occasion. Both the *Hartford Courant* and the *Hartford Times* gave extended coverage to the event. The *Hartford Courant* exuberantly announced that "Over 50,000 from Outside Hartford" attended, enjoying "splendid weather and a grand time." The coverage detailed the decorations between the Arsenal, where the flags had been stored, and their new home at the Capitol.[7]

Unlike its more negative coverage of Decoration Day in 1868, the *Hartford Times* anticipated that Battle Flag Day would be "An Interesting Ceremonial."[8] In its evening edition the newspaper rhapsodized about "the beautiful strains of a score of brass bands" and listed, in approving detail, the "Finest Display Ever Seen in Hartford. . . . Festoons, wreaths, bunting, eagles, Stars and stripes . . . seen on every side." The only significant difference in coverage between the two papers was that the *Hartford Times* gave a more conservative crowd estimate of "A Crowd of Thirty Thousand Visitors."[9] Before the year was out, an anonymous person (or group) compiled the speeches, sermons, and poems delivered on Battle

Flag Day, along with lists of participants, line drawings, reprinted newspaper articles, and narrative accounts of the day into a 256-page book, *History of Battle Flag Day, September 17, 1879.* That account shied away from a direct estimate of the Hartford turnout; rather, it suggested that "across the length and breadth of the State" the day "has been participated in, it is estimated, by not less than 150,000 people."[10] To this day, crowd estimation remains more art than science, so the discrepancy between the two Hartford newspapers' accounts may not have been a case of deliberate misrepresentation.

The next major Connecticut commemoration to receive extensive media attention did not even take place in the state itself. In general, regimental and, especially, battlefield reunions provided another means of Civil War commemoration for veterans. As long as the generation that had actually fought the war was still alive and active, those for whom memories of the war were not overwhelmingly painful still gathered together with their former brothers-in-arms to reminisce about battles fought and comrades lost. As the American railroad system became both faster and less expensive for passengers, battlefield reunions became popular among many veterans. These reunions were usually tied to the anniversary of particular battles: trying to gather any large group of people together is always an exercise in logistics, and having the reunions on the dates that the battles were fought not only provided a strong psychological pull but also ensured that the seasonal conditions would be similar (if not the weather itself). Gettysburg and Antietam were particularly popular sites for these reunions.

As reported in the *Hartford Courant*, on July 3, 1884, twenty-one years after the multiday battle at Gettysburg, members of the Fourteenth Connecticut Infantry gathered at Gettysburg to unveil and dedicate a monument dedicated to their fallen members, an event that was reported in the *Courant.* The paper gave its account only in a small paragraph, as part of a larger summary of regional events of that day.[11] Three years later, the *Courant* gave more attention to a similar expedition, reporting, "About one hundred survivors of the old Fifth regiment met at the Gettysburg battlefield yesterday to dedicate the monument which marks the spot where the Fifth hastily constructed earthenworks on the 2nd of July" in 1863. The report also included the final stanzas of a poem read at the ceremony and recorded the names and general remarks of the speakers at the dedication.[12] Interestingly, the *Hartford Times*, for reasons that can now only be guessed at, did not report on either of those events, although the omission may have been because each of those two occasions commemorated only a single regiment.

In 1894, however, both Hartford newspapers gave much more extended coverage to a group of "Antietam excursionists." Veterans of the Eighth, Eleventh, Fourteenth, and Sixteenth Regiments embarked on an odyssey that took them from their homes in Connecticut to New York City, where four hundred "members of those regiments and their friends" gathered to begin an itinerary that took them first to Gettysburg, where they were able "to visit the central and strategic points of the great battle and the many monuments erected by the surviving soldiers from many states." Gettysburg was, however, a prologue. The intent of the "Antietam excursionists" was actually to continue on to Antietam in order to bear witness to the unveiling and dedication of four monuments at the Maryland battlefield, one for each of those regiments.[13] The *Courant* even had a follow-up article about the return of the group, who reported that while their commercial accommodations had been "first class," the local "people opened their houses and entertained the visitors heartily" as well. At the dedication of the monument for the Sixteenth, Dr. Nathan Mayer of Hartford, who had been the regimental surgeon, read a poem that was considered the highlight of the day. "'There were many old soldiers standing shoulder to shoulder again,' said Captain William H. Lockwood yesterday, 'whose faces were wet with tears, called forth by the tender memories the poem awakened.'" The trip, concluded the *Courant*, "was a success from the beginning to the end."[14]

The *Hartford Times*'s coverage of the monuments' dedications did not include all the details of the "excursionists" odyssey to Antietam, but did carry a "Special to *The Hartford Times*" article about the ceremonies. The extensive article included illustrations of both the monuments and portraits of some of the attendees.

Although their adventures were not recorded in major newspapers, some of these "Antietam excursionists" of 1894 were already old hands at battlefield reunions. Members of the Fourteenth Regiment, for example, had, both individually and as a group, undertaken several trips to Antietam. The first group trip, in 1891, included "three hundred of us, as hopeful, happy, jolly a crowd as one can often see." The three hundred included veterans, and "ladies and friends, apparently as interested as the survivors themselves—for had not some of them suffered when we suffered in that long-ago time?" In fact, the voyage proved so moving that several participants asked H. S. Stevens, the regimental chaplain, to write a souvenir book about the trip. Stevens characterized the mood of the group as eager and enthusiastic as they contemplated the battlefield at Antietam and described to their noncombatant fellows how the battle had been fought. Even so, "[e]ach veteran thought of that former day this meeting commemorated, when the roar and panoply, the danger and havoc of battle were the things absorbing all attention . . . and the contrast of that with this peaceful, pastoral scene." In the end, however, "there was deep reluctance to break up that memorable, never to be repeated, meeting."[15]

Regimental reunions, whether on the battlefield or within Connecticut, tended to be relatively private and limited to survivors, families, and their closest friends. More publicly, commemoration began to be centered on Memorial Day rather than on anniversaries. In the case of Middletown, the majority of the town's historical memory of its participation in the Civil War was focused not on anniversaries of important Civil War dates but rather on the anniversaries of the town's founding.

In 1900, Middletown celebrated the 250th anniversary of its initial English settlement with parades, festivities, and various speeches on topics of local historical interest, including a lengthy address about the town in the Civil War. The speech, given by Wesleyan president Bradford Paul Raymond, recounted the general mood of unease and partisanship in Middletown immediately before the war, and the number of troops that the municipality sent to fight the war, as well as the number who died or suffered injury during its course. He carefully pointed out the home front contributions Middletown made to the war effort; in terms of finances, it had, he noted with pride, contributed the seventh-largest dollar amount of any municipality in Connecticut.[16] Overall, the speech was about local civic pride in a Civil War context.

Fifty years later, the Middletown tercentennial festivities included, among other activities remembering the Civil War, a historical pageant put on by students at Woodrow Wilson High School, who presented twelve "tableaux" relating to the town's founding and history, including a surprisingly frank acknowledgment of slavery in Middletown ("Under garb of sentiment / We don't speak of Yankee slave / Yet it was this kind of chattel / Brought by Indies trade"). When it came to the Civil War, however, the students retreated to a now-comfortable narrative of the war as a moral imperative to "free the slaves / And bind the union fast."[17]

The fiftieth anniversary of the Civil War, of course, came between those two local civic commemorations. April 12, 1911, passed largely without fanfare; the *New York Times* ignored the anniversary of the war's start.

The *Hartford Courant* offered a brief editorial suggesting that "it would be appropriate if Hartford's welcome to the veterans of the Civil War today included the lifting of the hat [when passing] one of the country's defenders of a half-century ago."[18] The specific "welcome to the veterans" was in the context of "the forty-fourth annual encampment of the Grand Army of the Republic of Connecticut," an event that, while ignored by the newspaper in both 1910 and 1912, received several column inches of coverage in 1911.[19] The next great milestone was the fiftieth anniversary of the Battle of Gettysburg, which included a battlefield reunion of troops from both sides and an address by President Woodrow Wilson. As with the "Antietam excursionists," the *Hartford Courant* followed the progress and encampment of Connecticut veterans attending the reunion. The centerpiece of this coverage was the article headlined "Blue and Gray Camp as Friends at Gettysburg," which gave an emotional testimony that underlined Wilson's message of national unity: "We have found one another again as brothers and comrades in arms, enemies no longer . . . our battles long past, the quarrel forgotten."[20] Wilson, of course, was being as optimistic about national unity as he would be about achieving world peace through founding the League of Nations four years later.

The next major milestone in public Civil War commemoration was not the fiftieth year of its ending in April 1915, which was barely remarked upon.[21] Rather, it was the one hundredth anniversary of its beginning, sixteen years after the end of World War II, and thus sixteen years into the Cold War. The story of the Civil War centennial, however, started long before the literal century mark. Ultimately, in all its successes and failures, the centennial is the most complex of all the Civil War commemorative exercises to date.

In his book, *Troubled Commemoration: The American Civil War Centennial, 1961–1965*, Robert J. Cook noted that the story of the Civil War centennial actually began in 1953, with a group of historical "buffs" who participated in Civil War round table discussion groups. Professional historians, such as Allan Nevins and Bruce Catton, as well as General Ulysses S. Grant III (grandson of the Civil War general and eighteenth president of the United States), joined forces with countless others to follow a truly torturous path, negotiating lingering sectional hostilities, which eventually led to the creation of the Civil War Centennial Commission in 1957. Cook admirably demonstrated the course the CWCC would take before its final report to Congress in 1968.[22]

Two of the largest obstacles that the CWCC attempted to overcome were continued American sectional disunity, particularly focused on the civil rights movement, and public reception, which was not always universally enthusiastic. Cook wrote extensively about the former, although there was a further nuance to that debate, as articulated by at least two separate southern clergymen. In 1961, Frank Ifird, a Lutheran pastor from North Carolina "with a record of opposition to racial bias," wrote a letter to the editor of a national denominational magazine that drew enough press attention that it was summarized in the *Hartford Courant*. "The Bible reveals no Hebrew commemoration of the way Cain slew Abel," Ifird insisted, further berating "both North and South" for having kept "holding onto and propagating prejudice and antagonisms and misunderstandings that continue to contribute to the disunity of the nation."[23]

Two years earlier, another clergyman, John Morris of Atlanta, had written to the *New York Times* in a similar vein, wondering why the Civil War "should be observed at all unless it be marked by a day of penitence for our failure to reconcile our differences peaceably." Morris was worried that "the Southern Press indicates that observances will be utilized for sounding off on present-day issues. . . . The passions that brought forth the war between Americans are not dead and will only be exploited by many who are still grieving that the South failed to win."[24] At the time, Morris was also working to help found the Episcopal Society for Cultural and Racial Unity in Atlanta, which was committed to desegregation.[25]

As antiracist southerners, they both viewed the national commemoration with alarm. Ifird and Morris also worried about the sentimentalization of warfare in general, another problem with public perception of the cwcc's work. Neither the summary of Ifird's letter in Hartford, nor the publication of Morris's in New York provoked further letters of support or refutation, but the desire to reflect on the Civil War was not always an exercise in excessive sentimentalization or in reflexive prejudice.

Robert Penn Warren certainly did not view the centennial as part of, as Morris had derisively described it, "our addiction to celebrating the one hundredth anniversary of everything."[26] A poet, novelist, resident of Connecticut, and member of the state's centennial commission, Warren published *The Legacy of the Civil War: Meditations on the Centennial* in 1961. In this deceptively slender volume, Warren tried to understand why, as his opening words would have us believe, "[t]he Civil War is, for the American imagination, the great single event of our history." In Warren's view, "the War gave the South the Great Alibi and gave the North the Treasury of Virtue." The Great Alibi excused southern prejudice and intransigence as noble traditionalism, while the Treasury of Virtue became a "plenary in-dulgence" by which northerners could both forgive and forget themselves for their racism before, during, and after the war. To Warren, a former segregationist and transplanted Kentuckian who came to Fairfield, Con-necticut, neither side was unblemished. Warren ultimately thought that, when it came to American national memory and the Civil War on its cen-tennial, "we may hazard that what Lincoln had in mind is a deeper and more complex communal involvement in the event, and in the history of the event" rather than a simple right-versus-wrong narrative, written by the winners.[27]

Warren's book was favorably reviewed by, among others, David Donald and Charles Poore, both in the *New York Times*. Donald wrote that "no mere summary could do justice to Mr. Warren's skillful and subtle analy-sis" and that "every Civil War student is bound to respect" Warren's book.[28] Poore described Warren's work as a "brilliantly searching soliloquy" but felt that "there may be no true mystery about the enduring appeal of the Civil War" because, for Poore, the Civil War's appeal was self-explanatory as "limitless escapism for man's insatiable, deplorably combattical na-ture."[29] Neither reviewer stopped to question Warren's underlying as-sumption that every American must necessarily be as fascinated by the Civil War as he was—or the reviewers themselves were.

Before too long, however, there was a far more critical examination of the centennial. In 1962, curmudgeonly critic Edmund Wilson published *Patriotic Gore: Studies in the Literature of the American Civil War.* "We have tried to forget the Civil War," Wilson moaned, "but we have had the defeated enemy on the premises and he will not allow us to forget it." Wil-son framed his praise of Warren's book in terms of "this absurd centen-nial."[30] Poore liked Wilson's book well enough, but his review (published one day short of a full year after his review of Warren's book) off-handedly demonstrated what had become a growing indifference to the centennial: "The Civil War centennials are proving to be rather sedate affairs. There probably have been louder rebel yells in committee rooms than on the fields of glory. Even the reliable tide of familiar essays on the war's appeal seems stuck at the ebb."[31] Poore articulated something that, by its very nature, few bothered to write about: public indifference. Cook identified other incidents of apathy, relayed from local centennial organizers to the CWCC.[32]

In light of these paradoxical themes of conflict and uninterest, Cook devoted an entire chapter of his history of the centennial to exploring how academic historians had to "take control" in order to save a beleaguered commemorative effort that was simultaneously succumbing to crass commercialism and bitter regionalism. Rather than being a somber reflection on a divided past that was going to forge a new national unity, particularly in the context of the Cold War, the national centennial efforts became littered with tchotchkes and hurt feelings.

The ongoing sectional squabbles about the commemoration came to a head in early 1961, when Everett Landers, the head of the New Jersey Civil War Centennial Commission, was trying to gain reassurance from Karl Betts, then head of the cwcc, that an African American member of its delegation would be able to participate fully in the cwcc convention to be held in Charlestown, South Carolina, a segregated city. Betts equivocated, and Landers finally wrote him a strong letter, also accusing Betts's approach to the centennial of being responsible for the "useless brochures and other trash" his state's commission was constantly receiving, writing that "[y]our continued emphasis on the 'fast buck' aspect of the Centennial is causing growing public discontent and considerable adverse press attention." Eventually, the convention was saved by relocating it from a hotel to a u.s. naval station which was, by its status as an American military installation, desegregated. Overall, however, the incident revealed deep fissures in the cwcc and the nation itself. Other states, including Virginia, also quarreled with Betts, and historians joined Landers in condemning Betts's commercial attitude. When the commission leaders voted to oust Betts in August 1961, Ulysses S. Grant III showed his support for Betts by immediately resigning from the commission he had worked so hard to create.[33]

Allan Nevins, a professor of American history at Columbia University, replaced Betts and immediately began addressing what he saw as the cheap commercialization of the centennial effort, with the help of James Robertson, editor of *Civil War History*. Their reforms were summed up in a new policy statement in which they vowed to "discourage observances that are cheap and tawdry. . . . Above all our centennial theme will be unity, not division."[34] Civil rights and slavery were still off the table as a theme for the cwcc, but there would be an increase in fostering academic projects over pageantry.

That was the national context of the cwcc's efforts over the years. From the start, however, Connecticut chose a different path in its pursuit of the Civil War centennial commemoration. On August 27, 1959, Governor Abraham Ribicoff formally announced the members of the Connecticut

Civil War Centennial Commission; six came from the Hartford Civil War Roundtable, including Albert Putnam, as well as Edward J. Lonergan, an assistant u.s. attorney; J. Doyle DeWitt, the president of Travelers Insurance; and John R. Reitemeyer, publisher and president of the *Hartford Courant*; along with other "students of the Civil War era" and "noted writers," including Robert Penn Warren, for a total of fifteen appointments to the commission.[35] After several preliminary meetings, all preserved for posterity and that demonstrate from the start that the ccwcc intended to pursue serious academic research as well as creating public interest in the Civil War, the ccwcc selected Putnam as its chair.[36] Putnam and the other members of the ccwcc were more than ready to begin promoting the Civil War centennial and promulgating information about Connecticut during the Civil War.

They quickly published *The Connecticut Civil War Centennial: A Manual for Its Observance in the Towns and Cities of the State of Connecticut*, a small (five and a quarter by seven and a half–inch) thirty-one page pamphlet filled with suggestions and organizational aids for any Connecticut town that was interested in taking an active part in the commemoration. The pamphlet began by posing the most basic question: "Why Commemorate the Civil War?" The answer was careful to point out that "the Civil War, like any other war, was a tragedy. Therefore . . . the Civil War Centennial is not a celebration. It is a commemoration."[37] Indeed, the distinction between "celebration" and "commemoration," which had already been addressed by the national cwcc, haunted the commemorations when critics began to take aim at both the national and state efforts to promote the study of the Civil War.

After trying to make that distinction clear, the ccwcc manual also stressed that the centennial was meant "to strengthen the unity of the country through mutual understanding," another theme that Connecticut took straight from the rhetoric of the national cwcc. The manual then claimed that "war is the ultimate test of character. The stories of the Civil War are full of lessons for present-day living. By these examples we can teach children and adults the moral values so needed in America today." If such strong invocations of moral declension and the need for the character-building lessons that only war can teach us seemed like a nostalgic hard sell, the ccwcc was willing to admit that they were, in fact, out "to sell Connecticut and her story to our countrymen. . . . The Centennial . . . is a turningback to the past" to learn "for ourselves the concepts upon which our democratic freedom depends . . . individual responsibility based on faith in God and service to country." At the same time, the manual cautioned, "We must avoid any display of bad taste."[38] To paraphrase a sentence that would become famous a few months later, the ccwcc was asking people both what they could do for the Civil War and what the Civil War could do for them.

More practically, the manual offered a tidy list of how towns could commemorate the Civil War, starting with "Publish a Proclamation" in order to "Get everybody involved" so that they could "Hold a public forum" and "Appoint a subcommittee on public relations" and so on, down to advising local groups to "Keep a scrapbook" of their activities. Oddly, the directive to create "a subcommittee on public relations" came *before* any suggestion of forming an executive or oversight committee. Throughout the manual, the emphasis was on either overtly or covertly selling history in general, the centennial in particular, and on the idea that both would be ideal for selling a broader agenda: "a chance to channel the natural interest of the young in the Civil War into an understanding [of] the philosophy and ideas of American democracy." Or the idea that "we find again the faith in God our fathers knew and that we recognize that our homes, schools, farms and business must be centers of strength and learning and that our lives much be based on concepts of unity, integrity and service."[39] Underpinning all of this patriotic training and retraining, of course, would be a reliance on organization, committees, checklists (helpfully provided), paperwork, and publicity. One might almost call the Civil War centennial a four-year plan for American democracy.

As easy as it might be to express cynicism about past enthusiasms, particularly with the hindsight knowledge that, nationally, the centennial was beset by problems of division, segregation, and racial tension, the ccwcc's efforts, in the end, were actually fairly effective. The degree to which individual cities and towns adhered to the *Manual for Its Observance* may not have been widespread, however. Although the ccwcc archives contain a fair amount of correspondence from town committees, a perusal of the archives for the Middlesex County Historical Society—whose president, William van Beynam, was also the president of the Middletown Civil War Centennial Committee—reveals that he did not save any correspondence or other material relating to that town's participation in the centennial.[40] That is not to say that Middletown did not participate, but rather that there is no surviving evidence that van Beynam kept the scrupulous records the ccwcc suggested. The Middlesex Historical Society did sponsor at least two documentary showings at the Middletown Public Library during the centennial years, as well as a handful of small-scale lectures, but that seems to have been the extent of its involvement—or at least of the records it maintained.[41] The ccwcc town correspondence archives reflect that there are only a few letters from Middletown. The town of Guilford, in contrast, wrote back and forth to the committee in much greater detail and volume.[42]

Furthermore, both state and local events designed to bring the Civil War centennial to the general public did not seem to have a lasting effect. People who lived in Connecticut at the time do not seem to have any specific memory of the Civil War centennial as such, including schoolchildren, former members of local historical societies at the time, or current members of Civil War roundtable discussion groups. This is not to say that their imaginations and interests were not sparked at the time, or that they did not engage with the Civil War in one way or another, just that the centennial did not leave behind strong impressions.[43]

As noted above, however, public apathy was a national problem. The ccwcc had already been working toward more academic goals. One of the ccwcc's earliest objectives was to commission an academic work about the role Connecticut played in the Civil War; a letter dated December 10, 1960, specifically discussed engaging John Niven to write his book, *Connecticut for the Union*.[44] While some members of the ccwcc worked on securing the funds and the talent to get the book written and published, others worked on gathering primary sources. For example, one member wrote to the American Anaconda Brass Works requesting that it send any material it had about its Civil War production; American Anaconda responded with detailed information.[45] That kind of information gathering, combined with the considerable academic and historic expertise of the members on the ccwcc eventually helped Niven complete *Connecticut for the Union: The Role of the State in the Civil War* by 1965. Published by Yale University Press, it was the most complete study of the subject until the publication of Matthew Warshauer's *Connecticut in the American Civil War: Slavery, Sacrifice, and Survival* in 2011, just in time for the sesquicentennial commemoration.[46]

In its focus on scholarly as well as public history, the ccwcc anticipated both the problems and the successes of the national cwcc early on, but that was not the only means by which Connecticut avoided some of the thornier national issues that plagued the cwcc. The *Hartford Courant*, for example, carefully followed the aforementioned issue of segregation at the cwcc convention in Charlestown, South Carolina, and reported that the

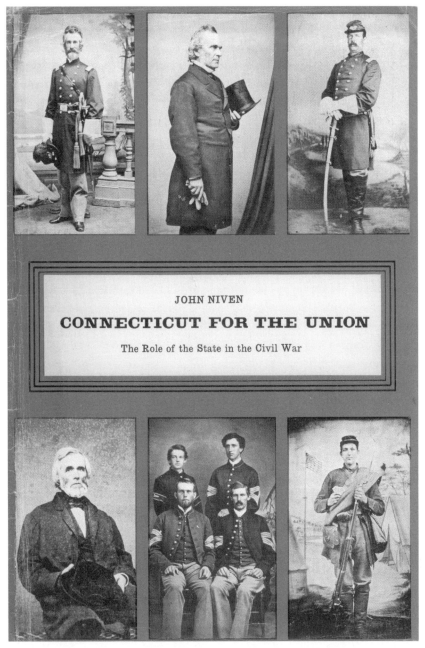

JOHN NIVEN

CONNECTICUT FOR THE UNION

The Role of the State in the Civil War

The Connecticut Centennial Civil War Commission focused on scholarship, commissioning John Niven's Connecticut for the Union. *Courtesy of the Connecticut State Library, Hartford*

Connecticut State Senate unanimously passed a resolution calling on the ccwcc to boycott that convention and any other events that might be segregated. Before the Connecticut House passed the resolution to be sent for Governor John Dempsey's signature, however, Edward Lonergan issued a statement that the commission was primarily interested in promoting education about Connecticut and the Civil War and had no intention of attending national conventions.[47]

Rather than getting embroiled in the messy politics that plagued the cwcc, the Connecticut group preferred to leave the issues of the national commemoration to the national commission. In keeping with its focus on accessible scholarship on issues relating to Connecticut in the Civil War, the ccwcc published ten pamphlets relating to the history of the Civil War in Connecticut. Some were about specific people, such as biographies of Generals Hawley, Terry, and Sedgwick; another was *Andrew Hull Foote, Gunboat Commodore*; and it also produced the compilation *Connecticut Military and Naval Leaders in the Civil War. So the War Came* by Peter Brett Schroeder, *Lincoln in Hartford* by J. Doyle DeWitt, and *Connecticut Physicians in the Civil War* by Stanley B. Weld were all self-explanatorily titled and rife with photographs and other visuals. Only a few other states' Civil War Centennial Commissions matched Connecticut in publishing these sorts of scholarly materials.[48]

In addition to the pamphlets, the ccwcc maintained a speaker's bureau of more than twenty historians and history buffs who were prepared to travel around the state, each speaking on a topic in his or her area of expertise. Dr. Philip Sheridan, for example, was ready to speak about "Surgery in the Civil War," while Catherine Doyle could educate audiences about "Women of the Sanitary Commission." Some speakers, like Professor Alice Brown of the University of Hartford, had academic affiliation, whereas some, like James Norris, were academically unaffiliated "buffs." Those two particular speakers were available to speak about "general topics."[49] Although the archives do not provide a full record of the degree to which schools, libraries, historical societies, or other local organizations engaged these speakers during the centennial years, small newspaper announcements occasionally show the speakers at work around the state. In October 1961, Lonergan, for example, addressed the South Windsor Historical Society on the topic of "Why We Commemorate the Civil War and Its Personages."[50] ccwcc chair Albert Putnam, meanwhile, was not too busy to attend an exhibit of Civil War memorabilia and give a lecture to put it in context in East Haddam in the late spring of 1962.[51]

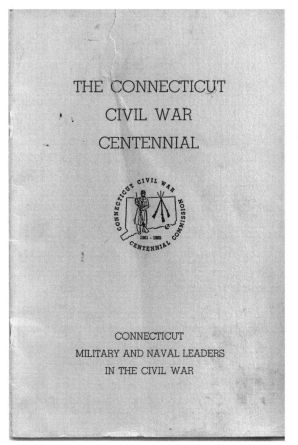

"Connecticut Military and Naval Leaders in the Civil War," one of many pamphlets created by The Connecticut Civil War Centennial Commission during the 1960s.

As difficult and divisive as racial issues were in both the country as a whole and within the national CWCC, and as much as participants might have wanted to ignore the subject as much as possible during the centennial years, the one hundredth anniversary of the Emancipation Proclamation, in September 1962, could hardly be ignored. On a national level, according to historian Robert Cook, proposals to observe the centennial of the proclamation "originated with blacks and their northern white allies and were clearly designed with the contemporary civil rights struggle in mind." Northern politicians of both parties, particularly from New York (which owned the original copy of the proclamation) and New Jersey, also wanted to use the occasion to avow their support for the civil rights movement. Southern participants in the CWCC, not unpredictably, were largely against celebrating that particular centennial, even issuing a "Reaffirmation of Policy," in which they asserted that, nationally, the cwcc must "continue to be non-political, non-partisan, non-sectarian and non-profit."[52] This proved to be difficult.

In Connecticut, meanwhile, the ccwcc organized a special event to celebrate the proclamation. One member of the ccwcc, Colonel Egbert White, proposed that it might be "fitting to have a Negro read the Proclamation," suggesting "Martin Luther King and Thurwood [*sic*] Marshall who is a Federal Judge. I am told Marshall is a talented speaker and of course King is also." There is no record of anyone from the ccwcc actually attempting to contact Marshall, King, or any other "Negro" to read the proclamation. Perhaps the tokenism of the gesture was a little too obvious, or perhaps other organizers realized the probability that both of those two potential readers had other things to worry about at the time that would preclude them from dropping by to read a proclamation that had only started a path for equality that each man was still fighting for daily. Instead, Ella Grasso (a Caucasian), then Connecticut's secretary of state and ultimately the state's first female governor, read the proclamation at the end of a program that included four speeches and a musical performance.[53]

The ceremony, held at the State Library's Memorial Hall, started at eleven in the morning and was over in time for participants and attendees to enjoy a two o'clock parade organized by the Hartford Council of the National Council of Negro Women. In addition to the parade, the council held an evening event at Weaver High School Auditorium that was a "celebration aimed at teaching all youth, regardless of race, of contributions made to our way of life by great Americans."[54] In a show of support for the event, the curator of the Old State House, Harold J. Egan, announced that his institution would offer free admission to those participating in or attending the parade.[55] The festivities on September 22, 1962, also marked the start of an exhibit relating to the Emancipation Proclamation, which included the table at which Lincoln signed the proclamation and, as the *Hartford Courant* delighted to inform its readers, "a photostatic copy of an article in The Hartford Daily Courant of Sept. 24, 1862, which comments favorably on the proclamation."[56]

Connecticut's observance was, understandably, not as grand as the national commemoration that the cwcc held at the Lincoln Memorial, with speakers including President Kennedy (through the means of a carefully distancing pre-videotaped message), u.n. Ambassador Adlai Stevenson,

Governor Nelson Rockefeller, and poet Archibald MacLeish, with a musical performance by Mahalia Jackson.[57] Nevertheless, Connecticut's efforts were well received by a respectable crowd of participants and observers, even meriting a follow-up account in the *Courant*.[58] On the other hand, according to Cook's account, the aftermath of the national event was brutal; the cwcc felt that civil rights activists had co-opted the ceremony, and, in internal correspondence, "cwcc officials revealed their hostility toward rising black assertiveness, derisively referring to Bishop Williams as 'De Law'd' and 'Holy Daddy.'"[59] While Connecticut's observance ultimately did not appear to have such a disastrous backlash, the ccwcc was hardly above the racial tensions of the times.

In early 1963, the ccwcc was short five seats, one of them owing to the death, in June 1962, of Edward Lonergan, who had been instrumental in establishing the commission.[60] Republican State Chairman A. Searle Pinney called on Governor Dempsey to fill at least some of the available seats with "some of the state's distinguished Negros," pointing out that "[t]he Negro soldier . . . played an important role in the war between the states" and that it would only be appropriate for increased Negro participation in the ccwcc. Pinney even suggested a few specific "splendid citizens" for the positions.[61] Pinney's request inspired Robert Maule to write a letter to the editor in support of the idea that, "as a Negro" he felt that the lack of representation on the commission, and in other areas of public life in Connecticut, was "the complete fault of the so-called Negro Democratic leadership." His brief letter raised many points, including his belief that it was up to the "Negro community" to suggest people for the commission; it was also significant because it represented one of the very few letters to the editor that anyone bothered to write in regard to the ccwcc's work.[62] Eventually, Governor Dempsey named eight new members to the ccwcc, including one from Pinney's suggested list: John E. Rogers. At least one other black resident was selected, Daniel I. Fletcher. Because newspaper reports of the appointments gave only names, not racial affiliation, it is possible that some of the other appointees may also have been African American.[63] If such a gesture was insufficient to alleviate African American concerns about the ccwcc and the centennial itself, and it may not have been, the historical record does not indicate that anyone considered the matter worth further pursuit.

While not without their own difficulties, the ccwcc spent the Civil War centennial years largely toiling away in trying to increase public education about Connecticut's part in the Civil War, with lectures and publications for the general public, as well as commissioning John Niven's more scholarly volume. The historians did not have to "take control" of the ccwcc as they did of the cwcc; historians had been in control from the start.

On the last weekend in June 1965, the ccwcc participated in a final three-day event of commemoration and remembrance. While neither the *Hartford Times* nor the *Hartford Courant* reported on the event, which was attended by Governor Dempsey, the weekly *Shoreline Times* gave it a nice write-up on page 4.[64] The *New Haven Register* also reported briefly on the event.[65] The lack of coverage by the *Hartford Courant* gives one pause. Throughout the life of the ccwcc, the *Courant* had followed its progress fairly regularly. During 1961, it ran a series of sixteen articles about the Civil War in its weekly magazine section. But on May 30, 1965, the *Courant* declared the Civil War centennial to be over "with the final commemorative event to be sponsored by the capital's Civil War Centennial Commission."[66]

What, then, are the lessons that can be learned from studying all of these modes of Civil War commemoration? Those exercises that seemed to carry the most emotional urgency, unsurprisingly, were related directly to people whose experience of the Civil War was within living memory. Perhaps that so little fanfare was attached to the fiftieth anniversary of the start of the Civil War in 1911 was due to continued hard feelings between the two sides. Another possible explanation, given the fiftieth anniversary held at Gettysburg in 1913, which was attended by survivors of both sides, is that the Civil War was still enough a part of living memory that commemorating its start was not seen as particularly necessary at the time. People in Connecticut had spent forty-five years commissioning and dedicating monuments, observing Decoration Day, and remembering the Civil War as part of an ongoing national, regional, and local history; re-reporting on its start may have seemed redundant.

By the hundredth anniversary, however, the Civil War was no longer a living memory, and while in no danger of falling out of public awareness, it continued to be perceived as a point of contention between North and South. The national commemoration, which was meant to unify, ended up failing in that goal, as the civil rights movement highlighted ongoing problems of racial inequality, problems that Civil War centennial commissions, both national and state, ended up having to confront despite their efforts to avoid them. Sectional rancor was still alive and at times vitriolic. The ccwcc was spared some, if not all, of the drama that plagued the national cwcc, in large part because of its strong emphasis on research and education. Because the ccwcc began as an attempt to increase both interest in and research on Civil War topics, it managed to keep to its mission. As we are now in midst of the sesquicentennial of the Civil War and Connecticut has been engaged on many levels—academic, statewide, and locally—it remains to future historians to assess the focus, impact, and any controversy that arises in remembering an event that has and continues to shape the nation.

NOTES

1. Ernest F. Faehtz, compiler, *The National Memorial Day: A Record of Ceremonies over the Graves of the Union Soldiers*, May 29 and 30, 1869 (Washington, DC: Headquarters Grand Army of the Republic, 1870), 5, 1056–57.

2. "Decoration Day," *Hartford Courant*, May 28, 1868.

3. "The Soldiers' Graves," *Hartford Times*, May 29, 1868.

4. "Should Middletown Have a Monument?" *Middletown Sentinel and Witness*, April 9, 1872.

5. Cummings quoted in Ray Organek, "Monuments of Middletown," *Veterans' Corner*, November 24, 1996.

6. David Ransom, "Connecticut's Monuments: An Essay," Connecticut Historical Society, http://www.chs.org/finding_aides/ransom/overview1.thm.

7. "The Veterans' Day!," *Hartford Courant*, September 18, 1879.

8. "An Interesting Ceremonial," *Hartford Times*, September 16, 1879.

9. "The Battle Flags," *Hartford Times*, September 17, 1879.

10. History of Battle-Flag Day, September 17, 1879 (Hartford, CT: Lockwood & Merritt, 1879), 219.

11. "News of the State," *Hartford Courant*, July 4, 1884.

12. "The Fifth at Gettysburg," *Hartford Courant*, August 10, 1887.

13. "Off for Antietam," *Hartford Courant*, October 8, 1894.

14. Back from Antietam," *Hartford Courant*, October 16, 1894.

15. H. S. Stevens, *Souvenir of Excursions to Battlefields by the Society of the Fourteenth Connecticut Regiment and Reunion at Antietam, September, 1891: With History and Reminiscences of Battles and Campaigns of the Regiment on the Fields Revisited* (Washington, DC: Gibson Bros., 1893), 5, 64.

16. Bradford Paul Raymond, "Middletown in the Civil War," text of speech in unindexed archive at the Middlesex County Historical Society, Middletown, CT.

17. "Middletown in Review: Woodrow Wilson High School Pageant for the Tercentenary Celebration of Middletown," manuscript, Middletown Room Archives at Russell Library, Middletown, CT.

18. Editorial, *Hartford Courant*, April 12, 1911.

19. "Veterans Meet in Annual Reunion," *Hartford Courant*, April 13, 1911.

20. "Wilson Speaks at Gettysburg," *Hartford Courant*, April 13, 1911.

21. The *Chicago Tribune* did mention Lee's surrender in its daily "Fifty Years Ago Today . . ." feature on April 9, 1915, but the *Hartford Courant* did not have that sort of reminiscence column at the time, and it did not bother to run a special editorial or any other observance of the date.

22. Robert J. Cook, *Troubled Commemoration: The American Civil War Centennial, 1961–1965* (Baton Rouge: Louisiana State University Press, 2007), 15–30.

23. "Better to Pray: Civil War Centennial Deplored by Lutheran," *Hartford Courant*, June 3, 1961.

24. Rev. John B. Morris, "Letters to the Times," *New York Times*, June 1, 1959.

25. Although Morris did not identify this institutional affiliation in his letter, his work at the time has been documented: "Exhibit Honors a History of Civil Rights and Celebrates Donation of ESCRU Archives," April 3, 2003, Archives of the Episcopal Church, www.episcopalarchives.org/escru.org.

26. Morris, "Letters to the Times."

27. Robert Penn Warren, *The Legacy of the Civil War: Meditations on the Centennial* (New York: Random House, 1961), 1, 54, 59–64, 105.

28. David Donald, "When the Smoke of Battle Cleared, an Ideal Had Been Born," *New York Times*, May 14, 1961.

29. Charles Poore, "Books of the Times," *New York Times*, April 27, 1961.

30. Edmund Wilson, *Patriotic Gore: Studies in the Literature of the American Civil War* (New York: Oxford University Press, 1962), xxxi.

31. Charles Poore, "Books of the Times," *New York Times*, April 26, 1962.

32. Cook, *Troubled Commemoration*, 200–211.

33. Cook, *Troubled Commemoration*, 93 (Landers quoted), 107, 138–39.

34. Nevins quoted in Cook, *Troubled Commemoration*, 147.

35. "Six Appointed to State Group on Civil War," *Hartford Courant*, August 27, 1959.

36. "Putnam to Head Group on Civil War Centennial," *Hartford Courant*, January 21, 1960. The minutes of the meetings can be found in box 1 of the Connecticut Civil War Centennial Commission archives at the Connecticut State Library, Hartford. Hereafter referred to as CCWCC Archives.

37. Connecticut Civil War Centennial Commission, *The Connecticut Civil War Centennial: A Manual for Its Observance in the Towns and Cities of the State of Connecticut* (Hartford: Connecticut Civil War Centennial Commission, 1960), 7.

38. CCWCC, "The Connecticut Civil War Centennial," 7, 8, 21.

39. CCWCC, "The Connecticut Civil War Centennial," 10–12, 16, 20.

40. The town's participation and correspondence for the CCWCC can be found in CCWCC Archives, boxes 1 and 2.

41. "Annual Reports of the Middlesex County Historical Society, 1960–1969," Middlesex County Historical Society, Middletown, CT.

42. CCWCC Archives, box 2.

43. Although certainly anecdotal, after asking many people of the kind described in the body of the paper, the author has found few people who remember particular Civil War centennial–related activities, unlike other similar efforts, such

*as the Freedom Train or the American Revolution Bicentennial. This does not mean, of course, that they did not experience them.

44. Letter from William Mills Jr. to Rolling G. Osteweiss, ccwcc Archives, box 3.

45. ccwcc Archives, box 1.

46. John Niven, *Connecticut for the Union: The Role of the State in the Civil War* (New Haven, CT: Yale University Press, 1965); Matthew Warshauer, *Connecticut in the American Civil War: Slavery, Sacrifice, and Survival* (Middletown, CT: Wesleyan University Press, 2011).

47. "State Unit Asked to Skip Segregated Centennials," *Hartford Courant*, March 29, 1961.

48. Within given limitations, it is difficult to research precisely what each of the other thirty-five states that participated in the Civil War centennial commemoration produced. Searching sources like World Cat, however, indicates that most states produced only two or three pamphlets at most, usually a general history of the state in the Civil War, and one or two general reports on their commissions' specific activities. Ohio and Michigan, however, both produced more research-oriented pamphlets than Connecticut, and New Jersey only a few less.

49. ccwcc Archives, box 1.

50. "War Centennial Set as History Unit Topic," *Hartford Courant*, October 15, 1961.

51. "Committee Sets Talk, Exhibit on Civil War," *Hartford Courant*, May 11, 1962.

52. Cook, *Troubled Commemoration*, 148, 149.

53. Correspondence and Official Program, ccwcc Archives, box 1.

54. "Negro Women Slate Emancipation Rally," *Hartford Courant*, September 13, 1962.

55. "Old State House Fee Dropped for Parade," *Hartford Courant*, September 20, 1962.

56. "Exhibit to Mark Emancipation Proclamation," *Hartford Courant*, September 22, 1962. It is worth noting that the celebration of the proclamation actually focused on the announcement of Abraham Lincoln's Preliminary Emancipation Proclamation, which promised freedom to slaves on January 1, 1863, when the actual Emancipation Proclamation was issued.

57. "Kennedy and Stevenson Sound Call to Continue Human Rights Fight," *Hartford Courant*, September 23, 1962. For details on Kennedy's videotaped message, see Cook, *Troubled Commemoration*, 174–75.

58. "Parade, Program Commemorate the End of Slavery," *Hartford Courant*, September 23, 1962.

59. Cook, *Troubled Commemoration*, 178.

60. "Attorney E. J. Lonergan Dies; Held Federal Post," *Hartford Courant*, June 14, 1962.

61. "Dempsey Urged to Name Negroes to Commission," *Hartford Courant*, February 2, 1963.

62. "The People's Forum: Let Negroes Pick Their Own Leaders," *Hartford Courant*, February 8, 1963.

63. "Dempsey Names 8 to Civil War Centennial Group," *Hartford Courant*, September 28, 1963. See also Warshauer, *Connecticut in the American Civil War*, 216.

64. "Centennial Events Held under Clear Blue Skies," *Shoreline Times*, July 1, 1965.

65. "Colorful Ceremonies in Guilford Mark Civil War's Centennial," *New Haven Register*, July 27, 1965.

66. "Centennial Ends for Civil War," *Hartford Courant*, May 30, 1965.

9 : Teaching the Past's Perspective of the Past

CIVIL WAR REENACTORS

IN CONNECTICUT

n the novel *Meet John Trow* by Thomas Dyja, the protagonist, Steven Armour, gets roped into joining a living history organization portraying the Second Connecticut Heavy Artillery. At an event, he and another Union soldier named "Lummer" engaged with a young spectator.

A boy of six or seven shook Lummer's canteen. The old man leaned over. "You know, son, slavery wasn't really the cause of the Civil War; it was states' rights. No one cared about slavery; the men of the Second fought to preserve the Union. They don't teach that nowadays." Steven's stomach turned. As much as the men of the 2nd knew about their weapons, the history of the regiment, and the War in general, the lives of soldiers and the movements of the War, so too did many profoundly misread the larger movements of history. He walked over. "Son, I for one am completely in favor of emancipation of the African."[1]

Dyja's fictional dialogue involving two reenactors and a child raises two critical questions about Civil War reenactors in Connecticut, and the "hobby" overall. First, what does the public learn from reenactors (or "living historians," as some prefer to be called) when they attend battle reenactments and living history events? This includes those portraying soldiers as well as civilians. The second question is closely related to the first. How, or to what extent, do reenactors' opinions about the Civil War mesh with those of academic historians?

The public engages with American history, including the Civil War, in myriad ways. They learn about their past in school, to be sure, but films, documentaries, popular media, and public demonstrations like those in which reenactors participate influence the public long after their seventh-grade u.s. history class, which is often little more than a footnote in their lives. In particular, Civil War reenactors have been educating the public for decades. The practice began in the 1800s and became more popular with America's centennial celebration in the early 1960s.[2]

Today, reenactors engage the public in Connecticut and around the country in battle reenactments both large and small, as well as in local, living history presentations. Reenactors may know a great deal about the Civil War from an experiential encampment perspective and may certainly be well-read, yet they are not professionally trained in historical methodology and rarely know the wider historiography of Civil War studies. In other words, historians know what other scholars have written over a long period of time, regarding many facets of the war, and have been trained to critically analyze the arguments. Still, academic historians rarely engage the public in ways that draw the kinds of sizable audiences that reenactors have the opportunity to influence. Hundreds and often thousands will attend Civil War encampments and spend time speaking with these living historians of the war period. Who, then, has the greater influence on the public's perception of the war?[3]

Considering that reenactors have the potential to be more influential than all but the most well-known academic historians, it is important to know what reenactors focus on when they teach the public. This includes their opinions on the causes of the war, the motivations of soldiers of the period, and other relevant topics. Is there a divide between the reenactors who engage the public, and historians who research and write professionally about the Civil War? Is what the public learns from attending reenactments and/or living history events "accurate" in terms of modern scholarship on the Civil War?

Civil War reenactors are a diverse lot, and even when a study is focused on a relatively small geographic area like Connecticut, one finds a kaleidoscope of opinions. The totality of the evidence though, sheds some light on these issues. On balance, Civil War reenactors in Connecticut, including those who portray both Union and Confederate, present a version of the Civil War that has more in common with the academic scholarship of fifty years ago than with the scholarship of today. Moreover, just as the scholarship prevalent during the Civil War centennial contains both strengths and weaknesses, so to do the reflections of Civil War reenactors in Connecticut. Connecticut reenactors focus heavily on the military side of the war (which should come as little surprise), with a secondary emphasis on the contributions of civilians, and the public can learn much about life during the Civil War era in these regards. In addition, reenactors' opinions on the motivations of Civil War soldiers are accurate, at least on the surface, when judged against what modern scholars have written.

Connecticut reenactors' approach also contains weaknesses. For one, although their opinions on what motivated Civil War soldiers are generally accurate, they often miss many of the nuances, especially with regard to how slavery acted as a motivator for Confederate soldiers. Reenactors, especially those portraying Confederates, also seem to underestimate the role slavery played in causing the war. Furthermore, though there are exceptions, Connecticut reenactors' focus on the lives of soldiers (with less emphasis on the causes and legacy of the war) places them in line with historians like Shelby Foote and John Niven, who both wrote around the time of the Civil War centennial. In part because of this military-centric focus, reenactors fall into what historian David Blight has called the reconciliationist tradition. This divide between what historians teach and what reenactors teach is at least in some part due to the fact that reenactors are more influenced by Civil War fiction or firsthand regimental histories or memoirs than by modern, academic histories.[4]

As a way of bridging this reenactor-historian divide, and to alleviate some of the internal problems associated with the hobby, both groups might consider the creation of a national umbrella organization, comprising both Union and Confederate groups. Such an organization may help build on the strengths that reenactors bring to the subject, bring them up to date on some of the latest research on the more nuanced and complicated aspects of slavery and the war, and, importantly, get some historians out of their offices and out into the public arena where a great deal of learning can take place. As much as reenactors might be educated by academic historians, scholars too have a great deal to learn from the experience and realism that living historians bring to an encampment.

Reenactors are not easy to study. Unlike the actual Civil War soldiers, there are not many written sources available. Perhaps for his reason, there is little scholarship on reenactors, and none that has focused on Connecticut in particular. The historiography of Civil War memory, or the study of how Americans, as opposed to historians, view and interpret the Civil War, is extensive, though the majority does not pertain to reenactors.[5]

To help fill this gap in historical scholarship, this chapter relies on two principal sources. The websites of reenacting groups themselves are one important source, but the most important resource was a survey conducted between November 17 and December 2, 2011. A total of

*Members of a Union reenacting regiment at Stanley Quarter Park, in New Britain,
Connecticut, part of the inaugural weekend encampment that began the 150th
anniversary commemoration of the Civil War. Courtesy of Matthew Warshauer*

102 reenactors from Connecticut and New England responded. Of these,
seventy-eight were either members of a Union reenacting group or identified themselves with the Union side. Twenty-four respondents were members of a Confederate group or identified themselves with the Confederacy. In the process of explaining the results of the research, a number of
prominent academic historians will be utilized to compare and contrast
the views of the two camps.[6]

It should be noted that reenactors were divided over whether they preferred the term "reenactor" or "living historian." This question is significant because of the differences in the connotation of the terms. "Reenactor" implies that the person engages in reenacting specific events, such
as battles; it sounds very participant-centered, as if they do what they
do for their own enjoyment and education. "Living historian" carries a
much broader and more professional-sounding connotation, and it implies a greater focus on educating the general public. Of those surveyed,
54 percent preferred the term "reenactor," while 46 percent liked "living
historian."[7]

At least one professional historian, Glenn LaFantasie, has taken umbrage with the term "living historian." "I've never understood why reenac-

Confederate reenactor, Colonel Joseph Pereira, Liberty Greys, Sixth Regiment,
First Division, Army of Northern Virginia. Courtesy of Matthew Warshauer

tors dislike being called reenactors," LaFantasie says. "They almost universally claim to be 'living historians' engaged in 'living history.' But I find these terms mystifying. For one thing, I think that I am a living historian; if not, someone should inform my loved ones of my passing." Even accepting LaFantasie's attempt at humor, his wider argument about reenactors is misguided. The majority, albeit a slight one, not only does not mind the term "reenactor," but prefers it. In addition, no one in the survey made any particular comments disputing either term.[8]

Reenactment groups from throughout the state engage in a variety of public events. Battle reenactments, of course, figure prominently. The Eleventh Connecticut Regiment, Company A is a representative example. The Central Connecticut State University Sesquicentennial encampment and reenactment on April 17–18, 2011, as well as the 150th anniversary reenactment of the Battle of Bull Run in July and Balls Bluff in September (the latter two held in Virginia) were listed on the Eleventh Regiment's events calendar for 2011. Yet the group also worked with the public at living history events, such as Camp Dutton in Litchfield, Connecticut, on May 14, 2011, and another at a school in Ridgefield on June 14, 2011. At such events, units typically engage in various drill and firing demonstrations, as well as set up a tented camp for the public to experience. Fires are going, food is often being cooked, and period games and music might be present. These are important events at which reenactors interact with the public, discuss a wide variety of topics with people, and often answer questions.[9]

Educating the public is, in fact, and important goal for reenactors. A plurality, 46 percent, said the primary reason they reenact is to educate the public. This ranked well ahead of honoring an ancestor (25 percent), or a desire to replicate the experience of soldiers (20 percent). Only 5 percent responded that their primary motivation was to spend time with others who share a common interest.[10]

Of the advantages that Civil War reenactors bring to the table when they interact with the public, their dedication to accurately portraying the military side of the war and the contributions of civilians of the period ranks highest. Indeed, when asked to briefly summarize what they wanted the public to learn about the Civil War, the most common response from both Union and Confederate reenactors related to the ordinary lives of soldiers and civilians. One Union reenactor from Massachusetts said he wanted the public to understand that "beyond the musketry and cannon they [Civil War soldiers] were real people with real families and real

Confederate reenactor cannon crew from the Richmond Howitzers.
Courtesy of Matthew Warshauer

dreams." Similarly, his favorite aspect of reenacting was "[p]ortraying a particular individual and conveying his story to spectators as well as other reenactors."[11] Nor are many doing this merely for their own enjoyment; they want to *teach* other people about those lives. One Union man said he enjoyed "[b]ringing life in the past to the people of the future." A Confederate from Massachusetts noted he "would like to remind people that this war was fought by citizen soldiers, the men next door, and that the damage of the war extended to every community in this Nation."[12]

If reenactors' primary focus is on the battle-oriented war experience, there are also a significant number who go to great lengths to re-create and teach the public about the home front and the challenges people faced there. One Confederate respondent from Connecticut taught for a time at a living history museum. She portrays a Confederate civilian, and elaborated on what she hoped to teach the public: "The soldiers fought in towns and cities and not just the wilderness. That there were civilians living in those towns and cities and that most civilians did not follow the armies around."[13] A Union respondent from Vermont specifically sought out women and children as her target audiences, saying her favorite aspect of reenacting was "[t]alking with people, more importantly the women, because a lot of the times, they are 'dragged' there by the hubby, so I make

Female reenactors take their attention to detail very seriously, and many are quite knowledgeable not only about the home front, but also about the lives of particular women from the Civil War era. From left to right: Carol Deleppo, Kathy Schmidt, Mary Lou Pavlik, and Marie Rogers, with Kevin Johnson as Private William Webb of Connecticut's Twenty-Ninth Regiment. Courtesy of Matthew Warshauer

it more personal for them. I like to make it real for them. I will tell them stories about lesser known people [or] kids of the Civil War, the stories you don't hear every day."[14]

A few respondents underscored not only the role reenactors play in educating the public but also the general and disturbing lack of knowledge the general public has about Civil War history. Profoundly, one woman enjoyed the "light that shines" in the eyes of people who "connect with their sense of history," and said, "If you have ever attended a large reenactment—you will discover how little Americans know about their own history—I've heard, 'Which ones are the British?,' 'Who won?' as an example."[15]

Such comments indicate the important role reenactors play in educating the public. Many spectators are attending reenactments and living histories with, perhaps an interest in history, but very little in the way of detailed knowledge. They often come out for entertainment but walk away with much more. Many reenactors go to great lengths in the effort to offer accurate presentations. One Massachusetts Union reenactor said that what he does is "a combination of educating the public BY experiencing the conditions of soldiers. One informs the other."[16]

Though the desire to educate is broadly shared, reenactors are often divided over their perceived degree of dedication to historical accuracy. On one hand are those who consider themselves "hardcore," or as some prefer, "progressive." These terms generally mean that they take historical accuracy very seriously. One of the best books to convey this outlook is Tony Horowitz's Pulitzer Prize–winning *Confederates in the Attic: Dispatches from the Unfinished Civil War*. When Horowitz attended an overnight camping excursion with a group of hardcore Confederate living historians, as they preferred to be called, he got an education about the lengths to which some will go to make their impression as authentic as possible. Horowitz wrote, "Young tossed me scratchy wool trousers, a filthy shirt, hobnailed boots, a jacket tailored for a Confederate midget, and wool socks that smelled as though they hadn't been washed since second Manassas. . . . Finally, he slung a thin blanket over my shoulder. 'We'll probably be spooning tonight.' He said." Later, one of the reenactors demonstrated how good he was at "bloating," which involved making himself look like a puffed-up corpse. Important to note is that this camping experience was not for the public. It was solely about personal enjoyment, historical authenticity, and thereby connecting with another time in American history.[17]

This desire for authenticity, at least as far as army accoutrements and camp life are concerned, is highly prized by many reenactors in Connecticut, with some willing to sacrifice comfort in the name of historical accuracy. Some 46 percent of the survey respondents identified themselves as "hardcore" or "progressive." In addition to issues like travel and cost of equipment, many survey respondents listed chores performed in the daily life of soldiers as aspects of the hobby they found most unpleasant. Still, there are some elements that some reenactors bear grudgingly. One Union man said his least favorite aspect of reenacting was "[s]leeping on the hard ground in dog tents during stormy weather." Another took umbrage at "the Heat," while another Connecticut Unionist disliked "eating hardtack."[18] Such responses surely could fit within the realm of historical authenticity, as Civil War soldiers often wrote home about the very same complaints.

The second reenactor category is known as "mainstream," which made up 49 percent of the respondents, and includes those who make sure that what the public sees is period-correct, but strict historical inaccuracies that are out of sight do not necessarily bother them. Look in some reenactor tents and one may find a hidden cooler or even a gas-powered portable heater for cold nights. A seemingly small issue for some, such modern accoutrements create controversy and debate among others. One Confederate reenactor from Maine objected to "[m]ilitary camps with more equipment than a tractor trailer can haul (less is more)." Another said he did not like "[p]articipating in poorly done (fake) battle demonstration[s]." Similarly, a Massachusetts Union respondent took umbrage with the "[l]ack of military discipline when on parade."[19] Some respondents were critical of those who were overly critical. One Massachusetts reenactor wrote, "I'm a big guy . . . and don't look like a starving private in the Union Army. There are some who really don't like this and let it be known. Authenticity at all costs. Which I believe to a certain point. But I would never make comments that I have heard. These are very few by the way."[20]

These issues of historical authenticity debated by the reenactors themselves is, perhaps, more hotly contested outside the community, by academic historians. Glenn LaFantasie has questioned both the authenticity and efficacy of battle reenactments. "In the first place, these pretend battles look and sound nothing like the real thing, although reenactors have convinced the public (and themselves) that they do. In the second place, these theatricals lose every bit of authenticity the moment the demonstration draws to a close and the faux dead and wounded on the field rise up in a mass resurrection resembling the Rapture, which is usually accompanied by the applause of the onlookers."[21] LaFantasie is, of course, correct. There is no way to truly recreate a Civil War battle. Reenactors, with both muskets and artillery, fire only partial gunpowder charges, and, thankfully, no one is bloodied or killed in the re-creations. Soldiers who "take hits" on the battlefield do indeed rise again and, as LaFantasie notes, often to the applause of onlookers. In many ways, that alone can be disconcerting for some who abhor war and shudder that spectators would applaud grown men making entertainment out of death.

Yet LaFantasie misses the more important point. Although the battles can never be perfectly accurate, they nonetheless offer the public a window into another period of time. It is something more than they can get in books and still images. Civil War historian Matthew Warshauer, the cochair of the Connecticut Civil War Commemoration Commission, has discussed this issue, noting that there is most certainly a "circus-like aspect to the encampments, especially the battle reenactments. What I mean is that people come out to be entertained by what to some is fantastic in almost a bizarre way. They've never seen anything like it before and they become entranced. Yet the real key is that their entertainment leads to interest, and interest may just lead to a teachable moment. Spectators walk away from their experience with an appreciation for the reenactors and a desire to learn more. That's the key." Historian Robert Isham added that reenactors are "a vital scholastic bridge that can connect the public to the 150th [anniversary of the Civil War]. An oft-quoted maxim of tutelage usually attributed to Confucius reads: 'I read and I forget. I see and I remember. I do and I understand.'" He noted further that scholarly histories are not, and perhaps should not be, the first step on the road to historical enlightenment but rather an end point. "Perhaps re-enacting is not really history," he said, "but it establishes a person's primordial connection with history." In other words, reenacting is "the first step" that average people experience, and it leads them to pick up a scholarly book and learn about the period.[22]

Reenactors' desire for historical authenticity also extends beyond their military uniforms, accoutrements, and camp life. Most also accurately portray the motivations of Civil War soldiers accurately when judged against what modern historians have written. The reenactor survey contained two questions asking respondents to identify the causes for which Union and Confederate soldiers fought. For each, several choices were given, and they could choose as many as they thought applied. Two additional questions asked responders to name their "most important" motive.

The range of choices offered to identify the causes for which men fought were based on the research of professional historians. Certainly the best such study is James M. McPherson's *For Cause and Comrades: Why Men Fought in the Civil War*, for which he studied more than twenty-five thousand Union and Confederate soldiers' letters and diaries. In fact, McPherson consciously avoided soldiers' accounts or memoirs published after the war. "They suffer from a critical defect," he wrote. "[T]hey were meant for publication. Their authors consciously or subconsciously constructed their narratives with a public audience in mind. Accounts written after the war present an additional problem of potential distortion by faulty memory or hindsight." McPherson strongly believed that if an accurate picture of what soldiers thought during the war is desired, one has to look at what they wrote in the midst of the conflict.[23]

McPherson also insisted that in addition to the bonds forged between soldiers in combat, men on both sides were motivated by a variety of

Connecticut reenactor color guard combined from several Federal Army reenacting units—the Second Connecticut Heavy Artillery, Eighth Connecticut Volunteer Infantry, Eleventh Connecticut Volunteer Infantry, and Fourteenth Connecticut Volunteer Infantry, Company G—at the 125th anniversary rededication of the Soldiers' and Sailors' Memorial Arch, September 17, 2011, Bushnell Park, Hartford. Courtesy of John Callahan

ideological causes that are largely absent from published accounts written decades after the war. For Union soldiers, they included values like patriotism, liberty, and of course, Union, all of which were intermeshed. McPherson wrote of one soldier who encompassed all three: "'I do not want to live,'" the soldier said, "'if our free Nation is to die or be broken [by] . . . the foul hand of treason.'" He fought for his "Nation" (patriotism), which is "free" (liberty), against it being "broken" (Union). One survey respondent, a Union reenactor, summarized McPherson's point nicely: "Based on extensive research of soldiers' letters home Union and patriotism are the causes I have seen documented the most in their own words. . . . Cause and comrades in McPherson's words."[24]

If there was one central theme for northern soldiers, according to McPherson, it was saving the Union. This was especially true for Connecticut soldiers. Warshauer argues precisely this in *Connecticut in the*

American Civil War: Slavery, Sacrifice and Survival. "What exactly was the glorious cause?" he asked. "For many, the answer was simple: the preservation of the Union." Indeed, 91 percent of Union respondents identified "to save the Union" as a motivation for Union soldiers. Of equal import was the second-most-common response: "they thought it was their patriotic duty," which was mentioned by 69 percent of respondents; the third-most-common response was, "They didn't want to let their comrades down."[25]

Such results might come as a great relief to one prominent historian. In a study of how the Civil War has been portrayed through film and art, Gary Gallagher noted that of the many possible Civil War themes, the cause of Union was the most inconspicuous in films. "No recent film," said Gallagher, "captures the abiding devotion to Union that animated soldiers and civilians in the North." Similarly, Earl Hess wrote that preserving "the republican heritage of the United States . . . was a potent force in mobilizing the Northern Population." Gallagher postulated that "most Americans take their form of government for granted and cannot imagine an internal threat of the kind that galvanized the northern people in 1861. . . . Yet anyone who does not appreciate that untold citizens believed Confederate independence would scuttle the American experiment in democracy cannot grasp what was going on in the North." Considering the survey results for those identifying themselves as Union reenactors, and in particular one who wrote that the most important Union motivation was "To keep the United States, united," or simply "Preservation of the union," it seems reasonable to conclude the today's reenactors have a solid grasp of why the men they portray went off to war.[26]

When it came to the motivations of Confederate soldiers, McPherson argued, "The urge to defend home and hearth that had impelled so many Southerners to enlist in 1861 took on greater urgency when large-scale invasions became a reality in 1862." A Tennessee captain after the Battle of Shiloh said "that his men were 'now more fully determined than ever before to sacrifice their lives, if need be, for the invaded soil of their bleeding country.'"[27] Connecticut reenactors also identified the defense of home and family as the primary Confederate motivation. Some 35 percent of respondents said that "to protect homes and families" was the Confederate soldier's primary concern. This was answer was given more than any other for the single question of motivation. One Confederate reenactor from Massachusetts, who was born and raised in the South, said, "I think that prior to the Civil War there was not an emphasis on 'the United States,' but rather an emphasis on 'home.' For that reason I believe the Confederate soldier fought to protect his home from what he believed were invading forces." Still, when asked to list all motivations, the defense of home and family placed a close second behind "State's Rights."[28]

Although reenactors in Connecticut and wider New England get soldiers' motivations right on the surface, one weakness is that they sometimes miss nuances presented by scholars. This is especially true with regard to how slavery motivated Confederate soldiers. Herein lies one clear difference between reenactors and modern, academic historians. A minority of Union respondents (30 percent) listed protection of slavery and white supremacy as one of the causes that motivated Confederates, and only four respondents (out of seventy-eight) thought it was the primary motivator. The responses of Confederate reenactors were even more lopsided. A mere 8 percent (two out of twenty-four) thought that the protection of slavery and white supremacy was a motivator for southern soldiers; not a single Confederate respondent thought it was the most important motivation. One announced plainly that it "was not the reason most of the soldiers fought." Even some Union reenactors held such views. "The average Johnny [Confederate soldier] didn't own slaves and didn't give a hang about that," responded one Union reenactor from Connecticut. "He was fighting for his home and because the Yankees invaded the South."[29]

Two prominent scholars of Civil War soldiers' motivations disagree with reenactors on this point. McPherson, in his study of unpublished letters and diaries of soldiers, said, "Indeed, white supremacy and the right of property in slaves were at the core of the ideology for which Confederate soldiers fought." Even non-slaveowners sometimes employed proslavery or white supremacist rhetoric. "I never want to see the day when a negro is put on an equality with a white person," quoted McPherson from one Louisiana artillerymen. "There is too many free niggers . . . now to suit me, let alone having four millions." McPherson identified only 20 percent of Confederates' letters and diaries expressing such views but pointed out that slavery was so engrained into southern consciousness that "[t]hey took slavery for granted as one of the 'southern rights' and institutions for which they fought, and did not feel compelled to discuss it." Historian Aaron Sheehan-Dean concurred with McPherson's assessment, noting, "The scarcity of references to slavery as an explicit motivating factor should not mask the fact that fighting to defend Virginia meant fighting to defend slavery." He noted further that as the war dragged on, "most [Confederate soldiers] became more committed to preserving slavery and expressed that through their eager capture of runaway slaves for return to masters."[30]

Historian Chandra Manning, like McPherson, relied primarily on un-published letters and diaries from the Civil War years, and also examined regimental newspapers in order to investigate soldiers' attitudes, focusing in particular on how both sides viewed slavery. She insisted that "no mat-ter which side of the divide a Civil War soldier stood on, he knew that the heart of the threat, and the reason that the war came, was the other side's stance on slavery." Such an assertion addresses a common misconception held by many in the general public, including reenactors.[31]

In actuality, it is easy to embrace the belief that most southerners had little explicit interest in slavery. The vast majority owned no slaves, had no direct economic ties to the institution, and no motivation to fight for someone else's property. Yet Manning accurately pointed out that "[s]lavery supplied an unambiguous mechanism of race control in a region where 40 percent of the population was black. Non-slaveholding Confederate soldiers' willingness to fight for slavery grew from a much deeper source than the calculation of economic interest to be expected among those who owned slaves. It grew from white southern men's gut-level conviction that survival—of themselves, their families, and the social order—depended on slavery's continued existence." In other words, the desire to protect their homes and families, which many reenactors regarded correctly as the most important of all Confederate motives, was itself enmeshed in the slave culture, and thus they perceived in the war a threat to that way of life. Many reenactors either miss this nuance or argue against it.[32]

Moreover, when reenactors consistently respond that states' rights was a key motivating factor for Confederate soldiers, they go against what modern scholars argue. Some 86 percent of respondents said that "state's rights" was a primary issue, even more so than "protection of home and family." Neither McPherson nor Manning had much to say about soldiers' dedication to states' rights; indeed, the term does not even show up in the index of either book. On the other hand, McPherson listed "slavery," "ven-geance," "liberty," and "duty" in his index.[33]

Another motive that reenactors underrated is the degree of contempt in which Civil War soldiers held their opponents. Only six respondents (all Union) identified "hatred of the South" as one of the motivators for northern soldiers, while fifteen respondents (again, all Union) believed that Confederates were motivated by hatred of the North. In actuality, McPherson insisted, hatred and bitterness were significant factors, espe-cially for Confederates. One Confederate artilleryman described with un-restrained jubilation the results at the Battle of Fredericksburg, where

Union soldiers were mowed down. "[I] enjoyed the sight of hundreds of dead Yankees. Saw much of the work I had done in the way of severed limbs, decapitated bodies, and mutilated remains of all kinds. Doing my soul good."[34] McPherson utilizes many such quotes. It seems reenactors underestimate, or at least downplay, this as an important motivation of, especially, Confederate soldiers.

Another point of interest in considering Civil War reenactors is that their priorities and views regarding the causes of the war are somewhat dated. Although reenactors do hold some common ground with modern historians, as has been discussed, they have more in common with the scholars of fifty years ago than the academics of today. The proof is in their priorities: both modern reenactors as well as historians writing near the time of the war's centennial were primarily focused on the military elements of the conflict. Survey respondents overwhelmingly listed the military as their favorite aspect of the Civil War, with 75 percent listing it as the most interesting aspect of the conflict. "Civilian" placed a distant second, with 17 percent. Subjects like the "Constitution," "Slavery," and "Politics" garnered a mere 5 votes out of the 102 who took part in the study. What is more, when asked to name the person "from the Antebellum or Civil War period" whom they most admired, the vast majority of respondents chose generals or other military figures. Although twenty-three did not answer the question, and the single most popular person was Abraham Lincoln (twenty votes, nineteen of them Union reenactors); forty-nine answered with Robert E. Lee, Joshua Chamberlain, or another military leader.[35]

The knowledge of and interest in the military side of war is certainly not a bad thing. Yet there is a vast history that leads up to the war, through it, and well after it that far exceeds the need for such a military-centric approach to engaging the conflict. This heavy reliance on combat and armies provides an incomplete picture and more accurately reflects the heavily military-focused scholarship of a half-century ago. Take, for example, the very popular three-volume history of the war by Shelby Foote, which was published between 1958 and 1974. Foote's massive tome is easily accessible to readers, and anyone looking for a narrative of the conflict will find an engaging story. Yet of the nearly three thousand pages, only a scant few engage the conflict's causes. In contrast, the Gettysburg campaign is told over 153 pages.[36]

In fact, Foote fell into much the same trap that many reenactors do today with regard to Confederate motivations. In his award-winning documentary *The Civil War*, Ken Burns related the story of a Confederate private who was asked what he was fighting for, and who responded wryly, "I'm fighting because you're down here." Foote deemed it "a pretty satisfactory answer." It is little surprise, then, that so many Confederate reenactors listed protection of home as a leading motivator, and one re-enactor wrote that the most important factor for Confederate soldiers was "[k]eepin' you northern invaders out."[37]

Connecticut historians writing near the time of the Civil War centennial took an approach similar to Foote's. John Niven, who published *Connecticut for the Union: The Role of the State in the Civil War* in 1965, is probably the best example of a scholar whose view of the war is most like that of today's Connecticut reenactors. As the title suggests, Niven's goal was to detail the contributions of Connecticut in the Union war effort. He made little attempt to explain to readers the underlying causes of the war, and the lack of discussion on slavery is conspicuous.[38] Even modern scholars who appreciate the important role the reenactors play in educating the public express concern over the dominating military focus. Historian Robert Isham, who wrote that reenactors are a "vital scholastic bridge" connecting with the 150th anniversary of the conflict, criticized their preoccupation with military matters to the exclusion of the larger meaning of the war, and noted that it caused them to misunderstand the war's key cause. "When it comes to educating the public, reenactors fail dismally," he said. Despite the benefits they bring to the table, Isham doubted whether reenactors would "say the correct thing" when asked a crucial question about the war's causes. "I cannot count how many times I have seen an interested spectator witness a flawless drill done by a Civil War re-enactment unit, then hold a rifle under a reenactor's supervision, ask question after question about the uniform and equipment, and then ask a reenactor: 'So what was all this about? Why did the nation fight the Civil War?' The reenactor, who to that point has put on an A+ performance, will then offer a deplorably uneducated answer about states' rights or tariffs, an answer that could have been contrived by any modern-day neo-Confederate society."[39]

How true is Isham's assessment as far as Connecticut reenactors are concerned? It is difficult to say. When one begins to look at how reenactors portray the broader picture of the war, and slavery's role in inaugurating it, it is difficult to accurately gauge the reenactors' opinions. This is largely due to a critical flaw in the survey itself. When asked how important the issue of slavery was in bringing on the conflict, respondents were given four choices. Slavery was either, "the most important cause," "somewhat important," "not very important," or "it was of no importance." Having only these four choices did not provide the best potential data. Specifically, the choice "somewhat important" is too vague, and the last two choices are far too similar. It would have been better to list five choices, as follows: "the only important cause," "the most important of several causes," "it was one of several causes of equal importance," "it was only a minor cause," and finally, "it was of no importance." It might also have been helpful to add a follow-up question asking respondents to elaborate on other salient issues that caused the war.[40]

Because of this flaw, conclusions about reenactors' beliefs regarding the importance of slavery are not entirely clear. Among reenactors, 31 respondents (out of 102) regarded slavery as the most important cause that started the war. Most striking was that of these, 29 were Union. The major problem is that 62 percent of respondents said that slavery was "somewhat important," which leaves a great deal of ambiguity. "Somewhat important" can mean different things to different people. It could mean that it was simply one of many causes, or it could mean that it was significant but ranked behind other, more important ones.

That being said, two conclusions are supported by the data. First, Union reenactors regard slavery as a more important issue than do their Confederate counterparts. This jibes with the fact that Union reenactors were far more likely to think that protecting slavery and white supremacy was a factor that motivated Confederates.[41] Some Confederate respondents were adamant in their belief that slavery was, at the very least, not *the* central issue of the conflict. One Confederate reenactor from Connecticut said he would like the public to learn from his organization that "Confederates were not all slaveowners and THAT was not the ONLY reason the war was fought" (emphasis in original). Another Confederate, from Massachusetts, disliked "[h]aving to justify why I portray a Confederate soldier when all they were doing was trying to perpetuate slavery!" A third Confederate, from Vermont, said he wanted the public to learn that "slavery was NOT the main issue of the war, the Yankee soldier was NOT fighting to free the slaves, and Lincoln used Emancipation as a political tool!" (emphasis in original).[42]

These three Confederate reenactors might give different answers if asked to elaborate on the importance of slavery in causing the war. The third respondent, certainly, did not regard slavery as an important issue; nevertheless, all three said the slavery issue was "somewhat important." Again, more clarity in the survey itself might have yielded clearer answers.

Additionally, although many Union reenactors believed that Confederate soldiers, on balance, did not fight to protect slavery, none felt compelled to elaborate, as some Confederates did, on the relative importance of slavery with regard to the cause of the war, regardless of whether they said it was "most important" or "somewhat important."

The second conclusion that the survey results support is that reenactors, as a whole, do not regard slavery with as much interest or think it is as important an issue, or a key cause, as modern scholars do. In this sense, they are, once again, presenting a Shelby Foote/John Niven version of the war. The view that slavery was not an important cause of secession is the result of what historian Sean Wilentz called, "one of the most consequential acts of falsification in American history," a strategy undertaken by Confederate leaders after the war.[43] Pulitzer Prize–winning historian Eric Foner argued that antislavery (not to be confused with abolitionism) was the dominant political ideology of the North. He said, ". . . southerners were coming more and more consciously to insist on slavery as the very basis of civilized life," and that "northerners came to view slavery as the antithesis of the good society." McPherson too, whose one-volume history of the war is regarded as the gold-standard of Civil War histories, spends close to three hundred pages detailing the causes that led to the conflict; quarrels over slavery's expansion figure prominently. "Everything," he insisted, "stemmed from the slavery issue."[44]

In short, Connecticut reenactors hold a view of the Civil War that is much closer to an earlier generation of historians. Both focus on the military and contributions of soldiers and civilians. They often miss, however, some of the nuances of soldiers' motivations, and they tend to downplay the slavery issue. What this translates into is that many reenactors, who identify educating the public as one of their main interests, are presenting what historian David W. Blight refers to as a "reconciliationist" version of the Civil War. Blight argues that in the decades following the Civil War, three competing versions, or memories, of the Civil War competed with one another. The emancipationist view identified slavery as the war's root cause and emancipation as its principal legacy. There was also the reconciliationist view, whose advocates sought to forget the political and social causes of the war, especially race and slavery, and focused instead on honoring soldiers and generals of both sides. Finally, the white supremacist vision sought to maintain as much of the antebellum, white supremacist social order as it could.[45]

In the end, argues Blight, white supremacists "locked arms with reconciliationists of many kinds, and by the turn of the century delivered the country a segregated memory of its Civil War on Southern terms." This was not just a southern phenomenon. Blight emphasized that the entire nation had to choose between "*healing* and *justice*," which meant Americans could heal the sectional divide between northern and southern whites *or* do justice for African Americans by recognizing the evils of slavery and advocating social and political equality. In the end, white Americans chose to honor the soldiers of both sides and remember the war as a great drama of American history in which both sides fought nobly and no one was to blame. At the same time, the causes and broader meaning of the war were swept under the rug. Matthew Warshauer applies this idea to Connecticut in great detail in *Connecticut in the American Civil War*.[46] Blight noted that this spirit of reconciliation manifested itself in the postwar era as veterans on both sides "relived and remade those experiences [during the war]; they reassembled the chaos and loss inherent to war into an order they could now control. While doing so, they cleaned up the battles and campaigns of the real war, rendered it exciting and normal all at once, and made it difficult to face the extended, political meanings of the war."[47]

Reconciliationist sentiments reveal themselves in the survey results. In addition to the similar preoccupation with the military aspect of the war and underrating the hatred felt by both sides during the conflict, as well as the role of slavery in causing the war, a spirit of "brother versus brother" exists among many reenactors on both sides. The key idea that both sides should be honored was an important theme for many. One Confederate respondent said, "That we were all Americans and the war wasn't just about slavery." In the same way, a Union respondent said that "the men and women who fought the war did what they did because they believed in what they were doing."[48]

Not all reenactors expressed reconcilationist sentiment. There are some who would fall into the emancipationist camp, principally those who thought that slavery, the most heated topic of debate, was the most important cause of the war. One Union respondent regarded slavery as the key issue of the war, writing, "The public should understand the reasons why the conflict occurred, what issues it resolved, and what issues (such as racism) persist today." On the Confederate side, the reenactor quoted earlier who disliked having to justify why he portrays a Confederate took a nuanced view of the conflict while acknowledging the role slavery played in bringing on the war. "While slavery was a very important issue in the mid-1800s, and is the reason that many states seceded, the war itself was fought over the right of those states to secede."[49]

There are a number of possible reasons for why reenactors tend to fall into the reconciliationist memory tradition. The most obvious factor correlates with the side they portray. More Union reenactors than Confederate, as was shown, regarded slavery as the most important cause. One can only speculate as to why, but one possible reason is that they view slavery and racism as purely "southern" problems, rather than as the national issues that they are and remain.

There are also very real logistical, local political factors. Reenactors pay hundreds of dollars for equipment and uniforms to encamp and reenact battles. Both sides have to work together to hold events, and things could quickly degenerate into heated shouting matches if the causes of the war were constantly at the forefront.

Another possibility is the contemporary political views of reenactors. According to the survey, reenactors, regardless of what side they portray, lean fairly strongly to the right. When asked how they would describe their political views, 51 percent indicated they were "conservative" or "very conservative," while 31 percent described themselves as "moderate." Only 16 percent listed themselves as "liberal" or "very liberal," and 2 percent were unsure. The results of the survey do not, however, reveal an especially strong link between political views and outlook on the cause of the Civil War. Those who believed slavery was the most important cause stretched across the political spectrum. Liberals, however, were more likely to identify slavery as the most important cause than were conservatives, with eleven of sixteen liberals identifying this belief.[50]

Reenactors may also adopt a more reconciliationist tradition as a result of popular films. For example, of the seven respondents who said that *Gods and Generals* did the best job of portraying the Civil War era, only one of them thought that slavery was the most important cause. Of the twenty-three who liked the film *Gettysburg*, five thought slavery was the most important cause. Finally, a noteworthy eight of twelve respondents who thought *Glory* was the best Civil War film also said slavery was the most important cause of the war.[51] Hardly conclusive determinations, the results are nonetheless interesting correlations. Within this circumstantial vein, though equally interesting, is the Union respondent who said of soldiers on both sides that "in the end was the fact that they fought for each other," which sounds suspiciously like Joshua Chamberlain's *Gettysburg* character who says, "In the end, we're fighting for each other."

The most likely origin of reenactors' outlook on the Civil War is what might be called their "source material." More so than films, books are seen as *sources* of information and learning, and just as historians' conclusions are influenced, at least in part, by the sources they employ, so too are re-enactors' opinions. This correlation between sources and memory tradition can be seen to some degree with reenactors. Not surprisingly, those who listed a modern, academic title as their favorite Civil War book were more likely to identify slavery as the most important cause of the war. Of the eighteen who regarded McPherson's *Battle Cry of Freedom*, Drew Gilpin Faust's *This Republic of Suffering*, or another scholarly work most highly, even if the book was not ostensibly about the war's causes, 67 percent thought slavery was the most important cause of the war. Out of those who listed an older historical work as their favorite, 43 percent thought slavery was the most important cause. For those who list a regimental history or other firsthand account written after the war, only 21 percent thought slavery was a major issue. Lastly, of respondents who liked *The Killer Angels* or *Gods and Generals* (the novels on which the movies *Gettysburg* and *Gods and Generals* were based), only 9 percent thought slavery was the primary cause of the war.[52]

Another clue can be found in the pages of reenactors' units' websites. Some have a list of suggested reading or reference sources. The website for the Twenty-Eighth Massachusetts Infantry contains a list of books that all deal directly with the Irish Brigade, of which the original unit was a part. Similarly, the website for the Second Connecticut Heavy Artillery lists works like William A. Croffut and John M. Morris's *The Military and Civil History of Connecticut during the War of 1861–65*. Indeed, scholars of Connecticut and the Civil War should know about Croffut and Morris, but what is missing from both lists is just as important as what is included. There are no entries for modern scholarship that deals with the causes of the war or what it means for Americans today.[53]

In sum, there is a divide between reenactors in Connecticut and modern academic scholars. One respondent from Connecticut illustrated this fact well. Identifying himself as a college professor and, not surprisingly, believing that slavery was the most important cause of the war, he also selected "to protect slavery/white supremacy" as a motivator for Confederate soldiers and did not choose "states' rights." He thought that "to end slavery" was a Union motivation, but he had difficulty naming a primary motive for either side, proclaiming, "The question is impossible to answer; there are too many reasons." He went on to succinctly summarize the attitude of the

North in a manner that would gain the approval of McPherson, Manning, or Foner. "Scholarship shows that the dominant political philosophy of the North was 'anti-slavery' (not to be confused with pro-African American), so I guess if I was forced to pick one answer [for what motivated Union soldiers] I would say that Union was the most important issue." He closed with these words: "As a 20 year veteran of reenacting, I am always fascinated by the wealth of knowledge my comrades have about battles or material culture. Sadly, I am also amazed at their almost complete lack of understanding of racial, political, or gender issues of the period."[54]

This divide between academic historians and reenactors begs an important question. How can it be fixed? One solution might be to form a national umbrella organization that encompasses Union and Confederate groups from around the country. To be sure, some organizations currently exist. The New England Brigade and Liberty Greys are groups composed of several individual Union and Confederate reenactment units in New England. Another is the National Regiment, which contains numerous Union units from the East Coast. Such organizations have authenticity standards by which member organizations must abide, and they play a key role in planning and organizing large events. They do not, however, set pedagogical guidelines for member groups. The authenticity standards of the National Regiment, for example, focus on the bric-a-brac of camp life as well as the rudiments of battlefield maneuvering. Individual unit's websites also have very specific guidelines for uniforms, rifles, and equipment, but neither the overall organization nor the individual units say anything about exactly *what* they teach the public.[55]

In order to work, an organization of the kind proposed here would need to have an executive board composed of both reenactors as well as professional historians. A model for such an organization is the National Council for the Social Studies. Its board of directors is made up of a combination of university-level educators as well as secondary school teachers and school administrators. They also set clear pedagogical guidelines for what local school districts should follow. This type of organizational structure, with the participation of those on both sides, might bridge the reenactor-historian gap and bring what reenactors teach in line with what historians write about.[56]

Part of the duties of this proposed organization should be handling issues of controversy among reenactors, especially those that lead to inter- and intra-unit fighting. A reoccurring complaint among reenactors was

"Political Divisions within the hobby," or something worded very similarly. Few elected to elaborate on the issue, so it is difficult to pinpoint exactly the kinds of issues that cause strife among reenactors, but it cut across the Union-Confederate divide. Another problem was, as one Confederate said, "individuals who do not follow the event rules and guidelines." An umbrella organization could be empowered to set standards of conduct and adjudicate disagreements between groups when necessary.[57]

Because such an organization would need the participation of both reenactors as well as professional historians, the cooperation of both groups is necessary. Reenactors with mixed or negative views of historians must come to the table with an open mind, and academics cannot walk in the door with the attitude described by one Rhode Island reenactor who detested "the lack of credit we receive among intellectuals and academics that look down their noses at us for not tak[ing] history 'seriously.'" One respondent from Massachusetts showed exactly what a little outreach effort on the part of historians can accomplish. "One of the best events I have participated in was the one in New Britain last spring. . . . It was also wonderful having the opportunity to meet and talk with [Central Connecticut history professor] Dr. Warshauer."[58]

A reenactor from Massachusetts wrote that he wanted the public "[t]o come away from an event and want to learn more about the Civil War." This sums up the strengths of Civil War reenactors in Connecticut. To allow someone to see, smell, touch, hear, and even taste the past is something that no textbook can do. When the public attends a living history presentation or battle reenactment, they are not, and cannot be, transported back in time to the 1860s, but through the work of Connecticut-area reenactors, thousands of spectators are given a glimpse of life in the 1860s. In this modern, Internet-driven era, this is an educational strength that absolutely cannot be overstated. Given the audience that reenactors often have, and the lack of knowledge among segments of the public, they have the potential to be a valuable educational asset.[59]

In closing, it is important to note that these conclusions are preliminary. So little has been researched when it comes to reenacting that the field of inquiry remains wide open. Moreover, as previously noted, some survey questions, if worded differently, might have yielded more accurate data. In addition, other sources can be used to either buttress or jettison the conclusions reached in this paper. For example, surveying the public after a major reenactment to get their perspective on what they learned, liked, and disliked would be valuable in helping understand what reenactors teach the public. My hope is that this paper leads to more research into this very interesting and important topic.

NOTES

1. Thomas Dyja, *Meet John Trow* (New York: Penguin Books, 2002), 236.

2. For a history of reenacting, see Gordon L. Jones, "Gut History: Civil War Reenacting and the Making of America's Past" (PhD diss., Emory University, 2007). In ProQuest Dissertations and Theses, http://0-search.proquest.com.www.consuls.org/pqdtft/docview/304741232/previewPDF/1336FE482443CE0993B/1?acc ountid=9970.

3. David Von Drehle, "150 Years after Fort Sumter: Why We're Still Fighting the Civil War," Time, April 7, 2001, http://library.williams.edu/citing/styles/chicago1 .php (accessed October 13, 2012). According to a Harris Interactive Poll taken in 2011 and referenced in the above *Time* article, a majority of respondents, and more than two-thirds of whites from former Confederate states, believed that the South was motivated not by the protection of slavery, but by states' rights.

4. David W. Blight, *Race and Reunion* (Cambridge, MA: Harvard University Press, 2001).

5. Paul H. Buck, *The Road to Reunion, 1865–1900* (Boston: Little Brown and Co., 1937). The literature detailing the various aspects of Civil War memory is extensive. I have chosen to focus on those works that have been especially influential or that deal in some fashion with Civil War reenacting. All of the following are good studies, but not directly relevant to this topic. For a study of the Lost Cause as a religion, see Charles Reagan Wilson, *Baptized in Blood: The Religion of the Lost Cause, 1865–1920* (Athens: University of Georgia Press, 1980). For a look at the connection between war memorials and memory, see James M. Mayo, "War Memorials as Political Memory," *Geographical Review* 78.1 (1988): 62–75. For work on the Grand Army of the Republic's role in shaping Civil War memory, see Stuart McConnell, *Glorious Contentment: The Grand Army of the Republic, 1865–1900* (Chapel Hill: University of North Carolina Press, 1992). For a look at the Civil War through bubble gum card cartoons, see Jan Baetens, "Civil War News: How Popular Culture Rewrites History," *Journal of American Culture* 20.1 (1997): 1–6. For an examination of why many southerners cannot let go of the Civil War and its consequences, see David Goldfield, *Still Fighting the Civil War: The American South and Southern History* (Baton Rouge: Louisiana State University Press, 2002). For a historian's view of Ken Burns's documentary, *The Civil War*, see Eric Foner, *Who Owns History: Rethinking the Past in a Changing World* (New York: Hill and Wang, 2002), 189–204. For a complete bibliography of Civil War memory, see Matthew J. Grow, "The Shadow of the Civil War: A Historiography of Civil War Memory," *American Nineteenth Century History* 4.2 (2003): 77–103.

A good collection of essays on various aspects of how Civil War memory was shaped can be found in Alice Fahs and Joan Wauch, eds., *The Memory of the Civil War in American Culture* (Chapel Hill: University of North Carolina Press, 2004). For an examination of the conflicts in the South over public commemoration of the

Civil War and its consequences, see Fitzhugh Brundage, *The Southern Past* (Cambridge, MA: Harvard University Press, 2005). For a very good discussion of how the issue of race crept into the national 1961 centennial commemoration despite efforts to prevent it, see Kevin Allen, "The Second Battle of Fort Sumter: The Debate over the Politics of Race and Historical Memory at the Opening of America's Civil War Centennial, 1961," *Public Historian* 33.2 (2011): 94–109.

6. CCSU Reenactor Survey conducted November 17, 2011, through December 2, 2011, under the auspices of Central Connecticut State University History Department, faculty adviser, Matthew Warshauer. Each survey submission was given a five-digit submission identification number. From this point forward, when I cite a specific submission, it will read CCSU Reenactor Survey, followed by the submission ID number. For data extrapolated from the whole of the surveys, or from a portion of them, the note will read simply, CCSU Reenactor Survey. Though this chapter is about reenactors in Connecticut, I have included reenactors from all of New England for two reasons. First, many reenactors from the surrounding area attend events within Connecticut, and second, their inclusion provided a much larger sample size. One can only speculate as to the overwhelmingly Union response, but geography surely played an important role. New England is in the North; consequently, most responders from that region identified with that side of the conflict. Two respondents provided unclear answers to the question of which side they identified with. Because both belonged to Confederate units, I elected to include them in that group.

7. Because the majority of respondents preferred the term "reenactor," I have elected to use that word throughout this chapter. Also, in retrospect, I realize that I should have asked for respondents' gender. In the absence of this information, I cannot always be sure of the gender of individual respondents. I will therefore use "he" unless I am sure the person being quoted is a female.

8. CCSU Reenactor Survey; Glenn W. LaFantasie, "The Foolishness of Civil War Reenactors," Salon.com, May 8, 2011, http://politics.salon.com/2011/05/08/civil_war_sesquicentennial.

9. 11th Regiment Volunteer Infantry Co. A, "11th Connecticut Events," 11th Regiment Volunteer Infantry Co. A: Averill's Rifles, http://www.11thcvi.org/events.html.

10. CCSU Reenactor Survey. Education might be even more important to reenactors than these statistics indicate. The question asked respondents for the "most important" reason they reenact. It is probable that there were those who did not say "educating the public" was the most important, but still regarded it as an important secondary motivation.

11. CCSU Reenactor Survey, 12015.

12. CCSU Reenactor Survey, 11955, 11902.

13. CCSU Reenactor Survey, 11928.

14. CCSU Reenactor Survey, 11935.

15. CCSU Reenactor Survey, 11936.

16. CCSU Reenactor Survey, 11869.

17. Tony Horowitz, *Confederates in the Attic: Dispatches from the Unfinished*

Civil War (New York: Vintage Books, 1999), 10, 16. There is a third category, known as "farb," though this is used more as a term of criticism of other reenactors and is not an expression that reenactors would generally use to describe themselves or their units. I therefore did not include it as an option on the survey.

18. CCSU Reenactor Survey, 11970, 11838, 11875.

19. CCSU Reenactor Survey, 11893, 11915, 11943.

20. CCSU Reenactor Survey, 11885. The remaining 5 percent of respondents answered "other" or "not sure."

21. LaFantasie, "The Foolishness of Civil War Reenactors."

22. Matthew Warshauer, comments made in "The Historical Imagination," a graduate course at Central Connecticut State University, fall 2011; Robert Matthew Isham, "Reconsidering Civil War Reenactors in the Sesquicentennial, or, the Insight and Foolishness of Glenn LaFantasie," Penn State University, Richards Center, May 18, 2011, http://www.psu.edu/dept/richardscenter/2011/05/reconsidering-civil-war-re-enactors-in-the-sesquicentennial-or-the-insight-and-foolishness-of-glenn.html.

23. James M. McPherson, *For Cause and Comrades: Why Men Fought in the Civil War* (New York: Oxford University Press, 1997), 11. There are several other studies on Civil War soldiers and their motivations. See also Reid Mitchell, *Civil War Soldiers* (New York: Penguin Books, 1988). For a look at Confederate soldiers, see Aaron Sheehan-Dean, *Why Confederates Fought: Family & Nation in Civil War Virginia* (Chapel Hill: University of North Carolina Press, 2007). For a study on how Union soldiers maintained morale despite the hardships of combat, see Earl J. Hess, *The Union Soldier in Battle* (Lawrence: University of Kansas Press, 1997). For a profile of the soldiers who participated in General Sherman's March to the Sea, see Joseph T. Glatthaar, *The March to the Sea and Beyond: Sherman's Troops in the Savannah and Carolina Campaigns* (Baton Rouge: Louisiana State University Press, 1985). See also Gerald F. Linderman, *Embattled Courage: The Experience of Combat in the American Civil War* (New York: Free Press, 1987). Linderman argued, unlike the others, that Civil War soldiers were not motivated by the type of patriotic and political causes that McPherson and others detailed. The difference is partially due to source material. Whereas McPherson used letters and diaries written during the war, Linderman employed memoirs and histories written decades later, by which time the mood of the nation had changed, underlying issues had been forgotten, and hard feelings were softened. For a window into the real motivations of soldiers on both sides during the war, therefore, McPherson's book is the more accurate.

24. McPherson, *For Cause and Comrades*, 99. Hess, in *The Union Soldier in Battle*, argued that some Union soldiers did still emphasize ideology during the era of reconciliation. He wrote, "The destruction of slavery was uppermost in these men's minds" (168). CCSU Reenactor Survey, 11850.

25. Matthew Warshauer, *Connecticut in the American Civil War: Slavery, Sacrifice, and Survival* (Middletown, CT: Wesleyan University Press, 2011), 93. Glatthaar, in *The March to the Sea and Beyond*, agreed that patriotism was important,

writing that "for most men it was patriotism that kept them in the service" (39). ccsu Reenactor Survey.

26. Gary Gallagher, *Causes Won, Lost, and Forgotten: How Hollywood and Popular Art Shape What We Know about the Civil War* (Chapel Hill: University of North Carolina Press, 2008), 12–13; Hess, *The Union Soldier in Battle*, 97; ccsu Reenactor Survey, 11885, 11899.

27. McPherson, *For Cause and Comrades*, 95.

28. ccsu Reenactor Survey; ccsu Reenactor Survey, 11852. It was the Union respondents who made "states' rights" come out as the top motive for Confederate soldiers. When asked to list all motives, 68 Union respondents identified "states' rights," whereas only 56 selected "protect homes and families." Among Confederates, 24 listed "protect homes and families," and 20 chose "states' rights."

29. ccsu Reenactor Survey, 11901, 11897.

30. McPherson, *For Cause and Comrades*, 108–10; Sheehan-Dean, *Why Confederates Fought*, 35.

31. Chandra Manning, *What This Cruel War Is Over: Soldiers, Slavery, and the Civil War* (New York: Vintage Books, 2007), 21.

32. Manning, *What This Cruel War Is Over*, 32. There are other studies that seek to explain the stake that non-slaveholders felt they had in slavery. For a discussion of how southern whites, regardless of whether they actually owned slaves or not, participated in slave patrols, see Sally E. Hadden, *Slave Patrols, Law and Violence in Virginia and the Carolinas* (Cambridge, MA: Harvard University Press, 2001); also, for a look at the connection between the widely held, antebellum concept of honor among white southerners and their support for slavery, see Bertram Wyatt-Brown, *Southern Honor: Ethics and Behavior in the Old South* (New York: Oxford University Press, 1982).

33. McPherson, *For Cause and Comrades*, 233–37; Manning, *What This Cruel War Is Over*, 339–50.

34. ccsu Reenactor Survey; McPherson, *For Cause and Comrades*, 150.

35. ccsu Reenactor Survey. This is another instance where formatting the question differently might have yielded different results. A better way of phrasing it would be to list all the choices, but to have respondents rank them from "favorite" to "least favorite." It is clear that the military aspect of the era is their primary interest, but the survey tells us little about whether, or to what extent, they have a secondary interest in other matters.

36. Shelby Foote, *Fort Sumter to Perryville*, vol. 1 of *The Civil War: A Narrative* (New York: Vintage Books, 1958); Shelby Foote, *Fredericksburg to Meridian*, vol. 2 of *The Civil War: A Narrative* (New York: Vintage Books, 1963); Shelby Foote, *Red River to Appomattox*, vol. 3 of *The Civil War: A Narrative* (New York: Vintage Books, 1974). Some did speak about the war's meaning and causes in the midst of America's centennial Civil War celebration. For a critique of the attitudes of both northerners and southerners, see Robert Penn Warren, *The Legacy of the Civil War: Meditations on the Centennial* (New York: Random House, 1961). For an example of a scholar who was critical not only of the celebratory nature of the

centennial but of reenacting battles in particular, see John Hope Franklin, "A Century of Civil War Observance," *Journal of Negro History* 47.2 (1962): 97–107.

37. Geoffrey C. Ward, Ric Burns, and Ken Burns, *The Civil War: An Illustrated History* (New York: Alfred A. Knopf, 1990), 265. ccsu Reenactor Survey, 11845.

38. John Niven, *Connecticut for the Union: The Role of the State in the Civil War* (New Haven, CT: Yale University Press, 1965); for Connecticut's role in the Civil War, see also Albert Van Dusen, *Connecticut: A Fully Illustrated History of the State from the Seventeenth Century to the Present* (New York: Random House, 1961). Van Dusen did elaborate on the lead-up to the conflict and how Connecticut tied into it, and in so doing, discussed how the expansion of slavery led to conflict. His primary focus, though, is on the contributions of soldiers and civilians, with a focus on the Fourteenth Connecticut Volunteer Infantry.

39. Isham, "Reconsidering Civil War Reenactors in the Sesquicentennial, or, the Insight and Foolishness of Glenn LaFantasie."

40. ccsu Reenactor Survey.

41. ccsu Reenactor Survey.

42. ccsu Reenactor Survey, 12153, 11852, 11939.

43. Sean Wilentz, *The Rise of American Democracy: Jefferson to Lincoln* (New York: W. W. Norton, 2006), 773–74.

44. Eric Foner, *Free Soil, Free Labor, Free Men: The Ideology of the Republican Party before the Civil War* (New York: Oxford University Press, 1970), 9; McPherson quoted in David Von Drehle, "150 Years after Fort Sumter: Why We're Still Fighting the Civil War," Time, April 7, 2011, http://www.time.com/time/magazine/article/0,9171,2063869,00.html. For a discussion of how commissioners from deep South states used the slavery issue to convince those in the middle South states to secede, see Charles B. Dew, *Apostles of Disunion: Southern Secession Commissioners and the Causes of the Civil War* (Charlottesville: University of Virginia Press, 2001). For a look at how slaves as well as slaveowners understood the cause of the war to be slavery, see Barbara Fields, *Slavery and Freedom on the Middle Ground: Maryland during the Nineteenth Century* (New Haven, CT: Yale University Press, 1984). For a modern historian's take on Connecticut as it pertains to the issue of slavery, see Warshauer, *Connecticut and the American Civil War.*

45. David W. Blight, *Race and Reunion: The Civil War in American Memory* (Cambridge, MA: Harvard University Press, 2001), 2. William Blair, in *Cities of the Dead: Contesting the Memory of the Civil War in the South, 1865–1914* (Chapel Hill: University of North Carolina Press, 2004), argued that Blight's construct was incomplete. He wrote that there were those who did not go along with reconciliation, at least on southern terms, and focused on the North's role in preserving the Union. Given how many reenactors who believe that preservation of the Union was the primary goal of Union soldiers, there are certainly those who would fall into this camp.

46. Blight, *Race and Reunion*, 2–3; Warshauer, *Connecticut and the American Civil War.*

47. Blight, *Race and Reunion*, 182–83; see also Jones, "Gut History." The abstract of Jones's dissertation says that reenacting is "firmly rooted in anti-modern,

reconciliationist culture." The full text of this dissertation, however, was not available during the writing of this chapter.

48. ccsu Reenactor Survey, 11900, 11955.

49. ccsu Reenactor Survey, 12199, 11852.

50. ccsu Reenactor Survey. Fifty percent of Union respondents identified themselves as conservative or very conservative, and 54 percent of Confederate respondents did the same. Six respondents chose very conservative, all of whom were Union. On the liberal side, fifteen of the sixteen were Union, including all five who were very liberal.

51. ccsu Reenactor Survey. Gallagher, in *Causes Won, Lost, and Forgotten,* argued that *Glory* presented an emancipationist view of the war, whereas *Gettysburg* and *Gods and Generals* adhered to a reconciliationist view. He added that *Gods and Generals* is the only modern film to depict elements of the Lost Cause Confederate myth.

52. ccsu Reenactor Survey; Michael Shaara, *The Killer Angels* (New York: Random House, 1974); Jeff Shaara, *Gods and Generals* (New York: Ballantine, 1996).

53. 28th Massachusetts Volunteer Infantry, "Recommended Reading," 28th Massachusetts Volunteer Infantry, http://www.28thmass.org/books.htm; Joe Santacroce, "2nd Connecticut Volunteer Artillery Regiment: Research Sources," The 2d cvha, http://www.the2dconn.com/research.htm; W. A. Croffut and John M. Morris, *The Military and Civil History of Connecticut during the War of 1861–65,* vols. 1 and 2 (New York: Ledyard Bill, 1868).

54. Forty-two percent of respondents had "mixed "views toward academic historians. Little, however, can be read into this, as 47 percent had a very positive or somewhat positive view of historians, and only six said they had a somewhat negative view (none had a very negative view). The question did not specify "modern" academic historians, it should be noted. Still, there are a sizable number who harbor mixed feelings. ccsu Reenactor Survey, 11863.

55. "The New England Brigade," http://www.newenglandbrigade.org/forums /content.php; "Liberty Greys Information Page," http://members.cox.net/rebmus; "The National Regiment," http://www.nationalregiment.com/; see also Company F, Fourteenth Connecticut Volunteer Infantry 1862–1865, "Unit Guidelines for Authenticity," Company F, Fourteenth Connecticut Volunteer Infantry 1862–1865, http://www.cof14thcvi.com/Authenticity/Authenticity.htm. This is a very good example of the kind of approved list of uniforms and equipment of a typical Union reenacting unit.

56. National Council for the Social Studies, "ncss Board of Directors," http:// www.ncss.org/about/board; National Council for the Social Studies, "Standards," http://www.ncss.org/standards.

57. ccsu Reenactor Survey, 11920, 11873. One issue that some reenactors felt strongly about was whether women should be allowed to participate as soldiers if they could hide their gender. Twenty respondents, all Union, took umbrage with the idea.

58. ccsu Reenactor Survey, 11867, 11852.

59. ccsu Reenactor Survey, 11878.

CONTRIBUTORS

DAVID C. W. BATCH is a resident of Coventry, Connecticut, and an instructor of English at Howell Cheney Technical High School. He holds a B.A. in English and secondary education from the University of Hartford and an M.A. in United States history from Central Connecticut State University, where his coursework focused on the American Civil War and Connecticut history. He is currently completing his post-master's degree in educational leadership and administration at Sacred Heart University. Batch's interest in the Fourteenth Regiment Connecticut Volunteer Infantry originated while living in Vernon and researching the role of Rockville in the Civil War for his master's thesis, "Their Lives and Labor: The Contributions of Rockville, CT, in the American Civil War." Most of his research focused specifically on Company D of the Fourteenth Regiment, of which the majority of soldiers originally mustered were from Rockville and Vernon.

LUKE G. BOYD holds a master's degree in public history from Central Connecticut State University. In the field, he has focused on first-person interpretation, portraying local and nationally known figures, including Sam Colt, Elihu Burritt, and Stephen Douglas. As an intern with the National Park Service, Boyd came to advocate the proposed Coltsville National Historical Park as a unique place where audiences might engage with the controversial gun culture of the United States and Connecticut's industrial heritage.

JAMES E. BROWN is a corporate attorney who, on sabbatical, spent a year taking graduate courses in history at Central Connecticut State University. This was his first venture into academic history. His work on Connecticut's approach to financing the extraordinary expenses incurred during the Civil War had not been the subject of previous work; though historians had explored issues directly or indirectly related to the financing of war-related expenses at the national level, little attention had been paid to comparable issues faced in Connecticut. Having served as a staff attorney to the Connecticut General Assembly, he was particularly interested in exploring the political and public policy aspects of this issue as documented through the legislative process. Brown presented his paper at a conference, "Connecticut at War," sponsored by the Association for the Study of Connecticut History. He received a B.A. in economics from Holy Cross College, a J.D. from the University of Connecticut School of Law, and an M.B.A. from the Barney School of Business, University of Hartford.

MICHAEL CONLIN is a master's degree student in history at Central Connecticut State University. His interests are in the American Civil War and Civil War memory. He is also a reenactor with Company F of the Fourteenth Connecticut Infantry, and his research grew from his involvement in, and fascination with, both reenacting and academic history, as well as the broader question of representation of the Civil War in popular culture. Conlin teaches middle school history and language arts at Saint Gabriel School in Windsor, Connecticut.

EMILY E. GIFFORD holds master's degrees from Yale Divinity School (in religion) and from Central Connecticut State University (in modern U.S. history). As a writer and researcher, she has contributed to the magazine *Connecticut Explored* and to the Connecticut Humanities website Connecticuthistory.org, writing on a variety of subjects, including religion, the arts, and social movements. She has also done extensive research on feature films as primary documents that reflect social attitudes and cultural mores during the twentieth century. As a specialist in twentieth-century history, she has enjoyed having the opportunity to study the Civil War in the context of memory and commemoration.

TODD JONES was born and raised in Connecticut, and he holds a master's degree in public history from Central Connecticut State University. As a Civil War enthusiast, Jones has visited Gettysburg, Pennsylvania, on a yearly basis for almost a decade, with each visit expanding his interest in monuments and commemoration. His history of a Connecticut monument to General John Sedgwick at Gettysburg was recently published in the *Gettysburg Magazine*, and he has contributed articles related to the Civil War to Connecticut History.org. He currently works in the field of historic preservation and lives in Washington, DC.

DIANA MORACO received a master's degree in public history from Central Connecticut State University and a bachelor's degree in history from Manhattanville College. Her interest in maritime history and industry led her to the Steamship Historical Society of America in Providence, Rhode Island, where she is the membership coordinator and a copy editor for its magazine, *PowerShips*.

CAROL PATTERSON-MARTINEAU's freelance work has appeared in an eclectic array of publications, including *Web Guide Magazine*, the *Connecticut Law Review*, and several Connecticut newspapers. Her familial ties to eastern Connecticut extend back seventeen generations and served in part as inspiration for her study of Windham County's Civil War experience. She has worked for the educational department of Mystic Seaport as an interpreter and a museum guide and is currently finishing her master's thesis in history at Central Connecticut State University in preparation for beginning doctoral studies at the University of Maine in 2013.

MICHAEL STURGES is a social studies teacher at Nonnewaug High School in Woodbury, Connecticut, where he teaches honors U.S. history and twentieth-century history. He has a bachelor of science in education degree from Central ✳ Connecticut State University and is currently a graduate student in CCSU's history master's program, focusing on the psychology of Civil War veterans. In addition to teaching, Sturges coaches the Nonnewaug debate team and serves as student council adviser. He has been a contributor to *Connecticut Explored* magazine, as well as to Connecticut History Online. He has found the opportunity to write history while also teaching it highly fulfilling.

MATTHEW WARSHAUER is a professor of history at Central Connecticut State University. He has written extensively on Andrew Jackson and the early republic, as well as Connecticut's role in the American Civil War. Warshauer currently serves as co-chair of the Connecticut Civil War Commemoration Commission and is helping to coordinate activities across Connecticut to focus on the importance and lasting legacies of the American Civil War and Connecticut's involvement in it.

Page numbers in *italics* indicate images.

abolitionism, 72, 75, 83–92, 183

Act to Indemnify the States for Expenses Incurred by Them in Defense of the United States, 30

Act to Provide a National Currency, 13

Adams, Herbert, 198

Adams, Peter, 76

African colonization movement, 87

Albatross, 48, 51, 61–62

Allen (sergeant, Fourteenth Connecticut), 124

American Anaconda Brass Works, 217

American Colonization Society, 88

American Journal of Insanity, 166

American Library Association, 2

American Revolution: expenses of, states reimbursed for, 29; influence of, on Civil War soldiers, 76; U.S. navy after, 47

Andersonville Prison, 171

Andrew Hull Foote, Gunboat Commodore (CCWCC), 219

Antietam excursionists, 209–10. *See also* Battle of Antietam

Anti-Slavery Almanac, 87

antislavery ideology, 246

antisubversion groups, 147

antiwar groups, 147

Armsmear, 146

Armsmear (Barnard), 145, 152

Arthur, Chester A., 194

Ashford Academy, 88

Association for the Study of Connecticut History, 2

Avon Free Library, 2

Ayers, Edward, 69, 87

Bacon, Elijah W., 117

banks, 7–8; national, 10, 13–14; tax on, 24

Barnard, Henry, 145

Batterson, James G., 192

Battle Cry of Freedom (McPherson), 249

battle exhaustion, 161

battlefield reunions, 208–10

Battle Flag Day Parade (Hartford, CT), 185, *188*, 207–8

Battle of Antietam, 101, 107–9, 171, 209

Battle of Bull Run (First), 83, 91

Battle of Chancellorsville, 101, 113–14, 124

Battle of Cold Harbor, 127–28

Battle of Fredericksburg, 101, 110–12, 159, 243

Battle of Gettysburg, 101, 114–19, 148, 208, 211

Battle of Mobile Bay, 59

Battle of Roanoke Island, 61

Battle of Spotsylvania, 126

Battle of Winchester (Second), 71, 83

battle recreations, 237. *See also* reenactors

Baughman, James B., 48, 55

Bayles, Richard, 76–77, 80

Beachdale Mill (Voluntown, CT), 79

Beauregard, P.G.T., 91

Bee, Robert L., 102

Beetham, Sarah Denver, 185, 192

Benson, George, 89

Benson, Helen Eliza, 89

Betts, Karl, 214

B. F. Hoxie, 51

Black Law, 88, 89, 99n89

black soldiers, payments to, 20, 36–37

Blackstone, 65n18

Blatchley, C. G., 128, 129–30

Blight, David W., 191, 230, 246–47

bonds, *18*, *21*, 23; campaigns for selling, 11–12; state's issuance of, 35, 37, 39; towns' issuance of, 35

borrowing: political aspect of, 8; as source of war expenditures, 9

bounties, 16, 19–20, 24, 33, 34, 36–39

Boys from Rockville: Civil War Narratives of Sgt. Benjamin Hirst, Company D, Fourteenth Connecticut Volunteers, The (Bee), 102

Bradley (sergeant, Fourteenth Connecticut), 126

Brady, Matthew, 69

Bridgeport (CT), 147

Bridgeport Standard, 150

Briggs, Ira, 79

Brooklyn (CT), 71, 72, 77, 78, 89

Brooklyn (CT) Unitarian Church, 89

Brooks, Preston, 84

Brown, Alice, 219

Brown, Dunn, 135n13

Brown, John, 3, 84

Brown, Thomas J., 185

Buckingham, William A., 14, 103, 146, 148; expressing Connecticut's loyalty to the Union, 45–46; financing the war, 15–16, 20–23; issuing call for troops, 15; on meeting obligations to the Union, 17; reporting on war claims reimbursement, 27; on secession, 41n21; as U.S. senator, 31

Bulkeley, Morgan, 201n12

Burns, Ken, 243–44

Burnside, Ambrose, 109, 159

Burpee, Thomas, 105

Bushnell, 48

Bushnell, Cornelius S., 52, 53, 54–56, 59, 65n25

Butler, Ithamar, 170–71

Caldwell, John, 107

Camp Dutton, 233

Camp Foote, 103

Canaan (CT), 72

Canterbury (CT), 72, 87, 88, 89

Carroll, Samuel, 125

Castle Pinckney, 91

Catton, Bruce, 211

ccwcc. *See* Connecticut Civil War Centennial Commission

Chalker, Allen, 173

Chamberlain, Joshua, 243

Chase, Salmon, 7, 8–9, 10, 11, 30

Christian Commission, 189

Christley, James, 54–55, 58

City of Hartford, 105

civil rights movement, 212, 220, 223

Civil War; appeal of, 213; centennial of, 2, 211–23; commemoration of, 1–2, 195–96, 205, 223–24 (*see also* Dedication Days; Hawley, Joseph R.; monuments); death toll of, 1, 93n1, 124; early enlistments in, 78–79, 83; films about, 240, 248, 257n51; financing, 6–9; historians of, 229; interest in, 228–29; length of, 7–8; paranoia during, 140, 144, 147; portrayal of, in film and art, 240; postwar accounts of, 238; public's perception of, 228–29; sesquicentennial of, 2, 3, 5; as struggle over national identity, 144; Union Navy in, role of, 45; versions of, 246–47

Civil War, The (Burns, dir.), 243–44

Civil War Centennial Commission (cwcc), 211–12, 214, 215, 220, 222

Civil War Connecticut, 146

Clark, C. C., 119

Cleveland, Grover, 194

coins, disappearing from the economy, 19

collective memory, 191–92

Colt, Elizabeth, 140–41, 143, 145, 146, 155

Colt, Samuel, 45, 140, 142–43, 145, 149, 151, 155

Colt: The Making of an American Legend (Hosley), 145

Colt Armory fire: chronology of, 140–41; conspiracy theories about, 140, 142, 143–44, 146–54; effect of, 154–55; historical narrative of, 144–45; historiography on, 145–46; interest in, 141–43, 149–50; newspaper accounts of, 141–42, 149–51; reconstruction after, 154–55. *See also* Colt Patent Firearms Company

Colt Band, 143

Colt Collections, 146

Colt Heritage (Wilson), 145

Colt Legacy, The (Grant), 145

Colt Patent Firearms Company, 63, *143*, 149

Coltsville (CT), 140, *141*, 142–43, 144

combat fatigue, 161

Confederates, sabotage by, 144

Confederates in the Attic: Dispatches from the Unfinished Civil War (Horowitz), 236

Confederate States: navy of, 53–54; subversion by, 152–54

Congregationalism, 94n17

Congress, 59

Connecticut: abolitionism in, 83–84; arms production in, 45, 46; banking and insurance industries in, 43–44n52; battle reenactments in, 233; calling for volunteers, 103–5; casualties for, of the Civil War, 6; Civil War centennial commemoration in, 214–23; Civil War monuments in, 1–2, 183; committing troops to the war, 17, 19; desertion rates for, 72; draft in, 19, 119, 148; espionage act in, 147; factory fires in, 148–49; fear in, of Confederate subversion, 146, 147; *Galena*'s importance to, 57; legislation in, war-related, 32–39; monetary costs to,

of the Civil War, 6; new constitution for, 74, 75; political landscape of, 14–15; racism in, 191; reenactors in, 229–30, 233–37 (*see also* reenactors); renewed support for the war in, 140; significance of, in the Civil War, 2; southern sympathy in, 146, 147, 148; textile factory work in, 79; veterans from, with psychological ailments, 167–75; war claims of, seeking reimbursement for, 27, 29–32; war expenditures and financing in, 14, 15–27, 28–29, 32–39

Connecticut Anti-Slavery Society, 89

Connecticut Civil War Centennial: A Manual for Its Observance in the Towns and Cities of the State of Connecticut, The (ccwcc), 215–16

Connecticut Civil War Centennial Commission (ccwcc), 205, 214–23

Connecticut Civil War Commemoration Commission, 2, 5

Connecticut Department of Mental Health and Addiction Services, 162

Connecticut for the Union: The Role of the State in the Civil War (Niven), 52, 102, 217, *218*, 244

Connecticut Hospital for the Insane, 112, 159–60, 162, 167, 171–74

Connecticut in the American Civil War: Slavery, Sacrifice, and Survival (Warshauer), 102–3, 217, 239–40, 247

Connecticut League of History Associations, 2

Connecticut Military and Naval Leaders in the Civil War (ccwcc), 219, *220*

Connecticut Path, 73

Connecticut Physicians in the Civil War (Weld), 219

Connecticut Valley Hospital, 162, 177n7

Connecticut Veterans' Home (Rocky Hill), 174, 175
Cook, Robert J., 211. 220, 222
Cooke, Jay, 11–12
Copperheads, 143, 146
Corning and Winslow, 66
cotton, 48, 49, 79
Cowden, Joanna, 15
Crandall, Prudence, 72, 75, *86*, 87–89, 92, 98n87
Croffut, William A., 52, 102, 105, 106, 107, 126, 249
Cummings, Joseph, 207
customs duties, 12
Cutler, Carl, 56, 57, 60

Daniel, John W., 196
Danielson, Joseph, 90
Danielsonville (CT), *70*, 81, 84
Davis, Jefferson, 145, 147, 152, 154
Davis, Samuel H., 112, 119
Dawes, Joel, 96–97n54
Day, Aaron, 84
Dean, Eric T., 165
Decoration Day, 181, 183, 205–6
dedications, 195–96. *See also* Hawley, Joseph R.
Deleppo, Carol, *235*
dementia, 165, 171
Democratic Party: in antebellum Connecticut, 74–75; weakening of, 14–15
Democratic-Republicanism, 74
Dempsey, John, 219, 222, 223
Department of Mental Health and Addiction Services (DMHAS), 177n7
desertions, 72, 119, 130
DeWitt, J. Doyle, 215, 219
Diagnostic and Statistical Manual of Mental Disorders III, 161. *See also* DSM III-R; DSM IV-TR
Donald, David, 213
Douglas, Benjamin, 206–7
Doyle, Catherine, 219
draft, 19–20, 119
Drake, William H., 109

DSM III-R, 178n19
DSM IV-TR, 178n19
Dudley Buck, 105
Dyja, Thomas, 228

Eagle, 48
Eaton, William, 15, 20, 41n21
Egan, Harold J., 221
Ellis, Theodore G., 113, 116, 119
emancipationist view, 246
Emancipation Proclamation, centennial of, 220–22
enlistments: brokers for, 19; incentives for, 16; towns encouraging, 19
Episcopal Society for Cultural and Racial Unity, 212
Ericsson, John, 55, 66n37

Fairfield (CT), 147
Falcon, 48
Falmouth (VA), 112–13
family payments, 15, 16–17, 19, 20, 24, 33, 35, 36, 38
Farragut, David G., 59, 61
Faust, Drew Gilpin, 249
Federal Conscription Act, 19–20
federal government: deficits of, 13; expenditures of, 12–13; financial structure of, 7–9; image of, as creditor, 9–10; national debt of, 8–9; revenues of, 12–13
federal income tax, 28
Federalism, end of, in Windham County, 74
Federalist Party, 73
Fessenden, Samuel, 27
Finney, Charles G., 96–97n54
First Great Awakening, 73
First World War, 199
Fish, Nathan G., 49, 56
Fisher, Barzillai, 76
Fisk, Ephraim, 76
Fiske, Samuel Wheelock, 106, 107, 111–12, 113, 117, 119, 121–22, 124, 125, 135n13, 159

Fitch, Benjamin, 171
Fitch's Soldiers' Home (Darien, CT),
    171–72, 174–75
Fletcher, Daniel I., 222
Flynn, Christopher, 117
Foner, Eric, 246
Foote, Shelby, 230, 243–44
*For Cause and Comrades: Why Men
    Fought in the Civil War* (McPher-
    son), 238
Fourteenth Connecticut Regiment,
    176n2; at Antietam, 101, 102, 107–9,
    209; at Bristoe Station, 121; camp
    life in, 110; at Chancellorsville, 113–
    14; at Cold Harbor, 127–28; compa-
    nies of, sources of recruits, 134n9;
    Company A, 108; Company B, 105,
    107, 108, 114; Company D, 105,
    107–8, 110–11, 122; Company I, 114;
    development of, 103–5; diversity of,
    105; first travel of, 106; flags of, *120*;
    at Fredericksburg, 110–12, 131, 159;
    at Gettysburg, 101–2, 114–19, *132*,
    208; last fight of, 130; maturation
    of, 101–2; at Morton's Ford, 123; at
    Petersburg, 128; recruitment poster
    for, *104*; recruits of, by town, 134n9;
    returning to Hartford, 131; sickness
    in, 110; at Spotsylvania, 126; train-
    ing of, 106–7; in Virginia, 120–30;
    at war's end, 131; in the Wilderness
    Campaign, 124–26; wintering at
    Fort Morton, 129
Fowler, William, 45
Fox, Hiram, 115
fractional currency, 19
Franklin, John Hope, 255–56n36
Freedmen's Bureau, 189
French, Parker, 147
French, William, 107, 108
Fundamental Orders, 41n19, 189

Galena, 45, 49–51, 53, 56–59
Gallagher, Gary, 240
Garfield, James, 194

Garrison, William Lloyd, 2, 72, 84, 89,
    92
Gay, Lusher, 76
*George Greenman & Co.: Shipbuilders
    of Mystic, Connecticut* (Stevens and
    Stillman), 49
Gettysburg (Maxwell, dir.), 248
Gettysburg (Sears), 115
Gettysburg: A Testing of Courage
    (Trudeau), 115
Gleason, Charles W., 172–73
Glory (Zwick, dir.), 248, 257n51
Gods and Generals (Maxwell, dir.),
    248, 257n51
Gods and Generals (Shaara), 249
Goldsborough, Louis, 57, 61
Goodrich, Lauren, 115, 116
Goodwin, Doris Kearns, 8
Government Hospital for the Insane,
    167
Grand Army of the Republic (GAR),
    184–85, 194, 205–6, 211
Grant, Ellsworth S., 145, 187
Grant, Ulysses, 101–2, 124, 125, 126–
    27, 128, 129, 152, 194
Grant, Ulysses S., III, 211, 214
Grasso, Ella, 221
Great Alibi, 212–13
Great Awakenings, 73, 80, 94n17
Greek fire, 153
Greenbacks, 10
Greenman (George) & Company, 48,
    49–51, 61–62, 65n18
Grimke sisters, 84
Guilford (CT), 217
Gunn Museum (Washington, CT), 2

Hall, Albert, 110
Hall, Jacob, 173
Hammond, Bray, 7
Harrison, Benjamin, 194
Hartford, 61
Hartford (CT), 96n54, 142, 144
Hartford & Providence Railroad, 76
Hartford Civil War Roundtable, 215

Hartford County (CT), free blacks in, 84

Hartford Courant, 1, 2–3, 16, 149, 187, 206, 207, 211, 223

Hartford Daily Courant, 141, 151

Hartford Press, 150, 155

Hartford Retreat for the Insane, 163, 167, 173

Hartford Times, 81, 150–51, 206, 207

Hartford war debt bond, *18*

hatred, as motivator for soldiers, 242

Hawley, Harriet Foote, 191

Hawley, Joseph R., 181, *182*, 219; anti-slavery outlook of, 190–91; concerned about the future, 195; consoling elderly veterans, 195; death of, 197–99; life of, 183–84; love of, for God, 189–90; monument-building activities of, 185; monuments as muse for, 192–94; on patriotism, 196; patriotism of, 187–89; Roswell, 199; on soldiers as citizens, 195; speaking at commemorative events, 185–94; speaking outside Connecticut, 197; veterans' affairs activities of, 184–85; on women during war, 191

Hawley (Joseph R.) Medallion, *198*

Hawley, William H., 122

Hayes, Rutherford B., 194

Haze, 48

Hazen, George, 174

Henney, W. F., 199

Hess, Earl, 240

Hill, A. P., 109

Hincks, William B., 105, 116, 117, *118*

Hines, Blaikie, 72, 112

Hirst, Benjamin, 101, 107–9, 114, 116–17, 119, 124

Hirst, John, 114, 117–30

History of Battle Flag Day, September 17, 1879, 208

History of the Fourteenth Regiment, Connecticut Vol. Infantry (Page), 102

Hitchcock, Frederick L., 113–14

Holmes, Oliver Wendell, Jr., 196

home, protection of, as motivator for soldiers, 240–41, 244

Hooker, Thomas, 73, 189

Hoote, Andrew Hull, 103

Hormats, Robert D., 28

Horowitz, Tony, 236

Hosley, William, 145

Hoyt, Heusted W.R., 196

humors, 164

Huntington, Charles, 59

Huxam (corporal, Fourteenth Connecticut), 115

Ifird, Frank, 212

impoverished agricultural theory, 79

income tax, 11

Indiana Hospital for the Insane, 165–66

inebriation, 165

Ingersoll, Jared, 77

insanity: ancient Greek concepts of, 165; concept of, during the Civil War, 165; discharge for, 167; as moral issue, 174; pensions and, 170; sin and, 164; social consequences of, 162–63, 176

insurers, tax on, 24

interest expense, 12

Internal Revenue Bureau, 28

In the Presence of Mine Enemies (Ayers), 87

Irish Brigade, 107

Ironclad Board, 54–55

ironclads, 45, 53–59

Isham, Robert, 238, 244

Isherwood, Benjamin, 52

Jackson, Thomas J. "Stonewall," 113, 114

Jeffersonians, in Connecticut, 74

Jewett, Levi, 105, *106*, 108

Johnson, Andrew, 152

Johnson, Kevin, *235*

Johnson, Lyndon, 6
Judson, Andrew T., 88

Keech, Ephraim, 71
Kennedy, John F., 221
Kensington Congregational Church
    Monument, 1–2
Killer Angels, The (Shaara), 249
Killingly (CT), 71, 74, 93n11
Knights of the Golden Circle, 147
Kox, E. K., 141

LaFantasie, Glenn, 231–33, 237
Landers, Everett, 214
Larned, Ellen, 76–77, 80, 87
Lee, Robert E., 102, 103, 107, 110, 126–
    27, 128, 130, 159, 196, 243
*Legacy of the Civil War: Meditations
    on the Centennial, The* (Warren),
    212–13
Legal Tender Act, 10
Lenthall, John, 52
Libby Prison, 71, 91
Liberator, The (Boston), 84, *86*
Liberty Greys, 250
Liberty Party, 89
"Life among the Contrabands" (Dan-
    ielson), 90
"Life among the Rebels" (Wilkinson),
    91
Lincoln, Abraham, 7, 144, 243;
    announcing naval blockade, 46;
    authorizing ironclad purchase,
    54; calling for troops, 15, 17, 45,
    103; on early enlistment in Union
    Army, 69; opposition to, 15; recog-
    nizing Connecticut's Fourteenth,
    105–6
Lincoln administration, 8, 143–44
Lincoln in Hartford (DeWitt), 219
Linderman, Gerald F., 254n23
liquid phosphorus, 153
Litchfield County (CT), 84
living historians, 231–33. *See also*
    reenactors

Lockwood, William H., 209
Logue, Larry M., 194
Lonergan, Edward J., 215, 219, 222
Lost Cause mythology, 196
Lounsbury, George, 196
Lucas, Walter, 121
Lyon, Nathaniel, 78

MacLeish, Archibald, 222
Mallory, Charles, 49, 54, 55
Mallory, Stephen, 54
Mallory (Charles) & Sons, 48–49, 51,
    52, 53, 60, 62, 65n25
*Mallorys of Mystic: Six Generations
    in American Maritime Enterprise*
    (Baughman), 48
mania, 165
Manning, Chandra, 242
Mansfield (CT), 72, 82
Maule, Robert, 222
Maxson, Fish & Company, 48, 49, 52–
    53, 55–56, 63
Maxson, William Ellery, 49, 52, 53, 55,
    56, 57, 58–59
May, Samuel Joseph, 89
Mayer, Nathan, 209
Mayo, James M., 192
McClellan, George, 57, 59, 81, 82–83,
    103
McGregor, John, 91–92
McPherson, James M., 69, 111, 124,
    238–39, 240, 241, 242, 246, 249
Meade, George, 130–31
Meet John Trow (Dyja), 228
melancholia, 165
Memorial Day, 197, 205–6, 210
memory, 191–92
mental illness: approach to, religion's
    influence on, 164–65; categorizing,
    165; moral cure for, 163–64; somatic
    approach to, 164; stigma of, 162;
    treatments for, 164
Merrick & Sons, 66n37
Merrimac, 53
Meyer, David R., 79

Middlesex County Historical Society, 216–17

Middletown (CT), 105, 210, 216

Military and Civil History of Connecticut during the War of 1861–65 (Croffut and Morris), 102, 249

military units: Buckingham Rifles, 90; First Cavalry, 71; First Company of Union Guard, 78; First Connecticut Light Battery, 185; First Connecticut Regiment, 103, 183; First Corps, Army of the Potomac, 122; First Regiment Heavy Artillery, 71; Second Brigade, 106–7, 114; Second Connecticut Regiment, 86, 103; Second Corps, Army of the Potomac, 106–7, 125; Second Division, 123; Third Connecticut Regiment, 91, 103; Third Division, 106–7, 114; Fourth Connecticut Regiment, 84; Fifth Connecticut Regiment, 71, 208; Sixth Alabama Regiment, 127; Sixth Connecticut Regiment, 71, 103, 185; Seventh Connecticut Regiment, 71, 103, 183, 184, 185; Eighth Connecticut Regiment, 71, 103, 176n2, 209; Eighth Ohio Regiment, 125; Ninth Connecticut Regiment, 103; Tenth Connecticut Regiment, 103, 185; Tenth New York Regiment, 125; Eleventh Connecticut Regiment, 71, 82, 103, 176n2, 209; Eleventh Corps, 113; Twelfth Connecticut Regiment, 71, 103; Twelfth New Jersey Regiment, 115; Thirteenth Connecticut Regiment, 85, 103; Fourteenth Connecticut Regiment (*see* Fourteenth Connecticut Regiment); Fourteenth Tennessee Regiment, 137n; Fifteenth Connecticut Regiment, 176n2; Sixteenth Connecticut Regiment, 109–10, 170–71, 176n2, 209; Seventeenth Connecticut Regiment, 176n2; Eighteenth Connecticut Regiment, 71, 72, 76, 79, 82–83, 84, 92, 96n54; Twenty-First Connecticut Regiment, 71, 72; Twenty-Seventh Connecticut Regiment, 111, 159, 176n2; Forty-Second North Carolina Regiment, 127; Fifty-Fourth Massachusetts Colored Regiment, 196; Eighty-Fourth Massachusetts Regiment, 84; 108th New York Volunteers, 106, 107, 111; 130th Pennsylvania Regiment, 106, 111

Milroy, Robert Huston, 71, 81, 83

modernism, 76

Monitor, 55, 57, 59, 66n37, 67n58

monuments, 183, 185, 191–94, 206, 207

Moore, S. A., 122, 123, 125, 126

moral cure, 163–64

Morgan, George D., 51, 59, 65n25

Morris, Dwight, 107, 110, 119

Morris, John M., 52, 102, 105, 106, 107, 127, 212, 249

Mystic (CT): history of, 46–48; industries in, 49; role of, in Union's naval strength, 45, 46, 48, 63

Mystic Built: Ships and Shipyards of the Mystic River, Connecticut, 1784–1919 (Peterson), 46–48

Mystic Iron Works, 49

Mystic Pioneer, 51

National Banking Act, 13

national banks, 13–14, 28

National Council for the Social Studies, 250

national currency, 28

National Freeman's Relief Association, 90

National Home for Disabled Volunteer Soldiers (Dayton, OH), 175

National Regiment, 250

Naval History of the Civil War (Porter), 61

naval warfare, changes in, 53

nervous disorders, 165, 170

neurasthenia, 165

Nevins, Allan, 211, 214
New Bedford (CT) *Mercury*, 88
New Britain (CT), dedicating Soldiers' Monument, 181
New England Anti-Slavery Society, 89
New England Brigade, 250
New Haven (CT), 147
New Haven Palladium, 150
New Haven Propeller Company, 52
New Ironsides, 66n37
New Jersey Civil War Centennial Commission, 214
New London, 48, 51, *62*
New London County (CT), 88, 96n54
New Orleans, capture of, 59–60
New York Chamber of Commerce, 9
New York Times, 10–11, 210
Nickols (captain, Fourteenth Connecticut), 126
Nightingale, 51
Niven, John, 14, 46, 52, 71, 75, 78–80, 96–97n54, 102, 217, 230, 244
Norfolk Navy Yard, 53
Norris, James, 219
North Atlantic Blockading Squadron, 59, 61
Norwich Academy, 88
Norwich (CT) *Bulletin*, 78
Norwich Courier, 88
Norwich Morning Bulletin, 150
Norwich & Worcester line, 76
nostalgia, 165, 166

Oneida, 59
Order of the American Knights, 147
O'Reilly, Francis Augustin, 111
Owasco, 48, 51, 53, 54, 55, 62, 65n18

Page, Charles D., 102, 105, 107, 109, 110, 112–13, 115, 119, 121, 124, 125, 130, 131, 132
Palmer, Oliver H., 111
paper coins, 19
Patent Firearms Company. *See* Colt Patent Firearms Company

Patriotic Gore: Studies in the Literature of the American Civil War (Wilson), 213
Patterson, Robert, 81, 83
Pavlik, Mary Lou, *235*
Peace Democrats, 14–15, 41n21, 85, 143–44
peace resolutions, 146
Pearl, Phillip, 89
Pension Act of 1862, 170
pensions, 194
Perkins, Sanford H., 107, 108, 110, 111, 112, 119, 159–61, 166
Perry, Samuel, 173
Peterson, William M., 46–48, 52
Pettegrew, John, 197
Phillips, Hannah, 98n76
Phillips, J. T., 85
Pickett, George, 101
Pickett's Charge, 116–17
Pinney, A. Searle, 222
Plainfield (CT), 72, 89
Plainfield Academy, 88
Plainfield Anti-Slavery Society, 89
Pomfret (CT), 89
Pook, Samuel H., 55, 66n38
Poore, Charles, 213
Port Royal Experiment, 90
Porter, David D., 61
post-traumatic stress disorder (PTSD), 161; defining, 165–66; effects of, 165; handling of, during Civil War, 166–67, 172–76; responding to certain stimuli, 163; underreporting of, 161
Press Association (Confederate), 151
Preston (CT) war debt bond, *21*
Price of Liberty: Paying for America's Wars, The (Hormats), 28
prisoner parole system, 82
property tax, 11, 24, 33
psychiatry, status of, during the Civil War, 163
psychological combat disorder, 165
PTSD. *See* post-traumatic stress disorder

Puritans, 73, 94n17
Putnam, Albert, 215, 219
Putnam, Israel, 72, 77, 78
Putnam (CT), 81

racism, 84
Ramsdell, W. P., 108
RAND Corporation, 161
Ransom, David, 1, 207
Raymond, Bradford Paul, 210
reconciliationist tradition, 230, 246–
    47
Red Cross, 199
reenactors, *231, 232, 234, 235, 239*;
    accuracy of, 229–30, 235–37, 243;
    categories of, 236–37; controversies
    among, 250–51; education of, 229;
    as educators, 233–36, 244, 246, 250;
    female, *235*; identification of, with
    different causes, 238–41, 243; influ-
    ence of, 229, 237–38, 251; influences
    on, 230; military focus of, 229–30,
    243, 244; politics of, 248; questions
    about, 228; reconciliationist tradi-
    tion and, 247–49; separating from
    modern scholarship, 229–30, 241,
    242, 243, 249–50; source material
    for, 249; umbrella organization for,
    230, 250–51; websites of, 249
regimental reunions, 210
Register (New Haven, CT), 75
Reitemeyer, John R., 215
Reliance Machine Company, 49, 60
religion, influence of, on approach to
    mental illness, 164–65
religious dissent, 73–74
Relyea, William, 109–10
remembrances, 195–96
Remling, Jeffrey, 53
Republicanism, birth of, in Connecti-
    cut, 74
Republican Party, in antebellum Con-
    necticut, 75
reunions, 208–10
Revere, Paul, 77

revivalism, 80, 96n54
Ribicoff, Abraham, 214–15
Richardson, Israel, 107
Richmond Daily Dispatch, 151
Roberts, Henry, 199
Robertson, James, 214
Rockefeller, Nelson, 222
Rockville (CT), 105
Rodgers, John, 57–58
Rogers, John E., 222
Rogers, Marie, *235*
Roulette, William, 107
Rush, Benjamin, 164

Salisbury Prison, 91
Sanitary Commission, 189
Savage, Kirk, 191
Schmidt, Kathy, *235*
Schroeder, Peter Brett, 219
Scientific American, 56–57, 151
Scotland (CT), 72
Sears, Stephen W., 115
sea warfare, changes in, 45
Second Great Awakening, 73, 94n17
secret societies, 147
Sedgwick, John, 219
Seymour, Thomas, 15, 74
Shackel, Paul A., 191–92
Sharps rifles, 63, 108, 115, 127
Shaw (Robert Gould) Memorial (Bos-
    ton), 196
Sheehan-Dean, Aaron, 241
shell shock, 161
Sheridan, Philip, 219
Sherman, William Tecumseh, 189
Shook over Hell: Post-Traumatic Stress,
    Vietnam, and the Civil War (Dean),
    165
Simpson, E. S., 82
slavery, 2, 190; conflicts over, 87; fight-
    ing against, 85; reenactors' presen-
    tation of, 230; reenactors' view of,
    230, 241–42, 244–49; soldiers' atti-
    tudes toward, 241–42
Smith, James, 146

Society of Civil War Historians, 2
soldiers: considered "special class,"
    194; disillusionment of, 81, 82;
    Hawley on, 195; as standard for
    American manhood, 197; statues
    of, 192
Soldiers' and Sailors' Memorial Arch
    (Hartford, CT), 185, *186*
soldier's heart, 161
Soldiers' Monument (Brooklyn, CT),
    185
Soldiers' Monument (Middletown,
    CT), 206–7
Sons of Liberty, 147
So the War Came (Schroeder), 219
southern sympathizers, 82
Spanish-American War, 196–97
Stamp Act, 77
stamps, as currency, 19
Standing Order, 73, 94n17
Stannard, J. E., 126
Stars and Stripes, 48, 51, 52, 53, 60–61,
    65n18, 65n25
states' rights, soldiers' attitudes
    toward, 242
steam vessels, sold to the government,
    64n10
Sterling (CT), 72
Stevens, Henry S., 108, *109*, 111, 115,
    122, 209–10
Stevens, Thaddeus, 10
Stevens, Thomas, 49, 63
Stevenson, Adlai, 221
Stillman, Charles, 49, 63
Stone, John Quincy Adams, 78, 80–83,
    84, 90, 92
Stoughton, Frank, 110–11
Stowe, Harriet Beecher, 3
Stroud, Edwin, 121
substance abuse, 164–65, 166, 174–75,
    180n20
substitutes, 20, 27, 37, 38, 72
Sumner, Charles, 84
*Surgical and Medical History of the
    War of the Rebellion*, 166

Tappan, Arthur, 88–89
tariffs, 12
taxes, 8, 20, 23, 24; on businesses, 34,
    38–39, 42n32, 43n42; increasing,
    10–11, 28; property, 33; structure of,
    11; raising, reluctance about, 9
Team of Rivals (Goodwin), 8
Telegraph, The (Windham County,
    CT), 80–81
temperance movement, 80, 89
Terry, Alfred H., 183, 219
Thames Bank (Norwich, CT), 15
This Republic of Suffering (Faust), 249
Thompson (CT), 88
Thoreau, Henry David, 84
Times (London, CT), 88
Todd, Eli, 163–64
Torrington (CT) Soldiers' Monument,
    193
towns, taxes on, 24
Transcript. See *Windham County
    Transcript*
Treasury of Virtue, 212, 213
*Troubled Commemoration: The Ameri-
    can Civil War Centennial, 1961–1965*
    (Cook), 211
Trudeau, Noah Andre, 115
Twichell, Joseph H., 189, 199
Tyler, E. B., 114–15
Tyler, W. S., 125

Underground Railroad, 89
*Under Two Flags: The American Navy
    in the Civil War* (Fowler), 45
Union: counterrebellion in, 147; sup-
    port for, weakening, 146
Union Army: early enlistment in, 69;
    psychiatric conditions affecting, 166
Unionist, The (Brooklyn, CT), 89
Union Navy: activities of, 62–63; in-
    creasing ship production, 51–52;
    power of, 46; unprepared for con-
    frontation at war's beginning, 46
United States, military strength in,
    and national finances, 28

u.s. Armory (Springfield, MA), 148, 149

Vallandigham, Clement, 146, 148
Van Beynam, William, 216
Van Dusen, Albert, 256n38
Varuna, 48, 51, 52, 59–60, 65n18, 65n25
Vernon (CT), 105
Veterans' Administration, 171
Vicksburg, 49–51, 62
Virginia, 53, 57, 59, 67n58

Wade, Edward, 117, 119, 127
war claims, reimbursement for, 27, 29–32
War Democrats, 14, 15
war doctors, 166–67
warfare, sentimentalization of, 212
war trauma, 161, 162
Warren, Gouverneur K., 122
Warren, Robert Penn, 212–13, 215, 255n36
Warshauer, Matthew, 102–3, 133n4, 217, 237–38, 239–40, 247, 251
Washington, Booker T., 196
Weld, Stanley B., 219
Welles, Gideon, 46, 47, 74; asking for ironclads, 54–55; on the capture of New Orleans, 60; matching Confederate threat, 53–54; ordering ships for the navy, 51–52; strategy of, 64n7

West, Richard S., 51
Whig Party, 75
white supremacist view, 246–47
White, Egbert, 221
Whitney, Eli, 45
Wilderness Campaign, 124–26
Wilentz, Sean, 246
Wilkinson, J. F., 81, 85, 90–92
Willimantic Journal, 82, 97n56
Wilson, Edmund, 213
Wilson, R. L., 145
Wilson, Woodrow, 211
Windham Academy, 88
Windham County (CT), 96n54; abolitionism in, 83–92; Civil War spirit in, 80–83; death toll for soldiers from, 72; desertion rates for, 72; farming in, 78–79; free blacks in, 84; history of, 73–76; map of, 70; nationalism of, 69–71; newspapers of, 80–85, 90–92; private academies in, 88; religious history of, 79–80; revolutionary ideology in, 76–78; social reformers coming to, 88–89; travel routes through, 76, 77, 88; uniqueness of, 69–71; as vacation destination, 88
Windham County Transcript, 80–85, 90–91, 97n56
Windham Peace Society, 89
Woodstock (CT), 71, 78, 89
Woodstock Academy, 88

Garnet Books

Garnet Poems:
  An Anthology of Connecticut
  Poetry since 1776
  Edited by Dennis Barone
Food for the Dead:
  On the Trail of New England's
  Vampires
  by Michael E. Bell
Early Connecticut Silver, 1700–1840
  by Peter Bohan and Philip
  Hammerslough
  Introduction and notes
  by Erin Eisenbarth
The Connecticut River:
  A Photographic Journey through
  the Heart of New England
  by Al Braden
Connecticut's Fife & Drum Tradition
  by James Clark
Sunken Garden Poetry, 1992–2011
  Edited by Brad Davis
The Old Leather Man:
  Historical Accounts of a
  Connecticut and New York Legend
  by Daniel DeLuca
Post Roads & Iron Horses:
  Transportation in Connecticut
  from Colonial Times to the Age
  of Steam
  by Richard DeLuca
Dr. Mel's Connecticut Climate Book
  by Dr. Mel Goldstein
Hidden in Plain Sight:
  A Deep Traveler Explores
  Connecticut
  by David K. Leff

Becoming Tom Thumb:
  Charles Stratton, P. T. Barnum, and
  the Dawn of American Celebrity
  by Eric D. Lehman
Westover School:
  Giving Girls a Place of Their Own
  by Laurie Lisle
Crowbar Governor:
  The Life and Times of Morgan
  Gardner Bulkeley
  by Kevin Murphy
Fly Fishing in Connecticut:
  A Guide for Beginners
  by Kevin Murphy
Water for Hartford:
  The Story of the Hartford Water
  Works and the Metropolitan
  District Commission
  by Kevin Murphy
African American Connecticut
  Explored
  Edited by Elizabeth J. Normen
Henry Austin:
  In Every Variety of Architectural
  Style
  by James F. O'Gorman
Ella Grasso:
  Connecticut's Pioneering Governor
  by Jon E. Purmont
Making Freedom:
  The Extraordinary Life of
  Venture Smith
  by Chandler B. Saint and
  George Krimsky
Welcome to Wesleyan:
  Campus Buildings
  by Leslie Starr

Barns of Connecticut
    by Markham Starr
Gervase Wheeler:
    A British Architect in America,
    1847–1860
    by Renée Tribert and
    James F. O'Gorman
Connecticut in the American
    Civil War: Slavery, Sacrifice,
    and Survival
    by Matthew Warshauer
Inside Connecticut and the Civil War:
    Essays on One State's Struggles
    Edited by Matthew Warshauer

Stories in Stone:
    How Geology Influenced
    Connecticut History and Culture
    by Jelle Zeilinga de Boer
New Haven's Sentinels
    The Art and Science of East Rock
    and West Rock
    by Jelle Zeilinga de Boer and
    John Wareham